PLANNING

GREENS CONCISE SCOTS LAW

PLANNING

By

Neil A. Collar, LL.B., LL.M., DIP.L.P., Solicitor
Brodies, W.S.
and
Part-Time Tutor, University of Edinburgh

W. GREEN/Sweet & Maxwell
EDINBURGH
1994

First published 1994

ISBN 0 414 01018 3

A catalogue record for this book is
available from the British Library

Printed in Great Britain by
Hartnolls Ltd., Bodmin, Cornwall

PREFACE

"Does the Englishman still fondly believe that his home is his castle when the Executive has the following powers over it?

(1) To knock it down.
(2) To take possession of it, without notice to the owner, but with 14 days notice to the occupier, and without previous payment of the price.
(3) To close the King's highway which gives access to his house.
(4) To direct the colour with which his doors and fences may be painted.
(5) To confiscate his property illegally if he, for example is fighting in Asia for his country and so unable to appeal to the Courts within 28 days from any illegal act.
(6) To seize it and pay as compensation less than its value."

(Mekie & Williams: *Town and Country Planning Law*)

The outrage at the growing power of the Executive felt by the authors of this statement is clear. Yet the basic premise of this statement which was written in 1946 remains valid today: the State has considerable powers over land under private ownership.

Town and country planning, to give its full title, is one of the powers exercised by the State to control building and other work on land which is in private ownership. Since 1947 any landowner wishing to develop his/her land must seek permission from the State before carrying out that development. If this permission is refused, the landowner is unable to carry out the development but has no right to claim compensation from the State as a result. In such circumstances, how can "the Englishman still fondly believe that his home is his castle"? It is therefore surprising, but perhaps a tribute to the results which it has achieved, that the planning system enjoys almost universal support.

This book is written as an introduction to Scots planning law, a subject which has grown in importance over recent years. It is intended for use by any person coming into contact with the planning system, whether in their professional or private life. In particular, Chapter 10 provides a guide to members of the public on the opportunities for participating in the system. Inevitably some readers will use this book as a general reference text. With this in mind, it is recommended that any reader unfamiliar with the operation of the planning system should first read Chapter 2, which describes the "nuts and bolts", before selectively reading other chapters.

For many years Young and Rowan-Robinson's *Scottish Planning Law and Procedure* has been the bible for those involved in the Scottish planning system. This book is not a replacement for their comprehensive work but is intended as an introduction for those who are unfamiliar with the subject. It should also be of use where a more up-to-date text is required, as many areas of planning law have changed since *Scottish Planning Law and Procedure* was published in 1985.

With one exception, the law is stated as at January 31, 1994. It has been possible to address the introduction of the plan-led system on March 7th, 1994, although this change in the law came too late in the publishing process for a detailed discussion on its implications to be included. The existence of other provisions of the Planning and Compensation Act 1991 which have yet to come into force, is also noted.

The starting point for this book was my LL.M. thesis, "The Effects of Judicial Intervention on Planning Conditions," for which I owe a continuing debt to my supervisor Sue Nott and the University of Liverpool for the award of a research studentship. I also thank Paul Watchman for guiding my first steps as a practising planning lawyer. Many people have assisted with the production of this book. Particular thanks must go to my parents for their constant encouragement. I am also grateful to the partners of Brodies, W.S. and my colleagues for their support. As a novice to legal publishing, I greatly appreciated the help offered by everyone at Greens. And to all my friends, thank you.

NEIL A. COLLAR,
Edinburgh,
February 1994.

CONTENTS

TABLE OF CASES

CHRONOLOGICAL TABLE OF STATUTES

CHRONOLOGICAL TABLE OF STATUTORY INSTRUMENTS

1971 Town and Country Planning (Minerals) (Scotland) Regulations (No. 778), as amended by 1982 Regulations of same name (S.I. 1982 No. 973) ... 367

1975 Town and Country Planning (Tree Preservation Order and Trees in Conservation Areas) (Scotland) Regulations (No. 1204), as amended by Amendment Regulations (S.I. 1981 No. 1385 and S.I. 1984 No. 329)—
  reg. 11 .... 336, 337

1980 Town and Country Planning (Inquiries Procedure) (Scotland) Rules (No. 1676) 272, 281
  Town and Country Planning Appeals (Determination by Appointed Persons) (Inquiry Procedure) (Scotland) Rules (No. 1677), as amended by Amendment Rules (S.I. 1987 No. 1522) 272, 281

1981 Town and Country Planning (Development by Planning Authorities) (Scotland) Regulations (No. 829), as amended by Amendment Regulations (S.I. 1984 No. 238) 369

1983 Town and Country Planning (Structure and Local Plans) (Scotland) Regulations (No. 1590) 44–45, 47–51, 53–58, 62–67

1984 Town and Country Planning (Control of Advertisements) (Scotland) Regulations (No. 467), as amended by Amendment Regulations (S.I. 1992 No. 1763) 77, 85, 91, 339–348

1987 Town and Country Planning (Listed Buildings and Buildings in Conservation Areas) (Scotland) Regulations (No. 1529) 317, 320, 332, 371
  Town and Country Planning (Determination of Appeals by Appointed Persons) (Prescribed Classes) (Scotland) Regulations (No. 1531), as amended by Amendment Regulations (1989 S.I. No. 577) 263, 346

TABLE OF SCOTTISH OFFICE GUIDANCE AND DIRECTIONS

Circulars

Circulars

National Planning Policy Guidelines

Planning Advice Notes

Directions

Directions

TABLE OF ABBREVIATIONS

A.C.	Appeal Cases (Law Reports)
All E.R.	All England Law Reports
B.P.P.	British Parliamentary Papers
Ch.D./Ch.	Chancery (Law Reports)
CLEUD	Certificate of Lawfulness of Existing Use or Development
CLOPUD	Certificate of Lawfulness of Proposed Use or Development
D.P.O.	Development Procedure Order
E.A.	Environmental Assessment
E.G.	Estates Gazette
E.G.C.S.	Estates Gazette Case Summaries
E.G.L.R.	Estates Gazette Law Reports
E.I.P.	Examination in Public
E.P.A.	Environmental Protection Act 1990
E.Z.	Enterprise Zone
F.	Session Cases 1898–1906 (8 Volumes), edited by Fraser
G.D.O.	General Development Order
G.D.P.O.	General Development Procedure Order
G.P.D.O.	General Permitted Development Order
G.W.D.	Greens Weekly Digest
I.P.C.	Integrated Pollution Control
J.L.S.S.	Journal of the Law Society of Scotland
J.P.L.	Journal of Planning Law
K.B.	King's Bench (Law Reports)
L.G.R.	Local Government Reports
L.J.(K.B.)	Law Journal Reports (King's Bench)
M.L.R.	Modern Law Review
N.H.A.	Natural Heritage Area
N.H.S.A.	Natural Heritage (Scotland) Act 1991
N.I.D.	Notice of Intention to Develop
N.P.P.G.	National Planning Policy Guideline
N.S.A.	National Scenic Area
O.J.L.S.	Oxford Journal of Legal Studies

P. & C.R.	Property and Compensation Reports
P.A.N.	Planning Advice Note
P.C.A.	Planning and Compensation Act 1991
P.D.O.	Permitted Development Order
P.L.	Public Law
P.L.I.	Public Local Inquiry
P.L.R.	Planning Law Reports
R.T.P.I.	Royal Town Planning Institute
Q.B.	Queen's Bench (Law Reports)
S.C.	Session Cases
S.C.L.R.	Scottish Civil Law Reports
S.D.D.	Scottish Development Department
S.Env.D.	Scottish Environment Department
S.I.	Statutory Instrument
S.L.T.	Scots Law Times
S.L.T. (Lands Tr.)	Scots Law Times Lands Tribunal Reports
S.L.T. (Sh.Ct.)	Scots Law Times Sheriff Court Reports
S.N.H.	Scottish Natural Heritage
S.O.I.R.	Scottish Office Inquiry Reporters
S.P.L.P.	Scottish Planning Law and Practice
S.P.Z.	Simplified Planning Zone
S.S.S.I.	Site of Special Scientific Interest
T.C.P.S.A.	Town and Country Planning (Scotland) Act 1972
T.P.O.	Tree Preservation Order
T.P.Rev.	Town Planning Review
U.L. & P.	Urban Law and Policy
U.C.O.	Use Classes Order
W.L.R.	Weekly Law Reports

ILLUSTRATIONS

Chapter 1

EVOLUTION OF PLANNING LAW

Planning law is the creation of statute, unlike many other areas of law. The development of the statutory provisions applicable to town and country planning is traced in the first part of this chapter and provides an historical perspective for the current planning system, which is examined in subsequent chapters.

The activity of planning initially evolved in tandem with the planning system, with statute setting out the objectives of planning. However, under the present system, statute provides the framework rather than the objectives for the activity of planning. The evolving planning profession and academic thought has led to many theories of planning. The second part of this chapter examines some of these theories, and considers whether there can ever be an answer to the question: "What is planning?."

Pre-1909 — Origins of Planning Law

Prior to the advent of state control of land use under the planning system, the feudal nature of Scottish land ownership provided an important facility for the private planning of land use. Feudal land tenure allows the feudal superior to impose restrictions on what the landowner may do on his own land. For example, the carrying on of trades and businesses likely to have an injurious effect on neighbouring landowners may be prohibited. One of the greatest feats of town planning — the creation of Edinburgh's New Town — was achieved almost a century before the introduction of statutory planning powers.[1] The uniformity of development was secured through

[1] Youngson, *The Making of Classical Edinburgh* (1966).

title conditions requiring the consent of the feudal superior to be obtained before development could proceed. However, title restrictions can vary considerably and not all feudal superiors in Scotland could be relied upon to impose such high standards. Events were to show that some form of state control was necessary.

The origins of planning law lie in the dramatic changes in nineteenth-century British society caused by the Industrial Revolution, with an influx of people from the countryside into the towns, attracted by employment in the expanding factories. Houses were hurriedly constructed to meet the demand, often close to the factories. There was no control over standards of construction, resulting in houses in close and unregulated proximity with little or no regard to the requirements of proper ventilation and sanitation. People were living in slum conditions.

Model industrial villages, such as New Lanark and Port Sunlight (close to Glasgow and Liverpool, respectively), provided a powerful precedent of how workers could be housed in pleasant and healthy surroundings, underlining the need for action to combat the existing slum conditions of many towns and cities. Organisations such as the Garden City Association, formed in 1899, promoted development of well-laid out towns, with extensive open spaces and houses with gardens. Well-designed and laid-out towns were seen as the way to assure human happiness and eradicate social problems.

Insanitary housing conditions were struck at by the introduction of the Public Health Acts. Local authorities were given powers to secure proper standards of drainage and sewage, and also to make bye-laws regulating the size of rooms, space between houses and width of streets.[2] Local authorities also had powers to remove insanitary dwellings and supply new houses for the working classes.[3] However, there was still a need for local authority powers to deal with more general land-use problems, such as the separation of incompatible uses.

[2] Public Health (Scotland) Act 1897 (60 & 61 Vict., c. 38) s. 181.

[3] Artisans Dwellings (Scotland) Act 1875 (38 & 39 Vict. c. 49), replaced and repealed by Housing of the Working Classes Act 1890 (53 & 54 Vict., c. 70).

By the beginning of the twentieth century, there was an increasing awareness of the ill-effects caused by the physical environment of the industrial towns and cities. With the political trend towards democracy and social equality, marked by the beginnings of the welfare state in the budget of 1909, action was required to improve living conditions. A healthy workforce was required to build the *Dreadnoughts*, the mighty battleships constructed in great numbers by Britain and Germany during the power struggle in the years leading to the First World War. It was recognised that urban conditions were inimical to health, and that degeneration of the population had led to reduced labour efficiency.[4] There was an increasing realisation that Britain had lagged behind other countries, including Germany, in the guidance of the growth of towns. As war became more likely, memories revived of the ill-health of British men enlisting to fight in the Boer War,[5] such ill-health caused by the squalid dwellings in British cities.

Two explanations therefore underlie the general acceptance of the principle of town planning in 1909.[6] First, it was a logical extension of earlier legislation concerned with housing and public health. Secondly, it was clear that the effect of rapid urban and industrial change required a more comprehensive approach than the public health bye-laws.

1909–1939 — Town Planning

Town planning was born in the Housing, Town Planning Etc. Act 1909, which conferred a power upon local authorities to prepare town planning schemes for their area[7]:

> "with the general object of securing proper sanitary conditions, amenity, and convenience in connection with the laying-out and use of the land, and of any neighbouring lands."

[4] Cd. 2175 (B.P.P., 1904, xxxiii).
[5] Cherry, *The Politics of Town Planning* (1982), Chap. 2.
[6] Ashworth, *Genesis of Modern British Town Planning* (1954), Chap. 7.
[7] 9 Edw. 7, c. 44, s. 54 — applicable to Scotland by virtue of s. 53.

The scope of town planning was therefore wider than that of the old sanitary and housing legislation, covering the additional objects of amenity and convenience.

The power conferred on local authorities by the 1909 Act was discretionary, and the cumbersome procedure for the preparation of town planning schemes provided little incentive for exercise of their powers.[8] Moreover, schemes could only be prepared for land about to be developed or likely to be developed, and the Act did not provide for control of building development in the countryside or redevelopment of built-up areas. Statutory town planning was confined to the physical layout of land and buildings, ensuring standards of amenity and convenience. However, local authorities had the power to take a comprehensive approach to development: where previously new buildings had to satisfy public health bye-laws, the impact of those buildings on the amenity and convenience of the surrounding neighbourhood now had to be considered. Town planning was born.

Town planning schemes were the principal instrument of town planning until 1947. The provisions of the operative scheme controlled development and the authority ceased to have planning control over individual development, unless zoning provisions required its consent for certain uses. The scheme was essentially a zoning plan, dedicating certain areas or zones to specified uses such as industrial use, open space and residential development. It left no doubts about what forms of development were permitted, but this certainty meant that the scheme was inflexible. To give more flexibility zones were often dedicated to a predominant use which was allowed without consent, while other specified uses were prohibited or required the consent of the local authority.[9] Schemes also provided limits on the number of buildings, the space around them, and their appearance. Planning schemes were entirely regulatory in nature, and did not secure that

[8] Fewer than 10,000 acres of land in England and Wales had been brought under planning control by 1919 — Griffiths, "The Law of Property (Land)" in *Law and Opinion in England in the Twentieth Century* (Ginsberg ed. 1959), p. 127.

[9] For detailed discussion, see Abercrombie *Town and Country Planning* (1st ed., 1933); Mekie and Williams, *Town and Country Planning Law* (1946).

development would take place, merely providing that if it did take place in any particular part of the area covered by the scheme it would be controlled in certain ways.

After the First World War, there was a desperate shortage of housing and calls for "homes fit for heroes." Social pacification through improved housing provision was a clear antidote to fears of bolshevism and industrial unrest following the Russian Revolution.[10] This was combined with increased planning powers in the Housing, Town Planning, Etc. (Scotland) Act 1919.[11] During the war there had been a considerable extension of Government powers, and it was felt safe to increase local authority planning powers in that light. The 1919 Act introduced compulsory town planning for the council of every burgh with a population of 20,000 or more. These councils were required to produce town planning schemes by January 1, 1926. Although some of the procedural obstacles on the preparation of schemes were removed, there was no attention paid to the most fundamental criticisms and, in particular, there was still no question of planning a town as a whole.

One innovation of the 1919 Act was the introduction of interim development control[12] for the period between the passing of a resolution to prepare a scheme until the scheme became effective, which could be several years. There was no obligation on developers to apply for permission, but a grant of planning permission under interim development control preserved the right to compensation if the development conflicted with the scheme eventually approved. Thus interim development control was purely negative in character, neither obliging nor assisting anybody to do anything. To avoid any liability to pay compensation, the authority would rely on the projected provisions of the planning scheme when granting planning permission.

The first statute to deal exclusively with town planning was the Town Planning (Scotland) Act 1925, which consolidated

[10] *Committee on Building Construction in Connection with the Provision of Dwellings for the Working Classes*, Cd. 9191 (B.P.P. 1918, Vol. vii).
[11] 9 & 10 Geo. 5, c. 60.
[12] s. 37. See Mekie and Williams *ibid.*, Chap. V "Interim Development."

existing planning law.[13] This was followed by the Town and Country Planning (Scotland) Act 1932,[14] which extended the planning powers of local authorities by providing that town planning schemes could be made over any land, urban or rural, containing buildings or not. The objects of town planning schemes now included[15]:

> "preserving existing buildings or other objects of architectural, historic or artistic interest and places of natural interest or beauty, and generally of protecting amenities whether in urban or rural portions of the area."

However, the 1932 Act also removed any requirement upon authorities to prepare town planning schemes, leaving planning as a voluntary activity. It also reintroduced the cumbersome procedures for preparing or modifying a scheme. The growing complexity of planning law was reflected in the size of the 1932 Act: 55 sections and 5 schedules, compared to the 22 sections and 4 schedules of the 1925 Act.

Post-1939 — The War Years

During the Second World War public opinion swung behind the need for effective town and country planning. As a relief from the struggle for survival, hopes had centred on the drive for reconstruction and it was increasingly expected that bold and imaginative planning would create a better Britain. After all, if the war could be planned, why not peace? State direction was seen as the way forward. At last, public opinion was prepared to subordinate private interests in land to the public interest in a planned environment.

[13] 15 & 16 Geo. 5, c. 17. The Housing Etc. Act 1923 (13 & 14 Geo. 5, c. 49) had extended planning powers to areas of aesthetic or historic interest, whether developed or not.

[14] 22 & 23 Geo. 5, c. 49. See *Encyclopaedia of the Laws of Scotland*. Vol. 14, "Town and Country Planning" (1933).

[15] 1932 Act, s. 1.

The Blitz saw the heart of many British cities and towns destroyed by bombing. Since extensive rebuilding was inescapable, there was an opportunity to improve cities as a whole. It was realised that unless proper planning was implemented, the end result would be a total lack of improvement. There was a need to treat the city as an entity, and not to concentrate on the devastated areas in isolation. Planning could deal with the enormous demand for housing and redevelop congested and inadequate areas of towns and cities.

The Government saw the possibilities of using the planning system as a political tool to achieve reconstruction of society after the war.[16] As a result it commissioned three reports to examine the future role of planning. The Barlow Report[17] recommended decentralisation of industry to allow redevelopment of congested urban areas, and a reasonable balance of industrial development throughout the country. This led to the establishment of the new towns. The Uthwatt Report[18] tackled the problem of compensation. Since planning powers were first conferred, the possible liability to pay compensation to landowners had left many authorities unwilling to control development. The report recommended that rights to development in all land outside built-up areas should be vested in the State on payment of fair compensation. This would allow local authorities in the future to divert land to uses not chosen by the owner, without automatic liability to pay compensation. It also recommended that control over development should be secured by speedy legislation bringing all land within interim development control, to prevent development prejudicial to post-war reconstruction plans. The Scott Report[19] called for local planning to become compulsory rather than permissive, and for the approval of the local

[16] See generally Cullingworth, *Peacetime History of Environmental Planning 1939–69* (1975), Vol. 1 "Reconstruction and Land-use Planning 1939–1947".

[17] Royal Commission on the Distribution of the Industrial Population, Cmd. 6153 (1940) (B.P.P. 1939–40, iv, 263).

[18] Reports of the Expert Committee on Compensation and Betterment, Interim Cmd. 6291 (1941) (B.P.P. 1940–41, iv, 205); Final Cmd. 6386 (1942) (B.P.P. 1941–42, iv, 15).

[19] Report of the Committee on Land Utilisation in Rural Areas, Cmd. 6328 (1942) (B.P.P. 1941–42, iv, 421).

authority to be required for any development during the period of interim development control.

Following the recommendation of the Uthwatt Report, the Town and Country Planning (Interim Development) (Scotland) Act 1943[20] extended interim control of development throughout the country, through the statutory fiction that all authorities were in the process of preparing a town planning scheme. Local authorities were also given the power to enforce interim development control. Previously, enforcement action could only be taken once a town planning scheme was operative and a development did not conform with its provisions. The 1943 Act enabled the authorities to take enforcement action against development which threatened their planning proposals or was not in accordance with the terms of the grant of permission, before any scheme was approved. However, there was still no requirement for planning permission to be sought from the local authority before development could proceed.

The Town and Country Planning (Scotland) Act 1945,[21] known as the "blitz and blight" Act, empowered local authorities to undertake the actual development of their own areas. For the first time, local authorities could buy land simply and expeditiously for planning purposes, particularly for redeveloping as a whole war-damaged or obsolete and badly laid-out areas.

Thus by 1945, local authorities had extensive planning powers unheard-of before the war. The 1943 Act extended existing powers, while the 1945 Act introduced major new powers. However, a complete overhaul of the planning system was still necessary to allow reconstruction after the war.

1947 Act and Beyond

In dealing with the principal recommendations of the Uthwatt and Scott Reports, the Town and Country Planning (Scotland)

[20] 6 & 7 Geo. 6, c. 43.
[21] 8 & 9 Geo. 6, c. 33.

Act 1947[22] heralded a new era of planned society. For the first time, local authorities were given comprehensive planning powers, and the whole country was subjected to planning control. The Act had five main purposes[23]:

> (a) to provide a framework, or pattern, for land use against which day-to-day development could be considered (the development plan);
>
> (b) to bring all development under control, making it subject to the permission of local authorities or central government;
>
> (c) to deal with specific problems of amenity, including the preservation of trees and woodlands, and of buildings of special architectural and historic interest, and control of outdoor advertisements;
>
> (d) to solve the compensation and betterment problem[24]; and
>
> (e) to extend the powers of authorities to acquire and develop land for planning purposes, and the scale and scope of grants from central funds to local authorities carrying out the acquisition and clearing of land.

Perhaps the most important measure in the 1947 Act was the introduction of a universal requirement to obtain consent from the local authority for any development. This control was created by nationalising all development rights in land, leaving owners with the existing (1947) use rights in their land. As all development rights were vested in the State, its permission had to be obtained for any proposed development. Unlike the non-obligatory nature of interim development control, consent was required before development could commence. This was a considerable extension of the proposals of the Uthwatt Report, which had restricted control to

[22] 10 & 11 Geo. 6, c. 53.

[23] Ministry of Town and Country Planning Report 1943–51, Cmd. 8204 (BPP 50–51, xx, 133).

[24] For a brief explanation of this problem, see Moore, *A Practical Approach to Planning Law* (1987), pp. 2–3. Also, Grant, *Urban Planning Law* (1982), pp. 18–20.

undeveloped land outside town areas. The effect of these provisions cannot be exaggerated. Owners were left with no absolute rights to develop their land, build upon it, or even change its use. This was a radical encroachment on rights of private property.

With the universal requirement for planning permission, the town planning scheme became meaningless, as there was no need to impose specific restrictions on the use of particular land. However, the advantage of the town planning scheme had been that the developer knew with considerable precision what development could be undertaken, and this advantage was retained with the introduction of development plans. Under the 1947 Act development plans had to be prepared for every area in the country, to outline the way in which each area was to be developed or preserved.

The development plan was conceived essentially as a statement of development proposals and the intentions of the local authority with regard to the development of their area, and was intended to show only broad land-use allocations. Unlike the town planning scheme, the development plan carried no guarantee that planning permission would be granted even if development proposals were in harmony with the plan. However, in considering an application for planning permission, the authority had to consider the provisions of the plan and "any other material considerations." In addition, the plan was not intended to be a final statement, even of the broad intentions of the authority. It was to be reviewed every five years, and amendments could be made at any time. It was hoped that the new system of flexible development plans would cure the rigid and static nature of town planning schemes.

The importance of the 1947 Act cannot be overstated. It made planning a compulsory function of all local authorities. Pre-war Britain had been largely free from any operative planning control, but following the 1947 Act every piece of land in Britain was under development control, with a universal requirement to obtain consent before development could commence. The Act imposed unheard-of limitations on the rights of landowners, and conferred unprecedented and largely unfettered discretionary power on local authorities. This was the true birth of planning.

Post-1947

Although the 1947 Act introduced the most sweeping planning powers yet conferred upon local authorities, disillusionment soon set in. The system rapidly became bogged down in details and cumbersome procedures. Development plans were too detailed and quickly became out of date. Changes to the system of development plans were proposed, to distinguish policy and strategic issues from detailed tactical issues.[25] This proposal was implemented through the introduction of the new two-part development plan in the Town and Country Planning (Scotland) Act 1969. Structure plans, which would require the approval of the Secretary of State, would set out and justify broad land-use policies for the area, policies for the management of traffic, and measures for the improvement of the physical environment. Structure plans would not contain detailed land allocations, which were left for the local plans to cover. Local plans were to set out the detailed plans for the area within the framework of the structure plans. The 1969 Act also provided for increased public consultation in the planning process.

The introduction of structure plans was seen as the opportunity for achieving more broadly based types of planning, stressing economic and social ends (theories of social and economic planning are discussed below). However, central government adopted a restrictive approach to social and economic policies in structure plans.[26] Social policies were rarely permitted to be incorporated as specific policies or proposals, and non-land-use criteria were excluded. Although the structure plan offered an opportunity to lay out broad policies and strategy, that policy and strategy related to land use. A similar approach is taken today.

The non-financial provisions of the 1947 Act, and the system of structure and local plans, still survive largely intact, consolidated in the Town and Country Planning (Scotland)

[25] Planning Advisory Group (PAG) Report, "The Future of Development Plans" (1965).

[26] Jowell and Noble, "Structure Plans as Instruments of Social and Economic Policy" [1981] J.P.L. 466.

Act 1972,[27] which remains the principal Scottish planning statute despite widescale amendment by subsequent statutes including the Planning and Compensation Act 1991.

Objectives of Planning

Since the 1932 Act no indication has been given in the Planning Acts of the objects for which planning powers are conferred. The Town and Country Planning (Scotland) Act 1972 (TCPSA) does provide guidance on the contents of structure and local plans (Chapter 3). When determining applications for planning permission, the planning authority are directed to have regard to the provisions of the development plan and to any other "material considerations."[28] As the power to determine such applications is conferred by the Planning Act, legal theory states that such considerations must be planning considerations. But what is "planning"?

Throughout the years, writers have suggested a variety of objectives, which have altered as the planning system has developed.[29] Every person involved in the planning process has a different conception of the objective of planning — a personal planning theory. Thus one of the problems of planning is that it promises to be all things to all men and therefore satisfies no one objective. However, the flexibility of the planning system has the advantage of being able to adjust to new philosophies and ideas as they arise, such as the concept of sustainable development, whereby planners may be seen as trustees of the environment for future generations.

In general terms, planning seeks to preserve the environment while improving it by careful control of development,

[27] c. 52. In England and Wales planning law was consolidated in 1990. There are plans to repeat this process in Scotland but proposals have yet to be announced.

[28] TCPSA, s. 26(1).

[29] *e.g.* Abercrombie, quoted in Hall, *The Containment of Urban England* (1973), Vol. 2, Chap. 1; Hall himself *ibid.*; Foley, "British Town Planning: One Ideology or Three?" (1960) 11 *British Journal of Sociology 211* and in Faludi, *A Reader in Planning Theory* (1973); Bruton (ed.) *The Spirit and Purpose of Planning* (1974); Simmonds, "The Conflicting Aims of Planning," in *Contemporary Issues in Town Planning* (Willis ed. 1986).

moving towards the ultimate goal of a healthy and civilised life. However, a more detailed analysis is required to explain the purpose of the planning system.

Town and country planning is predominantly about land use. However, writers have argued that interpreting "planning" as being concerned solely with land use is unduly confining, and that social and economic factors should be on a level par with land-use considerations.[30] In the sense that town planning is an activity carried out in the public interest, there must be a social element within it. The "public interest" must be an amalgam of the social values and interests of the population. Furthermore, the social origins of town planning lay in concerns for public health. Man's environment was conceived as the determinant of his happiness and behaviour, and early town planners believed that social problems could be eradicated by engineering the environment. Modern theories are less interventionist, providing a framework not to fashion behaviour, but rather to present the widest range of opportunities to enable individuals to fulfil their social objectives.[31]

There is also an economic dimension to planning, as it represents government intervention in the land market to correct deficiencies.[32] For example, the factory owner has no incentive to minimise pollution from the smoking factory chimney. The planning system therefore intervenes to balance the social costs of this pollution against the social benefits of the factory development, thereby providing for socially optimal use of land. The planning system also has the ability to change land values. Proposals for major developments such as roads can cause planning blight, with property values in the vicinity of the development plummeting. The reverse is also true: a grant of planning permission for a plot of land

[30] Faludi, *supra*, p. 291. The systems analysis approach of the 1960s viewed towns as complex systems where physical, economic and social environments were inter-related: see Ravetz, *The Government of Space — Town Planning in Modern Society* (1986).

[31] Cherry, *Town Planning in Its Social Context* (1970); Loughlin's social-needs model — "Planning Gain: Law, Policy and Practice" (1980) 1 O.J.L.S. 61 at pp. 74–5; Broady, *Planning for People: Essays on the Social Context of Planning* (1968).

[32] See generally, Broadbent, *Planning and Profit in the Urban Economy* (1977).

invariably increases its value. The Thatcher Government of the 1980s emphasised this economic dimension, believing that the planning system can be used to encourage economic prosperity.[33]

Various influences act as a brake on the pursuit of wider social and economic objectives,[34] and limit the extent of planning powers. Planning is a professional activity and must be influenced by the opinions and theories of the planning profession.[35] More importantly, planning functions within a political and legal structure, and this structure acts as a limiting factor. Planning is a political function, both in the sense that it is a power vested in government, central and local, and also because it is a process of choice and must therefore have an inherently political nature.[36] Planning powers are vested in local government, subject to the guidance of central government, which initiates all planning legislation. At every stage of the planning process, politicians take the final decisions, enabling the planners to claim political neutrality, although this claim is undermined by the reliance often placed on their advice by the politicians.[37] While the planner may argue that his advice is apolitical, it must be influenced by his own values and those of the planning profession.

The political influence on planning is demonstrated by the changes made to the planning system by the Thatcher Government. The political impetus was to promote economic

[33] Michael Heseltine, quoted in Cherry *The Politics of Town Planning* (1982), Chap. 4; Address by Mrs. Roe M.P., Parliamentary Under Secretary of State, D.O.E. [1988] J.P.L. 517.

[34] See generally; M.L. Harrison, "Development Control — Influence of Political, Legal and Ideological Factors" (1972) 48 T.P. Rev. 254; Regan, "Pathology of British Land-use Planning" (April 1978) *Local Government Studies*.

[35] For example, Healey, McDougall and Thomas (eds.), *Planning Theory — Prospects for the 1980s* (1982).

[36] See generally, Blowers, *The Limits of Power: The Politics of Local Planning Policy* (1980); Cherry *The Politics of Town Planning* (1982); Goldsmith, *Politics, Planning and the City* (1980); Hayward and Watson (eds.), *Planning Politics and Public Policy* (1975); Keating, *The City that Refused to Die — Glasgow: The Politics of Urban Regeneration* (1988).

[37] See Elkin, *Politics and Land-use Planning: The London Experience* (1974), Chap. 5; McAuslan, *Land, Law and Planning* (1974), p. 360 "The Role of Planning Officials", and p. 401 "The Actual Determination by the Committee."

growth by simplifying the planning system, and concepts such as the Urban Development Area, Enterprise Zones and Simplified Planning Zones represent political manipulation of the planning system to encourage industrial development.[38]

In general, the political will does not favour a truly comprehensive and broadly based planning system, as this is too reminiscent of communist planned economies. This philosophy is manifested in the government approach to the contents of structure plans, which confines policies to land-use factors. Writers may argue for planning to be given an explicit social and economic role, but this is resisted by the politicians. The political context of planning has limited it to a passive and negative character, responding to pressures for development rather than initiating development.[39] Local authorities have few positive planning powers enabling them to take active steps to achieve the policies promoted in development plans. Instead the development control function is emphasised and planning appears negative in character. Treating planning on this application-by-application basis provides no possibility for applying broad theories of social and economic planning. Thus the political framework within which planning operates has placed considerable limitations on what it may achieve.

Planning is also a legal activity, with its powers derived from statute and subject to judicial control, which is a further limiting factor on the extent of planning powers,[40] as will be demonstrated in later chapters. One writer concluded that the judiciary appear sympathetic towards individual property rights at the expense of the public control of land use represented by planning powers.[41] This serves as a reminder that the law and its institutions are not wholly neutral, and that the personal planning theories or values of the judiciary

[38] Redman, "Simplifying the System?" [1989] J.P.L. 563.

[39] Blowers, *supra*.

[40] See generally, McAuslan, *Land, Law and Planning* (1974), "Planning Law's Contribution to Problems of an Urban Society" (1974) 37 M.L.R. 134, "The Plan, the Planners and the Lawyers" 1971 P.L. 247. McEwan, *Planning Law and Ideological Disorder* (1982).

[41] McAuslan, *The Ideologies of Planning Law* (1980), and article of same name (1979) 2 U.L.&P. 1. See also, Griffiths, *The Politics of the Judiciary* (3rd ed. 1985), Chap. 9, in particular, p.202.

must influence its decisions on the breadth of planning powers.

As a result of these diverse influences, only general comments can be made about the extent of planning powers. The objectives attributed to planning powers reflect the prevailing political, legal, social and economic influences. Planning is predominantly concerned with the use of land, but social and economic considerations have a varying influence. Planning powers are exercised to preserve and enhance the environment, but only to the extent permitted by such influences as the political framework within which planning operates. The question "What is planning?" cannot be answered fully, because the activity of planning is not static and it changes or develops to reflect prevailing influences.

Conclusion

The evolution of planning law has not been a linear process, but a pattern of successive actions and reactions, with great leaps and small steps. Despite this fitful evolution, two trends have consistently influenced legislation. The preparation of town planning schemes and development plans has always been slow. Successive Acts have attempted to speed up the preparation process, as well as searching for a way of ensuring flexibility and comprehensiveness. The solution has yet to be found. The problems identified with the present system have changed little since the beginnings of statutory planning: the consequence of the length and complexity of procedures for preparation of development plans is that policies are frequently out of date before the plan is adopted; and plans are excessively long, too detailed and contain policies irrelevant to planning.[42] The other problem has been the delays in the development control process, a consistent problem since 1947.

A criticism frequently made of statutory planning is that it has consistently promised far more than it could hope to

[42] One example of an irrelevant policy is the frequent statement in structure plans that the local authority has declared the area a nuclear-free zone.

deliver. However, this is a result of inflated claims of what planning can achieve, made when the powers available have been insufficient to attain the desired aims. Immediately after major town planning legislation has been passed there have been periods of optimism and enthusiasm in planning, for example, in 1909, 1947 and 1969. However, this has given way to disillusionment once it is realised that what could be achieved was much less than was expected. Since 1947, planners have sought an increased scope for town planning, but central government has consistently taken the view that planning and the development plan is solely concerned with land use and the quality of the physical environment.

After more than 80 years of statutory town planning, it is interesting to trace the evolution of development control. The first planning powers were permissive and geographically limited (1909 Act). After some compulsory planning (1919 Act), planning became voluntary once again, although planning control could be exercised over more areas of land. After the Second World War, planning became both compulsory and comprehensive, covering all land. Since 1947 this has remained the situation, although in the late 80s some control was removed from local authorities. The universal requirement to obtain planning consent for development has been a feature of development control since the 1947 Act. This process is modelled on the voluntary process of interim development control which existed, in some form, since the 1919 Act. The tools of development control have been in existence since 1919, and only their function and importance have changed.

Chapter 2

THE PLANNING SYSTEM

Subsequent chapters examine in detail the important elements of the planning system. However, to appreciate its full magnificence and complexity, one must understand the basic "nuts and bolts" of the system, including the personnel who operate the system, and the tools which they use.

Territorial Limits

Planning control extends only to the mean low water mark around the coast.[1] From this point to the 12-mile limit of British territorial waters, there is no control over activities other than that exercised by the Crown Estate Commissioners in their capacity as landlords of the seabed. This creates an inherent weakness in statutory designations such as National Scenic Areas (Chapter 9), which cannot extend to the seabed and inshore waters beyond low water mark, and arguably prevents effective coastal management. An extension of the jurisdiction of planning authorities to the 12-mile limit has recently been recommended.[2]

Personnel

(a) Parliament

Much of the basic structure of the planning system comes from legislation passed by Parliament in the form of Acts of Parliament and statutory instruments (below).

[1] *Argyll and Bute D.C.* v. *Secretary of State for Scotland*, 1976 S.C. 248; 1977 S.L.T. 33.

[2] Report from the Select Committee on the Environment (1992; H.C.).

(b) European Community

It is an objective of European Community (now European Union) policy to preserve, protect and improve the quality of the environment. The competence of the Community to adopt measures concerning planning has been recognised,[3] subject to the principle of subsidiarity whereby it can only act if Member States cannot achieve the objectives of the proposed action. European Community law has already introduced environmental assessment (Chapter 5) and several statutory designations protecting areas of land (Chapter 9), and further initiatives from Europe can be anticipated.

(c) Secretary of State for Scotland

The Secretary of State for Scotland has executive responsibility for the planning system in Scotland, and is the Scottish equivalent of the Secretary of State for the Environment. This responsibility includes:

(i) initiating new legislation governing the planning system and piloting it through Parliament;

(ii) taking ministerial responsibility for the activities of the Scottish Office Environment Department (S.Env.D.) and the Scottish Office Inquiry Reporters (SOIR) (below);

(iii) drawing up national planning policies and issuing guidance on policy matters in the form of National Planning Policy Guidelines (NPPGs), Planning Advice Notes (PANs) and circulars (see below);

(iv) giving strategic or regional guidance to be taken into account by authorities drawing up development plans (Chapter 3);

(v) approving structure plans and considering, and if necessary calling-in for decision, proposed local plans (Chapter 3);

[3] Maastricht Treaty, art. 130s.

(vi) determining appeals against a range of planning decisions (Chapter 8), normally by delegating the decision to a reporter;
(vii) calling-in applications for planning permission for decision (Chapter 5);
(viii) listing buildings of historical and architectural interest (Chapter 9).

Of course, many of these functions are not carried out by the Secretary of State personally, but on his behalf by the Scottish Office Environment Department, the Scottish Office Inquiry Reporters and Historic Scotland.

In determining appeals and called-in applications, the Secretary of State considers the planning merits of the matter and generally has the same powers, and is subject to the same legal restrictions, as the planning authority.

(d) Scottish Office Inquiry Reporters

The Scottish Office Inquiry Reporters (SOIR) are responsible for administering planning appeals and the public inquiries system (both for planning and other statutory regimes). Where the Planning Acts require an appeal against a planning decision to be submitted to the Secretary of State, the notice of appeal should be forwarded to SOIR who will advise on further procedure and organise the administrative aspects of the appeal.

SOIR maintain a list of reporters to hear appeals, either by written submissions or at a public inquiry, and to chair public inquiries. There is a small core of full-time reporters supplemented by part-time reporters. All reporters are professionally qualified, and have experience in planning or a related discipline. SOIR appoint a reporter to each appeal or inquiry, and the parties have no say in this process.

A wide range of planning appeals has been delegated by the Secretary of State to reporters for decision, to the extent that over 90% of appeals are now decided by reporters. The Secretary of State retains the right to "claw-back" for his decision any appeal within these delegated classes. In a delegated appeal, the reporter hears the evidence at the inquiry or considers the written submissions and issues his decision letter. Where the decision is to be made by the Secretary of State, the reporter hears the case and reports to the Secretary of State, usually with a recommendation on its disposal. The decision on the appeal is made by the Secretary of State who can reject any recommendation made in the report.

The reporter is the master of procedure at a public local inquiry. He is entitled to adopt an interventionist role and to ask witnesses questions, rather than merely note the evidence brought out during examination by the parties. In reaching conclusions, the reporter is entitled to make use of his planning experience and expertise.[4] In common with the planning authority, the reporter is obliged to take account of all material considerations and not merely those raised by the parties at the inquiry or in their written submissions.[5] Where the reporter identifies a planning issue which he considers may be material to the decision, but which has not been addressed by either party, the reporter is not entitled to reach a conclusion on that issue and found upon it as a factor material to his decision without giving the parties an opportunity of commenting upon it.[6]

(e) Planning Authorities

It is left to the planning authorities to operate the grass-roots level of the planning system. They are responsible for implementing the policies of the Secretary of State, preparing development plans, determining applications for planning permission, and enforcing planning controls.

The division of functions between the planning authorities in Scotland is more difficult to describe than it is to operate in practice. In general, the district councils are responsible for the preparation of local plans (Chapter 3), the determination of applications for planning permission (Chapter 5), and enforcement (Chapter 7), while the regional councils have responsibility for structure plans and may call-in for decision

[4] *Narden Services* v. *Secretary of State for Scotland*, 1993 S.L.T. 871.
[5] But see *Anwar* v. *Secretary of State for Scotland*, 1992 S.C.L.R. 875.
[6] *Anduff Holdings* v. *Secretary of State for Scotland*, 1992 S.L.T. 696; *cf. Ladbroke Racing Ltd.* v. *Secretary of State for Scotland*, 1990 S.C.L.R. 705.

planning applications which have either regional or strategic significance. However, Highland, Borders, and Dumfries and Galloway Regional Councils, and Western Isles, Shetland and Orkney Islands Councils, are general planning authorities and within their areas exercise the powers vested in both the district and regional councils in other areas.[7] (Unless an indication is given to the contrary, in this book the term "planning authority" is used to refer to both district and general planning authorities.)

This division of functions is not without tensions. While the district councils have most of the planning powers, a special procedure must be followed if these powers are to be exercised contrary to the provisions of the structure plan. Following the introduction of the plan-led system (see development plans, below), they will be obliged to act in accordance with the provisions of the structure plan unless material considerations dictate otherwise.[8] Also, district councils are often required to consult the regional councils, which have the power to call-in applications for their decision or to act following any default by the district councils. However, this two-tier system has generally operated well. The Scottish Office proposals announced in July 1993 for the reform of local government introduce an element of uncertainty about the future shape of the planning system at grass-roots level.

(f) Councillors

The planning powers vested in the district, regional and islands councils are exercised by the elected councillors, either in a full meeting of the council or a planning sub-committee. Although more minor decisions may be delegated to planning officers for decision, the councillors will typically take decisions involving adoption of planning policies and development plans (see below and Chapter 3), determination of applications for planning permission (Chapter 5), and decisions on enforcment action (Chapter 7).

In making decisions on the exercise of these powers, the councillors are advised by the Director of Planning and the

[7] Local Government (Scotland) Act 1973, s. 172, as amended.
[8] TCPSA, s. 18A.

officers in his department. However, they are not bound to follow the recommendation of the professional planners.

There is (and will always be) a continuing debate about the wisdom of conferring the final say on planning decisions to councillors. Some argue that the decisions are best left to the professional planning officers, rather than councillors who may have little or no knowledge of the planning system. However, others would respond that these officers are too hidebound by their professional theories and that the councillors can be relied upon to bring common sense into decision-making, if necessary acting contrary to the advice given by the planning officers. Furthermore, our democratic ideals of government frown upon vesting power in unelected officials. However, the democratic pressures upon councillors, particularly from concerned local residents, may not always result in the best decision from a planning viewpoint. All that can be said with any confidence is that each side of the debate can be supported by examples of planning decisions proving the strength of their argument. Most of those involved in the planning system are comfortable with the present decision-making process, if perhaps not entirely happy.

Where planning powers are conferred by statute upon the planning authority, the power must be exercised by the authority and no other person or body. However, the authority can competently delegate its powers to sub-committees (of councillors) or planning officers.[9] Where a discretionary power is conferred, the authority can (or is sometimes obliged to) take into account the views of other bodies and persons on how that power should be exercised, but cannot allow those views necessarily to dictate its decision.[10]

The procedures for determining applications for planning permission vary between authorities. Some have delegated extensive decision-making powers to planning officers. Others operate a form of list system whereby the councillors sitting on the planning committee receive lists of applications and the officers' recommendations thereon. Unless a councillor

[9] Local Government (Scotland) Act 1973, s. 56, as amended.
[10] *Ynys Mon B.C.* v. *Secretary of State for Wales* [1993] J.P.L. 225.

indicates that an application should be discussed at the committee meeting, the application is deemed to be determined in accordance with the recommendations and the decision is issued under delegated powers. This form of system reduces the number of applications debated by the councillors. Many authorities still conform to the traditional approach of requiring all applications other than those of a minor and non-controversial nature to be decided at the committee meeting.

(g) Planning Officers

Councillors are rarely professional planners and may have limited knowledge of the planning system. Their council duties are not paid as a full-time job and they cannot be expected to attend to the administrative work required before decisions can be made. As a result, councillors require the advice and administrative assistance of the planning department.

Members of the planning department are responsible for administration of all planning functions up to the point at which a decision must be taken by the councillors, or appropriate delegates. In making the decision, the councillors must take into account the professional recommendation of the planning department, but may choose to reach a contrary decision. It is therefore vital to appreciate that any views or advice offered by a planning officer cannot dictate the eventual decision by the councillors and will not bind them.[11] However, officers normally have enough experience of the decisions reached by their councillors to be able to predict their decisions with a reasonable degree of accuracy, and their advice should be seriously considered. Planning officers and clerical members of the planning department have responsibility for:

(i) maintenance of the statutory registers which must be available for public inspection (below);

[11] *Western Fish Products Ltd.* v. *Penwith D.C.* [1981] 2 All E.R. 204; *cf. Camden L.B.C.* v. *Secretary of State for the Environment* [1993] E.G.C.S. 83.

(ii) drafting development plan proposals and organising publicity and consultation in relation to those proposals;
(iii) pre-application discussions with potential developers, which may include advising on relevant policies and possible alterations to proposals;
(iv) responding to communications or queries from members of the public (most authorities maintain a scheme whereby a duty planning officer is always available to speak to members of the public);
(v) preparing reports on applications for planning permission and, where appropriate, deciding these applications in terms of delegated powers (below);
(vi) preparing cases for appeals and giving evidence on behalf of the authority at inquiries (the Royal Town Planning Institute (RTPI) advise their members not to give evidence where a decision has been made contrary to their recommendation and their professional opinion will not allow them to support that decision, not least because their true opinion is likely to be exposed during cross-examination and used to support the opposing side);
(vii) checking compliance with planning consents or the need for planning permission to be obtained for works, and recommending to the councillors when enforcement action should be taken (Chapter 9).

The extent of the duties of the planning officers can be seen in the procedure leading up to determinations of applications for planning permission (Chapter 5). An application is submitted to the department. Compliance with the statutory requirements is checked, and the application registered. Responsibility for handling the application is given to a planning officer, who is a qualified planner. The officer will consult the appropriate bodies in connection with the application. He will prepare a report to the councillors, taking account of the development plan, consultation responses, representations received from the public and any other material considerations. This report will recommend to the councillors how they should determine the application. If the Director of Planning (the chief planning officer) does not have delegated powers to decide the application, the report is presented to the councillors who will make their decision.

Most councils have formally delegated the exercise of various planning powers in minor or uncontroversial circumstances to the Director of Planning. For example, the Director may be authorised to decide all applications for planning unless the application is either recommended for approval contrary to the provisions of the development plan, it raises controversial or major planning issues, a councillor requests that the application be decided by the committee, or objections to the proposed development are received.

Membership of the RTPI is usually a prerequisite for employment as a planning officer. The RTPI has laid down professional standards of conduct to be met by its members and will investigate complaints concerning failure to comply with these standards.

(h) Developers

Developers are the life-blood of the planning system. For all the views of the planning authority expressed in the development plan, there are few opportunities to put these views into practice unless and until developers seek permission for proposed developments. Although the requirement to obtain planning permission (Chapter 4) is an onerous burden placed upon landowners, the planning system protects them from over-restrictive control by providing rights to challenge planning decisions (Chapter 8) and imposing a policy in favour of development whereby planning authorities must justify refusals of permission (Chapter 5). The inability to obtain permission in some circumstances undoubtedly leads to dissatisfaction. However, the development control system also provides landlowner/developers with some guarantee that their amenity will not be adversely affected by development on surrounding land.

Although accepting the need for the planning system, developers complain that the process for obtaining permission is too slow, that planning officers and authorities have no sense of commercial reality, and that there is too much interference with matters of detail, such as design, which are not planning issues.

(i) Official Bodies

Depending upon the nature of a development, various official bodies must be consulted and asked for their views, such as Scottish Natural Heritage, the river purification boards and roads authorities. These bodies also have a role to play in the formulation of development-plan policies and proposals. However, their views cannot dictate the decision reached by the planning authority.[12]

(j) Public Interest

The planning system is broadly intended to control development in the public interest. Without interest and input from members of the public, the system cannot maintain the public confidence which it requires to function efficiently.

Chapter 10 examines public participation in the planning system in more detail. Both the development plan and development control parts of the system contain many requirements for matters to be publicised to alert members of the public to their opportunity to lodge representations and have their views taken into account as part of the decision-making process.

The weakness in the planning system perceived by members of the public is their lack of any right of appeal against a decision to grant planning permission. This omission confines them to use of the judicial review procedure (described in Chapter 8), which only allows the legality and not the merits of the decision to be challenged, and is therefore of limited value. As Chapter 10 explains, this omission can be linked to the presumption in favour of development. Put simply, to require a landowner to obtain permission before developing his land is restrictive enough, but to allow a member of the public to challenge any grant of permission would be going too far. However, this leaves the unsatisfactory position that members of the public have no means of reversing a decision which they consider to be wrong on planning merits, but which was made legally.

[12] *Ynys Mon B.C.* v. *Secretary of State for Wales*, see n. 10.

(k) New Towns

The new town development corporations have no planning powers as such. However, in terms of Special Development Orders made for each new town, other than Glenrothes, they are entitled to authorise development within land which they own or have previously owned which conforms with the proposals approved by the Secretary of State in those orders. This authorisation is equivalent to a grant of planning permission.

(l) Courts

According to British constitutional theory, Parliament makes laws and the courts apply those laws. The courts have been responsible for fleshing out many of the statutory planning provisions, through the process of statutory interpretation. For example, the seemingly wide discretionary power vested in planning authorities to impose "such conditions as they think fit" is now subject to a series of legal restrictions declared by the courts (Chapter 6). In addition, through the use of common-law concepts such as natural justice and fairness, the courts seek to secure procedural fairness within the planning system.

The role of the courts must be contrasted with that of the Secretary of State/reporter deciding an appeal. The jurisdiction of the courts is limited to reviewing the decision to ensure that all legal requirements have been met, and the judges are not entitled to intervene where they consider that the decision is wrong on its merits. Even where a decision is declared to be illegal, the court cannot change that decision but must quash it and return the matter to the decision-maker for a fresh decision to be made in a legal manner. In contrast, the Secretary of State/reporter determines the matter as if application had been made to him in the first instance, and is entitled to reach a decision on the merits of the matter.

The powers of the courts are examined in Chapter 8.

(m) Ombudsman

Complaints relating to both decisions and actions of planning authorities can now be made direct to the Commissioner for

Local Administration in Scotland—the Ombudsman (Chapter 8).

Law and Policy

The planning system is a mixture of law and policy.[13] Planning authorities and other participants must act according to the law, and compliance mechanisms, such as judicial review and prosecution, exist to enforce the law. The skeletal legal framework is fleshed out by policy, which is necessary to ensure that the wide discretionary planning powers are exercised consistently, both within districts and throughout the country.

One of the keys to understanding the planning system is appreciating the difference between law, which must be observed at all times, and policies, which are not binding, with departures from policy being competent in individual cases.

Law

The Act and Treaty of Union (1707) guaranteed the preservation of Scots law and a separate Scots legal system. The distinct nature of Scots law is carried into planning law, with different Acts of Parliament and statutory instruments applying to Scotland (some apply to the whole of Britain). However, despite separate legal provisions, the law in Scotland is very similar to that applicable to England and Wales, with many of the differences relating to the separate Scottish local government and court structure. Where appropriate, subsequent chapters highlight the differences, to avoid any confusion. In consequence of the similarities between the two sets of planning law, reference is made to court decisions from England and Wales in the absence of any decision of the Scottish courts.

[13] Henderson (ed.) *Scottish Planning Sourcebook* (1989), contains the text of selected items of planning law and national policy.

(a) *Acts of Parliament*

The basic framework of the planning system in Scotland is laid down by the Town and Country Planning (Scotland) Act 1972 (referred to in subsequent chapters as the TCPSA). This Act of Parliament has been substantially amended since 1972, most recently by the Planning and Compensation Act 1991 (the PCA), with few sections remaining unchanged. As a result, care must be taken to ensure that where any particular provision of the TCPSA is relevant to a case, all amendments to that provision are considered.[14] It should also be noted that several of the PCA amendments have yet to be brought into force. Subsequent chapters refer to the important forthcoming amendments. The law in England and Wales underwent a consolidation exercise in 1990, with the result that four updated Acts of Parliament replaced the Town and Country Planning Act 1971 which, like the Scottish Act, had been substantially amended. For several years now the Scottish Office have discussed a similar consolidation exercise for Scotland, but with no result. It is an unfortunate truth of our legal system that as soon as a consolidated Act of Parliament is passed it requires amendment. A suitable breathing space for consolidation to occur between amending statutes is rare.

In addition to the TCPSA, there are several other statutes which affect the planning system, such as the Local Government (Scotland) Act 1973 and the Wildlife and Countryside Act 1981.

(b) *Statutory Instruments*

The TCPSA and other statutes confer power upon the Secretary of State to prepare regulations (also variously known as statutory instruments or delegated legislation). These are placed before Parliament and published by HMSO. In many cases these regulations prescribe detailed procedural codes for various parts of the planning system. The principal statutory instruments affecting the planning system in

[14] Young (ed.) *Greens Scottish Planning Acts* (1993), contains an updated version of TCPSA, together with relevant parts of other Acts.

Scotland are the Use Classes Order, the General Permitted Development Order and the General Development Procedure Order (the latter two orders were previously contained in the single General Development Order).[15] Reference to these and other statutory instruments are made in subsequent chapters.

(c) *European Community Directives*

As noted above, the influence of the European Community (now the European Union) on planning is increasing. Directives, such as that on Environmental Assessment, oblige Member States to incorporate provisions into their national law within a specified period. If the provision has not been incorporated by the end of this period, an individual may be able to rely on the provisions of the directive when bringing an action in the Scottish courts.[16] This is known as the direct effect of European Community law.

(d) *Case law*

Under our unwritten constitution, Parliament is responsible for making laws, and the courts are responsible for interpreting those laws and declaring how they should apply in particular circumstances. Court decisions can therefore be used as authoritative statements on the meaning of legal provisions and their application in practice. Within the legal system, court decisions form precedents which often bind judges hearing future cases to decide those cases in a particular way. Previous decisions can therefore be used as an indication of how a future case might be decided. The weight to be given to a court decision depends upon various factors such as the position of the court in the hierarchy, the planning expertise of the judge(s), and the extent to which the decision is applicable only to the facts and circumstances of the particular case. Subsequent chapters refer to court

[15] Young, *supra* lists some 45 statutory instruments bearing on planning.
[16] For example, *Kincardine and Deeside D.C.* v. *Forestry Commissioners*, 1992 S.L.T. 1180.

decisions where these decisions explain or illustrate how a legal provision may be applied.[17]

Despite Scotland having a different legal system from the rest of Britain, there are few differences between the planning laws and widespread use is made in Scotland of case law from the English courts. While a decision of an English court (other than the House of Lords) is not binding on a Scottish judge, it will be very persuasive.

(e) *Comment*

It is of concern that the planning system, which is supposedly open to public participation, is regulated by such a myriad of legal sources. For example, the landowner who wishes to know whether planning permission is required for a proposed development must consult the TCPSA, as amended by several other Acts, the General Permitted Development Order and the Use Classes Order. Assuming the landlowner can obtain copies, he then has to interpret these provisions. It is a common criticism that the drafting of Acts of Parliament renders them impossible to read and difficult to understand, and planning law is one of the prime examples of this criticism. It is little wonder that our landowner gives up in disgust, only to be threatened by the planning authority with enforcement action for failing to obtain planning permission. When one of the underlying principles of Scots law is that ignorance of the law is no excuse, it seems unacceptable that an activity such as planning, which touches on the activities of so many members of the public, is regulated by laws which are often inaccessible to those persons, even after their best efforts.

Policy

Contrary to popular belief, the law supports the use of policy, within certain confines. Policies promote consistent decision-making which, in turn, ensures that every person is treated equally and in the same manner. Policies also provide a

[17] If fuller reference to case law is required, see Young and Rowan-Robinson *Scottish Planning Law and Procedure* (1985).

degree of certainty. What the law seeks to discourage is the blind, unthinking application of policy, which can lead to injustice in some cases. In every case, the decision-maker should consider whether the circumstances of that case justify making an exception to the policy. As has already been observed, one of the keys to understanding the planning system is appreciating the difference between law, which must be observed at all times, and policies, which are not binding, with departures from policy being competent in individual cases.

Consistency does not mean immutability of policies or their interpretation. The decision-maker need not adhere slavishly to a policy or a previous interpretation of it, but must clearly explain the reasons for not doing so in a particular case. Fairness may require notice of the change to be given to affected parties (Chapter 8 discusses the concept of legitimate expectations). For example, an appeal decision was quashed on the ground of unfairness where, by reason of the decision-maker's inconsistency in the interpretation and application of his policy, a person dealing with him had been taken by surprise and had had no adequate opportunity to meet the new approach before the relevant decision was made.[18]

(a) Development Plans

The development plan, consisting of the structure and local plan for the area, contains the policies and proposals of the planning authority with regard to use of the land in that area (Chapter 3). When exercising planning powers, the authority is generally required to have regard to the provisions of the development plan, so far as material, and to any other material considerations. From 7 March 1994, when the relevant provisions of the PCA are brought into force, the authority require to exercise such powers in accordance with the provisions of the plan unless material considerations dictate otherwise (commonly referred to as "the plan-led system").[19] This does not amount to a requirement to always

[18] *Barnet Meeting Room Trust* v. *Secretary of State for the Environment* [1993] J.P.L. 739.

[19] TCPSA, ss. 18A and 26(1).

follow the policies and proposals contained in the plan, as is recognised by provision of a procedure for granting permission contrary to the terms of the plan (Chapter 5).

Draft development plans are a material consideration in the planning process, but do not carry the full weight of a development plan until approved/adopted (Chapters 3 and 5).

(b) Scottish Office

The Scottish Office Environment Department (S.Env.D.) periodically issues statements of national planning policies to planning authorities.[20] These form one of the material considerations to which the planning authority must have regard in exercising its planning powers, but the authority is not bound to comply with the policy. As the policy will be applied by the Secretary of State/reporter in determining any appeal against the exercise of power by the authority, the sanction underlying such statements of policy is that by failing to comply with the policy the authority risks losing such an appeal and having to pay the costs incurred by the appellant (Chapter 8).

The national policy framework is undergoing a change. Previously circulars issued by the S.Env.D., and its predecessor the S.D.D., contained advice and guidance on both policy and procedural matters. In future the S.Env.D. intend circulars to be used primarily to explain the operation of new legislation and other administrative procedures. National Planning Guidelines are being replaced by National Planning Policy Guidelines (NPPGs), which provide statements of planning policy on land use and related matters. Planning Advice Notes (PANs) are intended to identify and disseminate good practice and to provide advice.

In the absence of any S.Env.D. policy, reference can be made to the policy of the Department of the Environment which, though it applies to England and Wales, often represents the policy which would be laid down by S.Env.D. (Chapter 5).

[20] These statements are not published, but are available on request from Scottish Office Environment Department; *The Scottish Planning Sourcebook* (see n. 13) contains copies of many policy statements.

(c) *Non-Statutory Policies*

While it is clearly preferable for all relevant policies of the planning authority to be contained in the development plan, there are instances where this is not possible. An urgent policy response may be required to an issue which has come to prominence since adoption of the plan. Alternatively, a policy may require to be stated in such detail as is not suitable for inclusion in the plan, such as development briefs for particular sites or design guides for certain types of development. As a result, policies other than those contained in the development plan may be applicable to an exercise of planning powers by the authority (such policies are commonly referred to as non-statutory policies). These policies form one of the material considerations to be taken into account by the authority.

(d) *Directions by Secretary of State*

The Secretary of State has power to issue directions to planning authorities restricting the grant of planning permission for a particular development or type of development.[21] A variety of directions have been issued authorising authorities to grant permission for certain types of development only after specified procedures have been followed. These often include notification of the proposed decision to the Secretary of State to allow exercise of his call-in powers (Chapter 5).[22] The directions are attached to circulars issued by S.Env.D., and are not published.

Development Plans and Development Control

The planning system can be divided into two parts: development plans and development control.

The development plan and its significance for the planning system is discussed in the next chapter. The development

[21] Town and Country Planning (General Development Procedure) (Scotland) Order 1992, art. 17.

[22] *Greens Scottish Planning Acts* (n. 14) contains the text of all current directions.

plan is an expression of the views of the planning authority with regard to the future use of land within its district. In this sense it operates as authoritative guidance to developers on the views of the authority. However, the plan does not relieve developers of the need to obtain planning permission, even in circumstances where the proposed development is entirely in accordance with the provisions of the plan. The development control process provides the authority with the opportunity to prevent development which is not in accordance with its views as expressed in the plan.

What authorities lack are positive powers to achieve the objectives outlined in the plan other than compulsory purchase powers. At present the function of the development plan is to encourage developers by showing which developments are likely to be given permission, However, if these developments are not attractive to developers, no application for planning permission will be forthcoming. The complete vision of the planning authority will be replaced by piecemeal development.

Unlike the passive development planning, development control is a negative process. If work amounts to "development" and does not enjoy permitted development rights, planning permission must be obtained before that work can commence. The development control process determines when permission is required (Chapter 4), the procedure for obtaining that permission (Chapter 5), the restrictions which may be placed on any permission granted (Chapter 6), and the enforcement action which may be taken if work commences without permission or in breach of the terms and conditions of a permission (Chapter 7). Where an application for planning permission is lodged, the development control process involves determination of that application according to the law, policy and the planning merits of the proposed development.

Effect of Planning Permission

The consequences flowing from a grant of planning permission are examined in Chapter 5. Every grant of planning permission carries a time limit for the commencement of development. If no start is made within that time limit, the permission expires. Once a start has been made, the permission exists in perpetuity and there is no time limit for completing the development, unless there is an express condition attached to the permission specifying such a time limit or the planning authority serve a completion notice. As a result, it is only possible to take enforcement action where a negative condition, such as a restriction on use, is breached or where there is a failure to comply with a positive obligation which is subject to an express time limit.

Planning Information

For the planning system to operate efficiently and maintain the confidence of all involved in or affected by it, information must be freely available. Planning authorities are required to keep registers detailing such matters as the progress and decision of applications for planning permission, enforcement action, and the progress with alteration or repeal and replacement of development plans.[23] These registers must be kept up-to-date and available for public inspection, along with copies of the development plan. Copies of the agenda for the planning committee meeting and any reports to committee must be available to the public at least three days prior to any meeting.[24]

In contrast to the availability of information from planning authorities, the various items of law and policy which are relevant to the planning systems are not easily obtainable and in many cases are difficult to understand even if an up to date copy can be obtained.

[23] For example, TCPSA, s. 31, as amended, and art. 10 of the Development Procedure Order 1992, as amended.

[24] Local Government (Scotland) Act 1973, s. 50B.

Chapter 3

DEVELOPMENT PLANS

Since 1947 the development plan has been a central feature of the planning system. This role will be heightened following the introduction of the plan-led system (below). The plan is an expression of the views of the planning authority (possibly as modified by the Secretary of State) with regard to use of the land within its district, formulated after consultation with official bodies and the general public. It also provides the framework within which the authority exercises its day-to-day control of development. Rather than being a prescriptive rulebook, the development plan provides authoritative guidance to those wishing to develop land.

The deficiency associated with development plans lies in the lack of any positive power conferred upon the planning authority to implement its views as expressed in the plan. Unless the authority has a legal interest in the land concerned, it cannot implement the proposals identified in the plan. These proposals therefore amount to no more than encouragement for developers to submit applications for planning permission for those proposed land uses. In this sense planning authorities have few positive planning powers and are restricted to the negative role of approving or rejecting proposals made by developers, which inevitably leads to piecemeal implementation of the development plan proposals. With the onset of the recession in the early 1990s, many authorities took a more active role in attracting potential developers to undertake development projects. This active role extended to assembling sites, often through use of compulsory purchase powers, and obtaining planning permission for the development.

With the exception of Borders, Highland, and Dumfries and Galloway regional councils and the islands councils in

Orkney, Shetland and Western Isles who are responsible for preparing both structure and local plans, the regional council is responsible for preparing the structure plan and the district councils prepare the local plans for the districts within the region. Structure plans require the approval of the Secretary of State, who may impose modifications, but local plans are approved by the initiating authority, although the Secretary of State has powers to call-in local plans for decision.

Plan-led System: Interaction Between Development Plan and Development Control

Although the development plan expresses the views of the planning authority with regard to the use of the land within its district, it does not remove the need to seek planning permission for development (Chapter 4). Indeed, even a development which conforms to the provisions of the plan is not guaranteed to obtain planning permission. The development plan system can therefore be distinguished from the rigidity of the zoning systems used by many other countries, whereby proposals in accordance with the zoning either cannot be refused consent or enjoy deemed consent without the necessity for an application (as in the British system of enterprise zones and simplified planning zones, Chapter 9).

When determining an application for planning permission, the planning authority is directed to have regard to the provisions of the development plan, so far as material to the application, and to any other material considerations.[1] When the amendments contained in the Planning and Compensation Act 1991 are brought into force on 7 March 1994 the application will require to be determined in accordance with the provisions of the development plan unless material considerations indicate otherwise.[2] This will introduce what is often referred to as the plan-led system. It will create a presumption in favour of permission being granted for development proposals which are in accordance with the provisions of the plan, but will not amount to a requirement

[1] TCPSA, s. 26(1), as amended.
[2] s. 18A.

that the authority decide all applications according to the terms of the plan. Instead, any relevant policies in the plan will be noted first. Attention then turns to other material considerations (Chapter 5). These may dictate that the application be decided contrary to the terms of the plan. A material consideration does not require any special weight to overcome the presumption in favour of the development plan.[3]

Until the plan has been approved by the Secretary of State (structure plans) or adopted by the authority (local plans), the policies and proposals in the plan are no more than a material consideration.[4]

The importance of the development plan is further emphasised by the special procedures which must be followed by the planning authority when it proposes to grant permission for a development which is contrary to the provisions of the development plan (Chapter 5).

Survey and Monitoring

Planning authorities have a duty to survey their districts as a first step towards preparation (and revisal) of the development plan.[5] Following the initial survey, fresh surveys may be carried out as the authority thinks fit. The matters to be examined as part of the survey and to be kept under review thereafter are those which may be expected to affect the development of the district or the planning of its development, including:

(a) the principal physical and economic characteristics of the district, including the principal purposes for which land is used, and of any neighbouring districts which might be expected to affect the district (the authority should consult with the authority responsible for that district about those matters);
(b) the size, composition and distribution of the population of the district (whether resident or otherwise);

[3] *St. Albans D.C.* v. *Secretary of State for the Environment* [1993] J.P.L. 370.
[4] *City of Glasgow D.C.* v. *Secretary of State for Scotland and William Hill (Scotland) Ltd.*, 1992 S.C.L.R. 453; S.P.L.P. 36:56.
[5] ss. 4, as amended, and 9(4A).

(c) the communications, transport system and traffic of the district (and of any neighbouring districts so far as they may be expected to affect the district);
(d) any other relevant considerations; and
(e) any changes already projected in any of these matters and the effect which those changes are likely to have on the development of the district or the planning of such development.

Following the initial survey and adoption of the development plan, the planning authority can anticipate the need to alter or replace the development plan by keeping these matters under review and monitoring changes in the environment, development pressures and political priorities, and the inter-relationships of these changes. As part of this monitoring process, some authorities prepare an annual or biennial monitoring statement indicating the extent to which the plan strategy and its component policies are still relevant and whether any alterations are required.

Development Plan

Although the TCPSA refers to "the development plan," there are actually two separate plans[6]:

(a) the structure plan, and any alterations to it, together with the notice(s) of approval by the Secretary of State; and
(b) the local plan, and any alterations to it, together with a copy of the resolution(s) of adoption by the planning authority or the notice(s) of approval by the Secretary of State.

As at November 1993, there are operative structure plans covering the whole of Scotland. Some are originals, often with alterations, while others have been replaced and the replacement altered. Replacement plans are in progress in Dumfries and Galloway, Fife, Grampian, Tayside and Lothian regions. The structure plans in Orkney and Shetland are under review. The Strathclyde Structure Plan 1992 Update is under way.

[6] s. 17, as amended.

Highland Regional Council is preparing an alteration to its structure plan in relation to the indicative forestry strategy.

In contrast, only 81 per cent. of Scotland is covered by an adopted local plan, even after 18 years. Although preparatory work is underway in most of the remaining areas, there are some areas where the work of preparing the local plan has yet to begin. The age of plans is a problem, as 80 per cent. of adopted local plans are over five years old, and 25 per cent. over 10 ten years old. 72 replacement plans are under preparation, and alterations are being made to a further 25 plans.[7]

STRUCTURE PLAN

The structure plan is intended to deal with strategic matters and statements of broad policy, the details of which will be fleshed out by the local plan. Responsibility for preparing the structure plan rests with the regional and islands councils.[8] With the consent of, or as required by, the Secretary of State, a structure plan may relate to part only of the district or consist of a series of plans relating to different parts of the district.[9] All structure plans require to be submitted to the Secretary of State for approval before the plan can take effect, and the Secretary of State can impose modifications contrary to the wishes of the authority.

Structure plans have two main functions:

(a) to indicate policies and proposals concerning the scale and general location of new development; and
(b) to provide a regional policy framework for accommodating development.

More generally, the structure plan provides a context for local plans, a framework for private and public sector investment and the promotion of development, and the basis for

[7] All statistics: "The Planning Bulletin" published by the Scottish Office Environment Department (Issue 7, May 1993 and Issue 8, November 1993).
[8] Local Government (Scotland) Act 1973, s. 172, as amended, and Sched. 22, Pt. I.
[9] TCPSA, s. 5(7), as amended, and Local Government (Scotland) Act 1973, s. 174(1).

decision-making on planning applications and appeals which, individually or cumulatively, raise issues of regional significance.

Structure plans are intended to be built around a vision of an area extending beyond currently programmed developments and provide a long-term perspective on the balance to be struck between development and conservation. This long-term view will normally require a time horizon extending at least 10 years beyond the expected date of approval of the plan.[10]

Content

Issues covered in the structure plan normally include urban and rural strategies; new housing; major industrial, business, retail and other employment-generating developments; regional transportation and infrastructure; urban and rural environments; mineral working and protection of mineral resources; waste disposal, land reclamation and re-uses; tourism, leisure and recreation; and indicative forestry strategies.[11] The plan may also identify action areas selected for comprehensive treatment by development, redevelopment or improvement, and the nature of the treatment selected.[12]

The structure plan is a written statement, accompanied by diagrams, drawings and other descriptive matter to explain or illustrate the proposals in the plan. These form part of the plan,[13] but in the event of any inconsistency the provisions of the written statement prevail.[14] The written statement is accompanied by a key diagram (not on a map base) which shows at a glance the policies and general proposals applicable to areas within the region, allowing reference to be made to these policies and proposals within the written statement, without reading the entire plan.[15]

[10] PAN 37, "Structure Planning," paras. 1, 2, 20 and 21.
[11] *Ibid.*, para. 17.
[12] TCPSA, s. 5(5). Provisions for comprehensive development areas have been repealed.
[13] s. 5(3) and (6), as amended.
[14] Town and Country Planning (Structure and Local Plans) (Scotland) Regulations 1983 (S.I. 1983 No. 1590), reg. 10.
[15] Reg. 9.

The written statement contains[16]:

(a) the authority's policies and general proposals in respect of the development and other use of land in the region, including measures for the conservation of the natural beauty and amenity of the land, the improvement of the physical environment and the management of traffic;
(b) the relationship of the proposals to general proposals for the development and other use of land in neighbouring regions which might be expected to affect the region covered by the structure plan;
(c) the existing social, economic and physical structure of the region to which the plan relates and the needs and opportunities for change;
(d) the resources likely to be available for the carrying out of the policies and general proposals formulated in the plan;
(e) the broad criteria to be applied as respects the control of development in the region, including guidance on the application of these criteria, where appropriate, in local plans; and
(f) such other matters as the planning authority considers relevant.

The written statement should be laid out so that the policies and proposals are clearly distinguishable from the other contents. A reasoned justification of the policies and proposals by reference to the results of the survey and any other information should also be included.[17]

In formulating its policies and general proposals, the planning authority must secure that the policies and proposals are justified by the results of the survey and by any other information obtained. It must also have regard to current policies with respect to the economic planning and development of the region as a whole and the resources likely to be available for the carrying out of the structure plan proposals.[18]

Procedure for Preparation or Alteration of Structure Plan

At various points in the procedure described below and in Fig. 3.1 the planning authority or the Secretary of State is

[16] s. 5(3), as amended; reg. 7.
[17] Reg. 6.
[18] s. 5(4).

required to give notice by advertisement. This requirement is satisfied by publication of a notice in the Edinburgh Gazette and, in each of two successive weeks, in at least one local newspaper circulating in the region.

Fig. 3.1 Preparation/Alteration of Structure Plan

Survey

↓

Notice of Intention to prepare plan published (publication of Issues Report)

↓

Consultative Draft Plan published

↓

Finalised Plan published and placed on deposit

↓

6 week period to lodge objections with Secretary of State

↓

Returned to Authority for additional publicity ⟵⟶ Consideration by Secretary of State ⟷ Examination in Public

↓

Approves, modifies or rejects plan

↓

Plan published

↓

6 weeks for Application to Court of Session challenging validity of plan

(a) *Survey*

The procedure for preparing a structure plan commences with the authority undertaking a survey of the area and publishing the report of the results of the survey. The information in the report forms the basis on which the policies and proposals to be contained in the structure plan are prepared.

(b) *Advertisement of Intention to Prepare/the Issues Report*

Notice is given by newspaper advertisement of the intention of the planning authority to prepare a structure plan.[19] Adequate publicity must also be given to the matters which are proposed to be included in the plan. The planning authority can comply with these requirements by publication of an Issues Report, seeking views on potential issues to be tackled by the plan. The Issues Report performs the dual function of stimulating interest and providing a structure for responses from the public.

(c) *Consultative Draft Plan*

The consultative draft plan is published by the authority after considering responses to the survey report and/or Issues Report. It is presented in substantially the same form that the written statement in the adopted structure plan will take, and contains the matters which the authority propose to include in that plan.

Notice of publication of the consultative draft plan will be given by advertisement, stating that representations in relation to the plan should be lodged with the authority within a specified period of not less than four weeks.[20] Copies of the plan are sent by the authority to all other planning authorities which are likely to be affected by the proposals

[19] Reg. 11.
[20] s. 6(1), as amended; reg. 3.

(including local authorities within the district to which the plan relates), the new town corporation (where the district includes a new town), and other appropriate bodies such as Scottish Natural Heritage and Historic Scotland.[21]

(d) Finalised Plan

All representations and responses from the consulted bodies are considered by the authority, together with all statements of government policy, and the finalised plan produced. If there are substantial changes to the draft plan, the authority may advertise the opportunity to lodge representations in connection with these changes and reconsult the various bodies for their views.

Following the adoption of the plan by resolution of the authority, the finalised draft plan and report of the survey are placed on deposit. Two certified copies of the plan are submitted to the Secretary of State for approval, accompanied by a report of the survey and a statement of the steps taken to publicise the report and the right to make representations thereon, the opportunity offered to make such representations and the consultations with other authorities and bodies.[22] The publicity and consultation statement should also clearly indicate which parts of the draft plan were amended to take account of representations received.

Notice is given by newspaper advertisement of the placing of the plan on deposit and its submission to the Secretary of State, and of the right to submit objections to the plan to the Secretary of State within a six week period.[23] Copies of the plan must be made available for public inspection, and be accompanied by a statement of this time limit for lodging objections to the Secretary of State.[24] An entry is made in all the planning registers in the district.

[21] Local Government (Scotland) Act 1973, s. 174(2); reg. 4.
[22] TCPSA, s. 6(3); reg. 12.
[23] Reg. 13.
[24] s. 6(2).

(e) *Approval by Secretary of State*

At the end of the six week deposit period the plan is considered by the Secretary of State. If he considers that the publicity procedures have not been carried out properly, the plan is returned to the authority with a statement of the reasons for its return and a direction to take remedial action and resubmit the plan within a given period (with modifications if appropriate). Any person who lodged an objection to the plan with the Secretary of State is informed that the plan has been returned to the authority. The authority publishes notice by advertisement of the return of the plan. After the required steps have been taken, the plan is resubmitted to the Secretary of State in the same manner as before, and notice of resubmission advertised and given to any party which lodged an objection with the Secretary of State to the original plan.[25]

If the plan is not returned in this way, the Secretary of State proceeds to consider its provisions, taking into account any objections which were properly lodged, and any matters thought relevant, whether or not these matters were taken into account in preparing the plan. The Secretary of State may also consult with any planning authority or other person or body, and consider their views on the plan.

An examination in public (EIP) may be held by the Secretary of State into any matter affecting his consideration of the plan,[26] although recent practice suggests that the EIP option has fallen into disuse. At least four weeks notice of the holding of the EIP must be given by advertisement.[27] Unlike a public local inquiry (Chapter 8), no person or body, including the planning authority, has an absolute entitlement to take part. It is for the Secretary of State to decide which bodies or persons should be invited to take part in the EIP, although the rules of natural justice might require that a party be heard (Chapter 8). The reporter conducting the EIP on behalf of the

[25] s. 6(4)–(7), as amended; regs. 14 and 15.

[26] s. 7(3)(b)–(6), as substituted; S.D.D. Circular 6/1985, "Code of Practice for the Examination in Public of Structure Plans."

[27] Reg. 17.

Secretary of State has the power to invite additional bodies or persons to take part, if this appears desirable to him.

Following consideration of the plan and any EIP, the Secretary of State issues his decision letter either approving the plan (in whole or in part and with or without modifications and reservations) or rejecting it, giving a statement of his reasons for the decision.[28] If any intended modification of the plan would materially affect its content, notice of the modification must be given by advertisement and to the planning authority, and to such other persons as the Secretary of State thinks fit, and an opportunity offered for representations to be made. The Secretary of State will consider any objections made to the proposed modifications, before making a final decision on the plan.[29] Notification of the decision of the Secretary of State on the plan is given to the authority, and such persons as he thinks fit, and notice given by advertisement.[30]

(f) Publication of Approved Plan

Following approval of the plan by the Secretary of State, the authority must arrange for the plan to be reproduced, incorporating the Secretary of State's decision letter and any modifications. Copies must be made available for public inspection and purchase. Each copy must contain the statement that the validity of the plan may be challenged by making an application to the Court of Session within six weeks (below).[31]

(g) Procedure for Alteration or Replacement of Plan

In contrast to the detailed procedure described above for adoption and approval of a structure plan, no procedure is specified for submitting proposals to the Secretary of State for

[28] s. 7(1) and (8).
[29] Reg. 18.
[30] Reg. 19.
[31] Regs. 43 and 44.

alteration, or repeal and replacement of the existing structure plan. The authority is simply required to give such publicity (if any), and undertake such consultations (if any), as they think fit.[32] The discretionary nature of this requirement makes it difficult to challenge in court the procedure adopted by the authority.[33]

It is anticipated that the full procedure will be followed for the repeal and replacement of a structure plan. However, an expedited procedure is often used for alterations to an existing plan. This is appropriate where the alteration involves a small change of planning policy with minor effects in the area and the public interest would not be prejudiced because of reduced publicity and consultation.[34] The publicity given to the alteration may be limited to notice of the right to lodge representations with the Secretary of State following adoption of the alteration by the authority and its submission to the Secretary of State for approval. If the authority opts for an expedited procedure, a statement explaining the absence (or limitation) of the publicity and/or consultation must be submitted along with the proposals, and the Secretary of State may return the proposals with a direction to publicise the application or consult relevant persons or bodies.[35]

The procedure for recent replacement structure plans has taken an average of 46 months from start to approval.[36]

Regional Report

The regional report consists of planning policy proposals and is prepared and submitted to the Secretary of State by a regional or islands council at any time prior or subsequent to submission of a structure plan.[37] The Secretary of State may require a regional report to be prepared and submitted, or prepare the report himself if the authority fails to do so. In

[32] s. 8(3), as amended; reg. 21.
[33] *Glasgow for People* v. *Secretary of State for Scotland*, 1991 S.C.L.R. 775; 1992 S.P.L.P. 35:16.
[34] PAN 37, para. 52.
[35] s. 8(4)–(8).
[36] PAN 37, para. 4.
[37] Local Government (Scotland) Act 1973, s. 173.

preparing the report, the authority must consult with every district planning authority within its region and every other planning authority likely to be affected by the report, and send a copy of the report to these authorities.

The Secretary of State makes observations on the report, and these are sent to all planning authorities which received a copy of the report, who then publish the report and observations within their own area. All planning authorities must have regard to the report and observations when exercising their planning functions.

Local Plans

Local plans are intended to apply the strategic guidance of the structure plan by showing the detailed land-use policies within a much smaller area. Except in Borders, Highland and Dumfries and Galloway regions and in Orkney, Shetland and Western Isles where it is the responsibility of the respective regional or islands council, every district council is required to prepare a local plan for all parts of its district as soon as is practicable.[38] Despite this requirement being almost 20 years old, only 81 per cent. of Scotland is covered by an adopted local plan.[39] As indicated above at p. 43, there have been problems in some areas in initiating plans and with the age of some existing plans.

The functions of the local plan have been described as[40]:

(a) stimulating and encouraging development where appropriate;

(b) indicating land where there are opportunities for change;

(c) applying national and regional policies;

(d) giving a clear locational reference to policies for the development, change of use or conservation of land, and to proposals for development;

[38] *Ibid.*, s. 176(1).
[39] "The Planning Bulletin" (n. 7, *supra*).
[40] PAN 30, "Local Planning," para. 1.

(e) showing how those who have an interest in the area, for example, the authority, private owners, residents, commerce, industry, developers and investors, could contribute to implementation of the plan;
(f) providing an adequate basis for development control;
(g) indicating the intended future pattern of land use and development in the area by showing how existing development and the policies and proposals of the plan fit together.

Different plans may be prepared for different purposes for the same part of any district. Where there is a contradiction between the provisions of any two or more local plans relating to the same area of the district, the provisions of the plan most recently adopted or approved shall prevail.[41] The trend is towards preparation of district-wide plans to avoid such inconsistencies or contradictions. Subject plans may be prepared to deal with a self-contained subject.[42]

Content

The local plan consists of a written statement and a key diagram based on the Ordnance Survey map, and known as the proposals map. This shows at a glance the policies and proposals applicable to individual areas of land within the district, allowing reference to be made to these policies and proposals within the written statement without reading the whole plan.[43] The plan may also include diagrams, illustrations and other descriptive matter, but in the event of any inconsistency, the provisions of the written statement will prevail.[44] Although not a statutory requirement, the written statement should also include a summary of the survey findings.

The written statement formulates the planning authority's detailed proposals for the development and other use of land within its district or for any description of development or other use of such land. It includes measures for the

[41] TCPSA, s. 9(4); reg. 27(2).
[42] For example, Forth and Clyde Canal, or mineral extraction
[43] Reg. 26.
[44] Reg. 27(1).

conservation of the natural beauty and amenity of the land, the improvement of the physical environment and the management of traffic. The statement specifies[45]:

(a) the character, pattern and function of the existing development and other use of land within the district or part of the district to which the plan relates, and the needs and opportunities for change;
(b) the implications of current policies and general proposals contained in the relevant structure plan for the district, or any part of the district to which the local plan relates;
(c) the resources likely to be available for the carrying out of the policies and proposals formulated in the plan;
(d) the criteria to be applied as respects the control of development within the district, or any part of the district to which the plan relates; and
(e) such other matters as the planning authority considers relevant.

The policies and proposals formulated in the local plan should be set out so as to be readily distinguishable from the other contents, and be accompanied by a reasoned justification.[46] The planning authority has a duty to ensure that the proposals contained in the local plan conform generally to the structure plan as it stands, whether or not it has been approved by the Secretary of State.[47]

Procedure for Preparation or Alteration of Local Plan

At various stages in the procedure described below, there is a requirement to give notice by advertisement. In most cases, this amounts to a requirement to publish an advertisement in each of two successive weeks in at least one local newspaper. However, in relation to publication of the finalised plan and of adoption of the local plan, advertisement in the Edinburgh Gazette is also required.

[45] s. 9(3), as amended; reg. 25.
[46] Reg. 24.
[47] s. 9(9), as amended.

Fig. 3.2 Preparation/Alteration of Local Plan

Survey

↓

Notice of Intention to prepare Plan published (publication of Issues Report)

↓

Consultative Draft Plan published

↓

Finalised Plan published and placed on deposit

↓

Local Plan Inquiry into outstanding objections

↓

Notice of Proposed Modifications published and 6 weeks allowed for representations

↓

Notice of Intention to Adopt published

↓

Secretary of State has 28 days to call-in plan for decision

↓

Adoption of plan by resolution and publication of adopted plan

(a) Survey

Planning authorities have a duty to institute a survey of their district for the purpose of preparing a local plan, taking into account any matters necessary for the formulation of their proposals. This duty extends to keeping those matters under review during and after the preparation of the local plan.[48]

It is open to the Secretary of State to direct a planning authority to prepare as soon as is practicable a local plan for (part of) its district, for which a structure plan has been or is in the process of being prepared. Such a direction can only be given before approval of the structure plan by the Secretary of State. The authority must be consulted prior to issuing the direction.[49]

(b) Advertisement of Intention to Prepare a Local Plan

The procedure for preparation of a local plan begins with the planning authority giving notice by newspaper advertisement of its intention to prepare a local plan.[50] This may be combined with publication of an Issues Report, identifying the key issues to be addressed in the plan, to stimulate public discussion. The Report also serves as a framework for responses from the public, which are considered as part of the preparation of the draft plan.

In preparing the draft plan, the authority must consult any other authorities whose areas form part of the district to which the plan relates, the new town development corporation (where the plan includes land within the area of a new town) and other appropriate bodies, and take their views into consideration.[51] The authority must also have regard to any relevant regional report and the Secretary of State's observations on that report,[52] and secure that the local plan conforms generally to the structure plan.

(c) Consultative Draft Plan

The consultative draft plan is published by the authority in substantially the same form as the final written statement will

[48] s. 9(4A).
[49] s. 9(7), (8) and (10), all as amended.
[50] Reg. 28.
[51] Reg. 4(2).
[52] Local Government (Scotland) Act 1973, s. 173(7).

appear. It serves to ensure that adequate publicity is given in the district to matters arising out of the survey and to those matters proposed to be included in the plan, and to give interested parties an opportunity of making representations in respect of those matters.[53] Notice of publication of the draft plan is given by advertisement and a period of not less than four weeks specified for representations to be submitted to the authority.[54] Representations received during that period are considered by the authority and may result in alterations to the provisions of the draft plan.

(d) Finalised Plan

The finalised plan is produced by the authority after considering the responses to the consultative draft plan. It represents their final view on the policies and proposals which should be contained in the local plan once adopted, and is therefore in the form of the plan which they propose to adopt. However, the finalised plan is subject to a period of public consultation, and the representations received may result in amendment of the policies and proposals. Included in or with the finalised plan is a statement of the steps taken by the authority to publicise the preparation of the plan, the opportunities given for representations to be submitted, the consultation process, and the authority's consideration of the views received.[55]

Notice is given by advertisement in both a local newspaper and the Edinburgh Gazette that the finalised plan has been placed on deposit and copies are available for public inspection and that representations may be submitted to the authority within six weeks from the first date of advertisement.[56] Forms for making objections should be made available at the places where copies of the plan are available for inspection. Objections should be made in writing, stating the name and address of the person making the objection, the

[53] TCPSA, s. 10(1), as amended.
[54] Reg. 3.
[55] s. 10(3), as amended; reg. 30(2).
[56] s. 10(2), as amended; reg. 30(1).

matters to which the objection relates and the grounds on which it is made.

Copies of the finalised plan are sent to the Secretary of State and other local authorities whose areas are wholly or partly within the district covered by the plan or whose interests appear likely to be affected.[57] Entries relating to the finalised plan are made in the register kept by the planning authority for public inspection and in the registers of other authorities to whose area the plan relates.

(e) Local Plan Inquiry

Where an objection to the finalised plan has not been withdrawn by an objector after resolution of the matter by the authority, that person or body can require a local plan inquiry to be held to hear that objection.[58] The inquiry is chaired by a reporter appointed by the planning authority from a list prepared by the Secretary of State, and therefore represents an opportunity for the objector to attempt to convince a planning expert independent of the plan preparation process of the soundness of the objection. The objector can either present his case at the inquiry, or in writing or request that the reporter considers the terms of the objection originally submitted. The authority has an opportunity to respond.

The procedure for local plan inquiries is similar to the broad outlines of the public local inquiry procedure (Chapter 8), but with some differences.[59] Responsibility for organising the inquiry lies with the planning authority rather than the Scottish Office Inquiry Reporters (SOIR). The authority must give notice of the inquiry by advertisement at least four weeks before the date of the inquiry and serve notice upon each objector (unless their objection has been withdrawn) and on such other persons as it thinks fit.[60] At the same time as

[57] Regs. 29 and 30.
[58] s. 11(1), as amended.
[59] S.D.D. Circular 7/1985, "Code of Practice for Local Plan Inquiries and Hearings." No procedural rules have been prescribed.
[60] Reg. 34.

publishing the advertisement, the authority must make available for public inspection at its office copies of the objections which are to be considered at the inquiry.

The reporter may hold a pre-inquiry meeting with the authority and objectors. Notice of this meeting will be served upon the authority and objectors, and given by newspaper advertisement. The purposes of the meeting are to agree a timetable for the inquiry, and identify the issues and the areas of agreement and disagreement between the parties. Objections can be divided into general policy issues and more site-specific matters, and an attempt made to group them together at the inquiry accordingly. A copy of the agreed timetable will be circulated to all parties.

Unlike public local inquiries, the advance circulation requirements applicable to local plan inquiries are minimal. The parties already have prior notice of the case to be presented by each other: the authority will rely on the provisions of the finalised plan, and the objector's case is contained in the objection. If the objection gives insufficient information to allow proper preparation for the inquiry, the reporter can request amplification. Where the parties propose to rely on other written material (known as productions) at the inquiry, agreement will normally be reached at the pre-inquiry meeting on the exchange of copies of this material. In the absence of such agreement, parties may adhere to the usual public local inquiry procedure of exchanging productions 10 days before the inquiry. Copies of all productions should also be sent to the reporter.

Where an objector proposes to refer at the inquiry to alternative sites for proposed development or suggest that a policy should apply to an area different from that shown on the plan, notification of this intention should be sent to the authority and the reporter as early as possible in advance of the inquiry.

The procedure at the inquiry is a matter for the discretion of the reporter, but is intended to be informal. For each objection or group of objections, the planning authority normally presents its case first and is followed by the objector(s). The evidence presented by the authority will take the form of testimony of witnesses, including planning officers. Objectors may present evidence through their own testimony, or lead witnesses, who may be concerned individuals or expert witnesses. Unless the testimony to be given by a witness is short, it is normal practice for a written statement of that testimony to be prepared (known as a precognition), and circulated to the reporter and other parties present at the inquiry immediately before the testimony commences. The use of precognitions in this manner aids the reporter's note-taking. Following his initial testimony, each witness may be cross-examined by the other parties, re-examined, and questioned by the reporter, in the same way as at public local inquiries. After all the evidence has been presented in relation to the objection or group of objections, the parties make their closing submissions, and the inquiry then moves to consider the next objection.

While the evidence presented at the inquiry should involve general policy issues, in practice these are often overshadowed by site-specific arguments in which developers seek to protect development proposals. This results in the case presented at the inquiry being more in the form of an appeal against a refusal of planning permission, leading to more detailed cases and longer inquiries. Landowners who are uncertain of their long-term development proposals will seek the widest possible allocation for their land in the plan to avoid restricting the available development options. These are inevitable consequences of the introduction of the plan-led system, whereby it is important for development proposals to be in accordance with the provisions of the development plan.

At some point during or after the inquiry, the reporter will make a site inspection which the parties are entitled to attend (the reporter will probably have made an unaccompanied inspection in advance of the inquiry). The purpose of the inspection is to confirm the physical characteristics of the site, and the reporter may ask the parties to confirm points raised at the inquiry in this regard. The reporter will not allow the parties to use the site inspection as an opportunity to reopen arguments on the merits of the objection, plan policy or proposal.

The cost of organising the inquiry and employing the reporter is paid by the authority. The objectors must bear their own costs, and there is no provision for an award of expenses (in contrast to public local inquiries).

Where an objector also has an outstanding appeal to the Secretary of State concerning a matter similar to the content of the objection, the SOIR may suggest to the objector and the authority that the appeal inquiry could usefully be conjoined with the relevant part of the local plan inquiry. Both parties must consent to conjoining the inquiries. As the same issues may underlie both the objection and the appeal (indeed, the objection is often submitted in support of the proposed development which is the subject of the appeal), the time and expense of two separate inquiries can be avoided.

Conjoining inquiries is not without its difficulties. For the local plan inquiry, the reporter is paid by and reports to the authority, but in the appeal inquiry the reporter is employed by the Scottish Office and reports to the Secretary of State. In the conjoined inquiry, the reporter would therefore be paid, at least in part, by the authority which initially refused or delayed in determining the application for planning permission which is the subject of the appeal. This raises an appearance of bias possibly rendering the decision illegal (Chapter 8). It is arguable that this potential illegality cannot be cured by the consent of the objector/appellant to the conjoining. One solution may be to hold both inquiries back-to-back, closing one before opening the other, and taking as read at the later inquiry the evidence presented to the earlier inquiry. Difficulties may be encountered with this solution if members of the public who were not present at the earlier inquiry, and therefore did not hear, or have an opportunity to challenge, evidence given at that inquiry, wish to participate in the later inquiry. A better solution may be for two reporters to chair the conjoined inquiry, one to report on the local plan objection and the other on the appeal. However, this solution negates much of the benefit offered to the SOIR by conjoining and is unlikely to be attractive to them.

Another problem is that confusion often reigns during a conjoined inquiry, with the participants finding it difficult to distinguish local plan from appeal issues.

Where the inquiry is conjoined, the authority must comply with the local plan inquiry requirements and SOIR is bound by the appeal inquiry procedural requirements, resulting in two sets of advertisements. At the inquiry itself, the appeal procedure takes precedence, and the objector/appellant presents his case first.

Following the local plan inquiry, the reporter prepares a report which is sent to the authority for consideration. The report will show the following matters for each objection or group of related objections: a summary of the arguments advanced by the objectors and by the authority, a summary of any other arguments or facts advanced at the inquiry which are relevant to consideration of these objections, the reporter's findings of fact, and his recommendation, if any, as to how the authority should deal with the objection.

On receipt of the report of the inquiry, the authority must consider whether to accept the recommendations made by the reporter. It is open to the authority to ignore the report completely, provided that reasons for this approach can be given. The authority may decide to adopt the plan without change, propose modifications, or abandon the plan. A reasoned statement of its decision whether or not to take action in light of the report is prepared and made available for public inspection along with copies of the report.[61] Each objector is notified by the authority of the decision in relation to his objection and sent a copy of the statement and report, or informed of the opportunity to inspect them.

(f) Modifications to Finalised Plan

Where modifications to the finalised plan (other than drafting or technical matters of a minor nature) are proposed by the authority following consideration of objections or an inquiry report, a list of the modifications and the reasons for proposing them is prepared by the authority and made available for public inspection. Notice of the proposed modifications is given by newspaper advertisement and served on all objectors who have not withdrawn their objections. A six-week period must be allowed for representations to be submitted with regard to the proposed modifications.

[61] Reg. 35.

Any objections made to the proposed modifications are considered by the authority and a further inquiry must be held to hear unwithdrawn objections which do not relate to matters considered at the previous inquiry. A further inquiry may also be held to hear other objections.[62] Even if no further inquiry is held, the authority is obliged to consider all representations received in relation to the proposed modifications.

(g) Adoption by Planning Authority

Prior to final adoption of the plan by the authority, notice of its intention to adopt the plan is given by newspaper advertisement and served on objectors whose objection has not been withdrawn. Copies of the plan in the form which the planning authority proposes to adopt are made available for inspection and sent to the Secretary of State and the regional planning authority. The authority must certify by recorded delivery to the Secretary of State that this notice has been given. The plan can only be adopted 28 days after sending this certification. Within the 28-day period the Secretary of State may direct that the plan cannot be adopted until the authority receives notification that the plan is not to be called-in for decision by the Secretary of State.[63] The procedure following call-in by the Secretary of State is considered below.

If no such direction is received, on the expiry of the 28 days the authority may adopt the plan by resolution.[64] Adoption of the plan is advertised (both in a local newspaper and in the Edinburgh Gazette), and notice served on those who have requested notification and on such other persons as the authority thinks fit, indicating where the plan can be inspected. Two certified copies of the adopted plan must be sent to both the Secretary of State and the regional planning authority not later than the date on which such notice is given.[65]

[62] Reg. 37.
[63] s. 12(2A)–(3), as amended; reg. 38.
[64] s. 12(1), as amended.
[65] Reg. 39.

Following adoption, copies of the plan must be available for inspection and purchase at the authority's offices and at the office of every other local authority to whose area the plan relates. Each copy must contain a statement detailing the right to question the validity of the plan by making an application to the Court of Session (below).[66]

(h) *Powers of Secretary of State*

At any time between receipt of the finalised local plan and its adoption, the Secretary of State has a general power to "call-in" the plan for decision whereby it will have no effect until approved by him.[67]

Following the call-in, if the Secretary of State decides not to reject the plan, he must take into account any objections to the plan made in accordance with the regulations. Objectors have no right to demand an inquiry unless no inquiry has been held by the authority. If an inquiry is to be held, an opportunity to participate must also be offered to the planning authority and such other persons as the Secretary of State thinks fit. At least four-weeks notice of the inquiry must be given by newspaper advertisement and notice served on the objectors and such other persons as the Secretary of State considers appropriate.[68] In considering the plan, the Secretary of State may consult with other planning authorities or persons, and take into account any relevant matters irrespective of whether such matters were considered in the plan.

After considering the plan, the Secretary of State may either approve it in whole or in part and with or without modifications, or reject it. The planning authority must be notified of any proposal to modify the plan, unless the Secretary of State is satisfied that the modifications will not materially affect any policy or proposal in the plan. On receipt of notification of proposed modifications, the authority must give notice of the modifications by advertisement (unless such advertisement was carried out previously) and serve notice on

[66] Regs. 42, 43 and 44.
[67] s. 12(3) and (4), as amended.
[68] Reg. 40(1).

such persons as it thinks fit. Any objections to the modifications are considered by the Secretary of State who decides whether or not to hold an inquiry.[69]

The Secretary of State notifies his decision in writing to the planning authority which gives notice of the decision by advertisement and serves notice on persons who have requested notification and such other persons as the Secretary of State may direct.[70] Copies of the local plan as approved by the Secretary of State are made available for public inspection and purchase at the offices of the planning authority.

In addition to the power to call-in the plan for decision, the Secretary of State may direct the authority at any time prior to the adoption of the plan to consider modifying it in specified respects. After such a direction, the authority cannot adopt the plan unless it either satisfies the Secretary of State that the necessary modifications have been made, or the direction is withdrawn.[71]

(i) Procedure for Alteration or Replacement of Plan

Similar procedures apply to the alteration, or repeal and replacement of a local plan.[72] If the planning authority regard the alteration as too minor to justify full publicity and consultation, when submitting the plan to the Secretary of State it should include a statement giving a brief account of the publicity and consultation undertaken or its reasons for not undertaking any publicity or consultation. The Secretary of State may call-in the alterations if the publicity and consultation carried out is unsatisfactory. The expedited procedure normally involves no publicity until the finalised alteration is placed on deposit. A change to a policy contained in a validly adopted local plan cannot be made by the planning authority merely issuing a different document without giving the public notice of the changes or an opportunity to lodge representations.[73]

[69] s. 12(4)(a) as substituted; reg. 40(2) and (3).
[70] Reg. 40(4).
[71] s. 12(2A) and (2B) as inserted.
[72] s. 13, as amended.
[73] *Falkirk D.C.* v. *Secretary of State for Scotland*, 1991 S.L.T. 553.

On average, replacement local plans take four years to prepare and adopt.[74]

Relationship between Structure and Local Plan

The planning authority has a duty to secure that the proposals contained in the local plan conform generally to the structure plan as it stands (whether or not it has been approved by the Secretary of State), and cannot adopt a local plan which does not conform to an approved structure plan.[75]

Borders, Highland, and Dumfries and Galloway regional councils and the island councils may prepare a local plan before a structure plan for the area is approved, subject to any directions given by the Secretary of State. A district planning authority cannot prepare a local plan before the structure plan for the area is approved unless it has obtained the consent of the regional planning authority, or this consent is deemed to have been given or is dispensed with by the Secretary of State. Consent may be withheld or withdrawn by the regional planning authority where a structure plan is in course of preparation or a decision is likely to be taken shortly by any authority and that plan or decision is likely to have a substantial effect on the contents of the local plan.[76]

Application to Court of Session Challenging Validity of Plan

An action may be raised in the Court of Session challenging the validity of a structure or local plan within six weeks from the date of publication of the first notice of the approval or adoption of the plan or its alteration, repeal or replacement.[77] No challenge will be possible outside this time limit (Chapter 8).

The action may be raised by any "person aggrieved" by the structure or local plan or any alteration, repeal or replacement of the plan. This includes a neighbouring regional planning

[74] "The Planning Bulletin" (n. 7 *supra*).
[75] ss. 9(9), as amended, and 12(2), as substituted.
[76] Local Government (Scotland) Act 1973, s. 176(2) *et seq.*, as amended.
[77] TCPSA, s. 232(1).

authority,[78] but not the planning authority responsible for preparing the plan where it seeks to challenge modifications made by the Secretary of State.[79] It has been suggested that the term will include objectors, persons selected to appear at an examination in public (structure plan) or who participated at a local plan inquiry, bodies which have to be consulted in the making of a plan, and any person whose property is affected by a plan.[80] It would also seem to include bodies consulted during the plan process.[81]

The grounds of challenge are that the plan is not within the powers conferred by the TCPSA in relation to development plans, or that any of the regulations made under the TCPSA have not been complied with in relation to the approval or adoption of the plan, alteration, repeal or replacement. These grounds of challenge are discussed in detail in Chapter 8.

The Court of Session has the power to suspend in the interim the plan, alteration, repeal or replacement, either generally or only in so far as it affects the applicant's property. Following a successful challenge, the court has the discretion to quash wholly or partly the plan, alteration, repeal or replacement, either generally or in so far as it affects the applicant's property.

Reading Development Plans

Planning authorities are obliged to make copies of the development plan available at their offices for public inspection free of charge. Copies can also be purchased for a small fee (typically between £5–£10, although copies of draft plans may be more expensive due to the cost of the limited print run). They are also obliged to maintain a register containing information on the development plan and any proposals to alter, repeal or replace it, together with an index map showing the plan boundaries.[82]

[78] *Central R.C.* v. *Secretary of State for Scotland*, 1991 S.L.T. 702; S.P.L.P. 33:49.
[79] *Strathclyde Regional Council* v. *Secretary of State for Scotland*, 1989 S.L.T. 821.
[80] Young and Rowan Robinson, *Scottish Planning Law and Procedure* (1985), P. 530.
[81] *Glasgow for People* v. *Secretary of State for Scotland* (n. 33, *supra*).
[82] Town and Country Planning (Structure and Local Plans) (Scotland) Regulations 1983 (S.I. 1983 No. 1590), regs. 42–45.

When consulting the provisions of the structure or local plan, reference should be made initially to the key map or diagram which shows the policies and proposals applicable to particular sites. This will allow the appropriate provisions to be found in the written statement without reading the entire text.

Attention should be paid to the term used to describe any particular provision, and to any glossary explaining the interpretation of that term. The weight to be given to the provision may depend upon which "label" is used. For example, "proposal" is used to denote action which the authority intends to take within the short term, whereas "policy" denotes a longer-term intention. A "recommendation" is made where the authority wishes to indicate its views to another body which has control over the result sought. Most of the written statement is not expressed in the form of proposals, policies or recommendations, and can be used for little more than background information. A proposed development is only contrary to the plan if it does not conform with a proposal, policy or recommendation. The general aims expressed in the plan cannot derogate from its specific policies.[83]

Objecting to Draft Plans

With the enhanced status of development plans resulting from the plan-led system, it is important for all persons, whether developers, landowners or members of the public, to monitor changes to development plans. Such monitoring has several different objectives:

(a) landowners/developers should ensure that any proposals for development of their land, even if uncertain or long-term will be consistent with the plan;

(b) landowners/occupiers will also be anxious to preserve land value and amenity by ensuring that the plan does not contain proposals which may have a negative effect on land

[83] *Bearsden and Milngavie D.C.* v. *Secretary of State for Scotland*, 1992 S.L.T. 917; S.P.L.P. 36:55, *per* Lord Justice-Clerk Ross.

value, such as allocating neighbouring land for a sewage works;

(c) members of the public should ensure that the plan makes provision for the proper planning of their neighbourhood, town or area, or any items or issues of special interest or concern to them.

It is important to note that publicity requirements attached to the plan process do not include notification to individual landowners of proposals to change policies applicable to their land. It is therefore conceivable that land previously allocated for housing could be reallocated for agricultural use without the knowledge of the landowner and to his financial loss. Although this would not necessarily prevent a successful application for planning permission for housing, under the plan-led system the agricultural zoning would give the authority an easy reason for refusing permission.

Monitoring draft plans in this way will inevitably lead to submission of objections. This can be done by completing the form obtainable from the authority, or submitting an objection in writing. The objection itself should specify the provision(s) of the plan to which the objection relates, and explain the reasons for the objection. For local plans, the form also seeks a (preliminary) indication of whether the objector wishes to appear at a local plan inquiry.

There are no limits to the content of the objection. It may relate to a provision contained in the plan, or point to something omitted from the plan. It may concern a minor error or a complex policy issue. No particular expertise is required, and a strong argument can often be made on the basis of general local knowledge. The only essential element is that the objection identify the provision in the plan and the result sought by the objector in relation to that provision (*i.e.*, removal, modification, etc.).

In pursuing the objection, one should be aware of the constraints on the authority. For instance, if the provision in the plan relates to a development which has already been granted planning permission, the authority cannot change that provision as it has no power to stop the development from proceeding, short of revoking the permission and exposing itself to a claim for compensation. Landowners or developers should also be realistic, and accept that authorities can rarely allocate sites for what amounts to any possible development idea which might arise during the next decade.

Campaigning against planning issues is examined in more detail in Chapter 10.

Chapter 4

DEVELOPMENT CONTROL I —
THE NEED FOR PLANNING PERMISSION

The keystone of the planning system is the requirement to obtain planning permission for any development of land. It provides a means for planning authorities to control unsuitable development either by refusing permission or granting permission subject to conditions (Chapters 5 and 6), and the other elements within the system flow from the requirement for planning permission. Development plans have little practical effect until their policies are applied in the determination of applications for planning permission. Unless there is a breach of planning control caused by the failure to obtain planning permission or to observe the terms and conditions attached to a grant of planning permission, planning authorities have few enforcement powers over land short of compulsory purchase.

To determine whether planning permission is required, the following questions must be asked of the proposed activity (fig. 4.1):

(a) Does it fall within the statutory definition of "development"?
(b) Is it an activity which is declared not to amount to "development", for example, in terms of the Use Classes Order (U.C.O.)?
(c) Is planning permission deemed to be granted for the proposed activity, for example, in terms of the Permitted Development Order (P.D.O.)?

Depending upon the answer to any of these questions, an application for planning permission must be submitted before the proposed activity can be commenced. In practice, these questions are asked in reverse, principally because of the ease of reference of the U.C.O. and P.D.O. as the main sources of exemptions. The thorny question of "development" is only considered if the U.C.O. and P.D.O. fail to exempt the proposed activity from the need for planning permission.

This may be expressed diagrammatically, thus:

Fig. 4.1 The need for planning permission

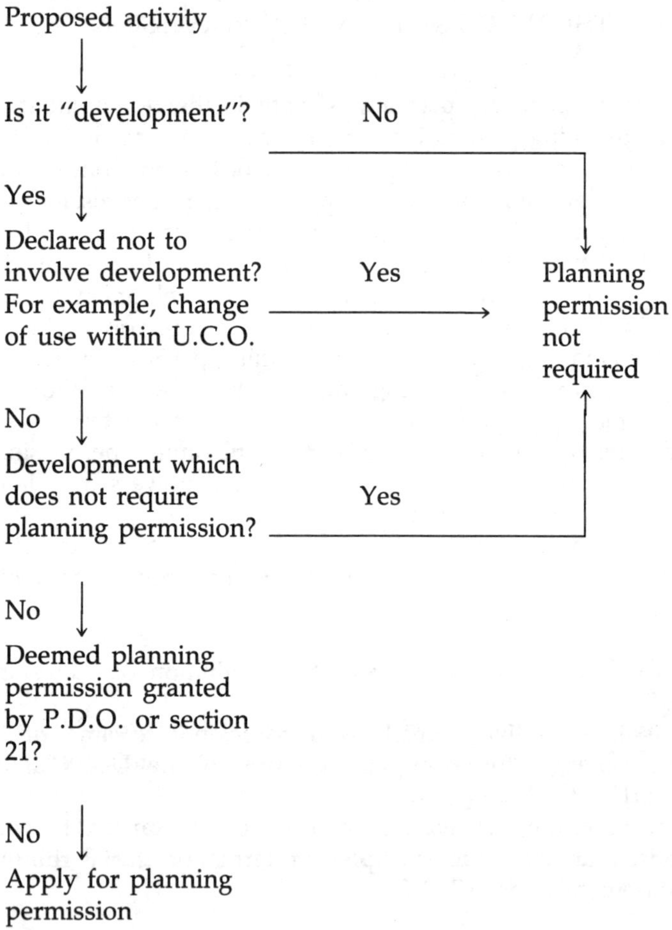

It is a question of the facts and circumstances of each individual case whether the proposal falls within the requirement for permission. There is a procedure for obtaining a formal answer from the planning authority on the need for planning permission, with a right of appeal to the Secretary of State.

Requirement for Planning Permission

Planning permission is required for the carrying out of any development of land or buildings,[1] which is defined as the carrying out of[2]:

(a) building operations,
(b) engineering operations,
(c) mining operations, or
(d) other operations in, on, over or under land, or
(e) the making of any material change in the use of any buildings or other land.

Building, engineering, mining or other operations are generally described as operational development. This description highlights the difference in character between these forms of development and material changes of use. It is possible for an activity to involve both operational development and change of use.

The question of whether what is proposed amounts to "development" and, therefore, requires planning permission is one of fact and circumstances for the planning authority, or the Secretary of State on appeal, to decide. As a result, the courts will be reluctant to interfere unless the decision is unreasonable.

The imprecise definition of terms such as "building operations," combined with the residual term "other operations," gives ample scope for disputes with planning authorities on this question. For example, prior to statutory intervention (below), the courts decided that demolition could be a building operation[3] or an engineering operation,[4] thereby

[1] TCPSA s. 20.
[2] s. 19(1), as amended.
[3] *Cambridge City Council* v. *Secretary of State for the Environment* [1991] J.P.L. 428 (reversed on appeal); *Glasgow District Council* v. *Secretary of State for Scotland*, 1982 S.L.T. 28, *per* Lord Justice-Clerk Wheatley at p. 32.
[4] *Coleshill* v. *M.H.L.G.* [1969] 1 W.L.R. 746.

requiring planning permission, or an operation for which planning permission was not required.[5] In a recent appeal decision the reporter held that provision of a limited number of unmarked and unfenced private graves did not constitute a material change of use from grazing land, and digging those graves by hand was not an engineering operation. Planning permission was therefore not required.[6]

Operational Development

(a) Building Operations

Planning permission is required for rebuilding operations, structural alterations of or additions to buildings and other operations normally undertaken by a person carrying on business as a builder.[7]

A "building" is defined to include any structure or erection, and any part of a building.[8] Size, permanence and degree of attachment of the structure are factors to be considered.[9]

As a result of the confusion caused by conflicting court decisions (above), once the relevant provision of the Planning and Compensation Act 1991 is brought into force, building operations will be defined as including demolition of buildings. However, the Secretary of State will have the power to direct that the demolition of any description of building shall not require planning permission.[10]

Internal maintenance or improvement works or other alteration of a building (other than structural alterations) do not require planning permission unless the works materially

[5] *Cambridge City Council* v. *Secretary of State for the Environment* [1992] J.P.L. 644 (C.A.).

[6] *The Scotsman*, December 3, 1992.

[7] TCPSA, s. 275(1).

[8] s. 275(1).

[9] *Barvis Ltd.* v. *Secretary of State for the Environment* (1971) 22 P. & C.R. 710. The concept of fixtures in property law may provide a useful parallel, see, for example, Gordon, *Scottish Land Law*, Chap. 5.

[10] TCPSA, ss. 19(1A) and (2)(g) to be inserted by P.C.A., s. 44; Scottish Environment Department consultation paper, "New Planning Controls over the Demolition of Houses" (September 1991).

affect the external appearance of the building.[11] The distinction between alteration, which does not require planning permission, and rebuilding works, which do need permission, may be difficult to draw. The statutory wording suggests that when assessing the effect of the proposed works on the external appearance of the building, no account should be taken of the appearance of the surrounding area. Canopies, grilles, roller shutters, stone cladding, and replacement windows are all works which may materially affect the external appearance of a building.

Planning permission is also required for works to provide additional space below ground, such as lowering the floor level or creating a basement.

The P.D.O. grants deemed planning permission for many forms of building operations, including those within the curtilage of a dwelling-house and agricultural buildings (see pp. 85–95). For example, planning permission is deemed to be granted for painting a building. This deemed permission does not extend to listed buildings and buildings situated in conservation areas. However, planning permission is only required if the painting of such a building amounts to development because it will materially affect the external appearance of the building.

(b) *Engineering Operations*

Engineering operations are defined as operations usually undertaken by or under the supervision of an engineer or which would require engineering skills, irrespective of whether an engineer is actually involved,[12] including the placing or assembly of a tank in inland waters for the purpose of fish farming[13] and the formation or laying out of means of access to roads.[14]

Planning permission is not required for the following works which might be considered to be engineering operations:

[11] s. 19(2)(a). Listed building consent is required for internal works which affect the character of a listed building (Chapter 9).
[12] *Fayrewood Fish Farms* v. *Secretary of State for the Environment* [1984] J.P.L. 267.
[13] s. 19(3B).
[14] s. 275(1), as amended.

works carried out on land within the boundaries of a road by the local roads authority for the maintenance or improvement of that road, and works carried out by the local authority or statutory undertakers for inspecting, repairing or renewing any sewers, mains, pipes, cables or other apparatus, including the breaking open of any road or other land for that purpose.[15]

(c) *Mining Operations*

Mining operations include the removal of material of any description from a mineral-working deposit, from a deposit of pulverised fuel ash or other furnace ash or clinker, or from a deposit of iron, steel or other metallic slags, and the extraction of minerals from a disused railway embankment.[16] For the purposes of the P.D.O., mining operations are defined as the winning and working of minerals in, on or under land, whether by surface or underground working.

Unlike building and engineering operations, mining is a continuous operation lasting for many years. Special controls apply to mining operations (Chapter 9). The removal of each shovelful constitutes a separate mining operation and it will therefore be rare for unauthorised mining operations to become lawful.[17]

(d) *Other Operations*

There is no definition of what amounts to "other operations." It has been suggested that these are operations of a positive, constructive and identifiable character[18] which result in some physical alteration to land.[19] Arguably the definition of development is not intended to comprehend every operation on land. Clearly there are some operations on land which should not require planning permission, for example, mowing

[15] s. 19(2)(b) and (c), as amended.
[16] s. 19(3A).
[17] *Thomas David (Porthcawl) Ltd.* v. *Penybont R.D.C.* [1972] 1 W.L.R. 1526.
[18] *Coleshill* (n. 4), *per* Lord Wilberforce at p. 765.
[19] *Parkes* v. *Secretary of State for the Environment* [1978] 1 W.L.R. 1308, *per* Lord Denning at 1311 E.

a lawn. The phrase "other operations," therefore, does not refer to all other operations.[20] Indeed, it has been suggested that this residual category may be restricted to operations similar to building, engineering or mining operations.[21]

For practical purposes, "other operations" will include any form of operational development which does not fall within the other categories, but which the planning authority or the Secretary of State may reasonably consider requires planning permission—for example, any excavation and levelling works which cannot be considered engineering or mining operations.[22]

Material Change of Use

Following nationalisation of development rights in 1947, owners were left with their existing (1947) use rights and required to obtain planning permission from the State for any material change of use of land or buildings.

Certain changes of use are declared to be material and therefore require planning permission[23]:

(a) Sub-division of a single dwelling-house resulting in its use as two or more separate dwelling-houses. In contrast to the P.D.O., this provision extends to sub-division of flats.
(b) Deposit of refuse or waste materials on land, notwithstanding that the land is already used for that purpose, if either the superficial area of the deposit is thereby extended or the height of the deposit is extended to exceed the level of the land adjoining the site.
(c) Use of any external part of a building for the display of advertisements, if it is not normally used for that purpose. However, if the advertisement is displayed in accordance with the Control of Advertisement Regulations (Chapter 9), planning permission is deemed to have been granted.[24]

[20] *Cambridge City Council* v. *Secretary of State for the Environment* (n. 5, *supra*).
[21] *cf. Coleshill* (n. 4), *per* Lords Wilberforce and Guest.
[22] Young and Rowan-Robinson, *Scottish Planning Law and Procedure* (1985), p. 123.
[23] s. 19(3) and (4).
[24] s. 62.

These changes of use should be distinguished from the changes of use which are declared not to involve development and, therefore, do not require planning permission[25]:

(a) The use of any buildings or other land within the curtilage of a dwelling-house (see pp. 88–89), for any purpose incidental to the enjoyment of the dwelling-house does not amount to a material change of use and, therefore, requires no planning permission. This does not extend to keeping up to 44 dogs as a hobby.[26] Subject to the provisions of the P.D.O. planning permission may be required for erection of the buildings.
(b) The change of use to agricultural or forestry use (including afforestation) of land and any building occupied together with the land does not require planning permission (Chapter 9).
(c) A change of use within any class specified in the U.C.O. (below).

Whether any other change of use is "material" and therefore requires planning permission is a question of fact and degree for the planning authority, or the Secretary of State on appeal, to decide and the courts will only interfere with an unreasonable decision. There is no general guidance on when a change of use will be considered "material." Some assistance is provided by case law, but much of this area of planning law remains conceptual in nature.[27]

The first step in assessing whether a material change of use has occurred is the identification of the area of land or the building to be used as the reference point against which the change can be judged. This area of land or building is known as the "planning unit."

The correct identification of the planning unit may be of crucial importance to the planning authority or the owner. In general, the larger the planning unit, the less likely that a change of use will be material. For example, a lean-to building

[25] s. 19(2)(d), (e) and (f).
[26] *Wallington* v. *Secretary of State for the Environment* [1990] J.P.L. 112.
[27] See Young and Rowan-Robinson *op. cit.*, p. 125 *et seq.*

in a car-breakers yard had been used as the yard office and for retail sales of car parts salvaged from vehicles broken up on the site. New owners used the lean-to for the sale of new vehicle parts and camping equipment. They appealed against an enforcement notice on the ground that the planning unit was the whole yard and that looking at the site as a whole, the intensification of the retail sale use was insufficient to amount to a material change of use. The Secretary of State held that the planning unit was the lean-to and there had been a material change of use. The court tended to agree with the Secretary of State, but found that he had applied the wrong test and returned the matter to him for re-decision.[28]

Identification of the planning unit is a question of the facts and circumstances of each case, but some broad criteria have been suggested.[29] If there is a single main use, perhaps with secondary activities which are incidental or ancillary to that use, the area of land occupied as a single holding (the unit of occupation) is the planning unit. Where the occupier carries on a variety of activities, the unit of occupation may still be the planning unit. However, if these activities occupy separate and distinct areas, each area which can be identified as being used for a different main purpose forms a separate planning unit (the unit of activity replaces the unit of occupation).

In general, the unit of occupation is the planning unit unless and until some smaller unit can be recognised as the site of activities which amount to a separate use both physically and functionally. Physical separation of plots of land within the same occupation may cause the individual plots to form separate planning units.

The planning unit may be larger than the unit of occupation, but only in exceptional circumstances.[30] This avoids the possibility of enforcement action directed against an occupier sharing a planning unit with others (except for joint occupiers) in respect of activities carried on by the other occupiers over which he has no control. Thus the Secretary of State on appeal rejected the argument that the whole group of

[28] *Burdle* v. *Secretary of State for the Environment* [1972] 1 W.L.R. 1207.
[29] *Burdle, ibid., per* Bridge J.
[30] *Rawlins* v. *Secretary of State for the Environment* [1989] J.P.L. 439; *Kwik Save* v. *Secretary of State for Wales* (1978) 37 P. & C.R. 170.

lock-up garages previously used for a taxi business, but gradually let singly or in groups to different persons formed a single planning unit. The appropriate planning unit was the unit of occupation and each garage individually occupied became a separate planning unit. Enforcement notices alleging a material change of use were validly directed against garages in separate occupation where vehicle repairing was being carried out.[31]

After the planning unit has been identified, it is possible to consider whether there has been a material change of use within it. Once again, this is a matter of fact and degree to be determined by the planning authority or the Secretary of State on appeal. Relevant factors in assessing the materiality of a change of use are the character and intensity of the various uses, the degree to which the uses are dependent on each other, the proportion of the planning unit devoted to each activity, and any planning effects on the locality.

If the general character of the use remains the same, but there is a change from one particular purpose to another particular purpose, there may not be a material change of use. Where land was used as a railway storage depot, there was no material change of use when it came to be used for storage of motor vehicles mainly destined for rail transport instead of coal for transport by rail. What should be considered is the character of the use of the land, not the particular purpose of a particular occupier.[32] However, a change from one leisure activity to another is capable of constituting a material change of use if the particular nature of the type of leisure activity has changed.[33]

The character of the use is determined by the primary or main use. Changes in ancillary or incidental uses do not involve a material change of use, provided the subordinate and dependent character of the ancillary use is preserved. Once an ancillary use is no longer subordinate and linked to the main use, or has become a main use in its own right, a material change of use may have occurred. Thus, in terms of a planning permission for a quarry operation, backfilling the

[31] *Johnston* v. *Secretary of State for the Environment* (1974) 28 P. & C.R. 424.
[32] *East Barnet U.D.C.* v. *British Transport Commission* [1962] 2 Q.B. 484.
[33] *Shepherd and Love* v. *Secretary of State for the Environment* [1992] J.P.L. 827.

quarry with waste material from the quarrying operation was ancillary to the main activity. When the quarry came to be used for dumping refuse from outside, the ancillary dumping use had become a main use. The character of the use had altered and a material change of use had occurred.[34] Similarly, keeping up to 44 dogs in a dwelling-house as a hobby amounted to a material change of use because it was not incidental to the enjoyment of the dwelling-house.[35]

The size of the area devoted to a use is not conclusive. The use of cubicles for viewing films in a sex shop was not ancillary to the main retail use.[36] Although residential use of a caretaker's flat in an office building may be ancillary to the principal office use, it is often considered that these are two physically separate and distinct primary uses, and the flat and the office therefore form separate planning units.

It may also be relevant to consider whether the change of use will have material or relevant planning considerations, such as adverse effects on the locality. The limited environmental health effects of the sale of heated food from a shop was a factor in the decision that there had been no material change of use.[37]

Creation of a new planning unit is not conclusive evidence of a material change of use. As the general rule is that the planning unit is the unit of occupation, a new planning unit is therefore formed when part of a site is sold or leased to another person. However, the primary use may remain as before, in which case there is no material change of use (with the exception of a subdivision of a dwelling-house into two or more dwelling-houses which is always a material change of use). In contrast, a material change of use caused by an ancillary use becoming a main use in its own right will not necessarily result in the creation of a new planning unit unless it occupies a separately identifiable part of the site.

If existing use rights are lost, the planning unit has a nil use and planning permission will be required for any new use or

[34] *Alexandra Transport* v. *Secretary of State for Scotland*, 1974 S.L.T. 81.
[35] *Wallington* (see n. 26).
[36] *Lydcare* v. *Secretary of State for the Environment* [1984] J.P.L. 809.
[37] *City of Glasgow District Council* v. *Secretary of State for Scotland*, 1985 S.L.T. 19.

resumption of the previous use. Confusingly, this is often referred to as the creation of a new planning unit, when what is meant is that there has been a fresh start or new chapter in the planning history.

Demolition of a building results in the right to continue its use being extinguished. Resumption of that use thereafter requires planning permission.[38] Rebuilding operations would probably require planning permission in any case, but there may be circumstances in which permission would not be forthcoming for a resumption of the use, for example, a disco in a residential area.

Loss of existing use rights may also occur when a planning permission is implemented. Where planning permission was granted for construction of retail units, but a unit was used as an air terminal in terms of a separate permission, resumption of the retail use required fresh planning permission.[39] If the existing use is supplanted or superseded by another use, the right to resume the existing use is lost and planning permission will be required for its resumption, even if the change to the supplanting use did not require planning permission.[40] The erection of a building will not of itself result in the loss of existing use rights.[41]

A temporary discontinuance of use does not lead to loss of existing use rights.[42] As a result, no planning permission is required to resume the discontinued use, unless the land has been used for some different purpose in the meantime. In contrast, where a use has been abandoned, the land has a nil use and planning permission will be required for any use, including resumption of the former use.[43] In distinguishing between a temporary cessation of use and abandonment, at least four factors should be considered: the physical condition of the land or building; the length of the period of non-use; whether there has been any other use; and evidence of the

[38] *Iddenden* v. *Secretary of State for the Environment* [1972] 1 W.L.R. 1433, Buckley L.J. p. 1440; see also App./6/90/p.4225/1 [1992] J.P.L. 579.
[39] *Regent Lion Properties* v. *Westminster* C.C. [1991] J.P.L. 569.
[40] *J.L. Engineering* v. *Secretary of State for the Environment* [1993] E.G.C.S. 24.
[41] *Jennings Motors* v. *Secretary of State for the Environment* [1982] 1 Q.B. 541.
[42] *Paul* v. *Ayrshire County Council* 1964 S.C. 116; S.L.T. 207.
[43] Planning permission for operational development can never be abandoned, but may be incapable of implementation (see Chapter 5).

owner's intentions.[44] Any action inconsistent with retention of the right to resume the use, such as removal of petrol tanks and pumps at a filling station, will also be relevant. Cessation of a car sales use for four years was sufficient grounds to find that the use had been abandoned.[45]

It is important to determine when a change of use occurs. Although land is converted to allow a new use, there is no change until the land is actually put to the new use.[46] If the change of use has occurred gradually over a period, it will be necessary to identify the point at which the change became material. At that point any failure to obtain planning permission results in a breach of planning control which may be the subject of enforcement action (Chapter 7).

Operations and Uses Declared Not to Involve Development

The following operations and uses are declared not to involve development and therefore will not require planning permission[47]:

(a) internal maintenance or improvement works or other alteration of a building (other than structural alterations), unless the works materially affect the external appearance of the building (see Building operations, above):
(b) works required for the maintenance or improvement of a road which are carried out by a local roads authority on land within the boundaries of the road;
(c) works carried out by a local authority or statutory undertaker for the purpose of inspecting, repairing or renewing any sewers, mains, pipes, cables or other apparatus, including the breaking open of any road or other land for that purpose;
(d) use of any buildings or other land within the curtilage of a dwelling-house for a purpose incidental to the enjoyment of

[44] *Trustees of Castel-y-Mynach Estate* v. *Secretary of State for Wales* [1985] J.P.L. 40.
[45] *Hartley* v. *M.H.L.G.* [1970] 1 Q.B. 413.
[46] *Caledonian Terminal Investments* v. *Edinburgh Corporation*, 1970 S.C. 271; S.L.T. 362.
[47] s. 19(2), as amended.

the dwelling-house as such (see Material change of use, above);
(e) use of any land for the purposes of agriculture or forestry (including afforestation) and the use for any of those purposes of any building occupied together with land so used (Chapter 9);
(f) a change of use within the terms of the U.C.O. (below);
(g) demolition of any description of building specified in a direction given by the Secretary of State to planning authorities generally or to a particular planning authority (see Building operations, above).

Development Which Does Not Require Planning Permission

Notwithstanding the definition of "development," planning permission is not required in certain restricted circumstances.[48] In consequence of the substitution of the 10-year immunity period for changes of use without planning permission, for the previous rule that only changes prior to 1965 were immune (Chapter 7), the only important categories are:

(a) if on July 1, 1948 land was used on occasions for a purpose other than its normal use, whether or not at regular intervals, permission will not be required for use of the land for that other purpose on similar occasions on or after December 8, 1969 if the land has been used for that other purpose on at least one similar occasion between July 1, 1948 and before the beginning of 1969;
(b) planning permission is not required for the resumption of the normal use of the land on the expiry of a temporary planning permission (Chapter 5), provided that use was not in breach of planning control (Chapter 7);
(c) where planning permission has been granted by a development order, such as the P.D.O. (below), planning permission is not required for resumption of the normal use of the land, provided that use was not in breach of planning control; and

[48] s. 20.

(d) where an enforcement notice has been served in respect of any development of land, planning permission is not required to change the use of the land to any use which would have been lawful if that development had not been carried out. Uses which are immune from enforcement action are deemed to be lawful (Chapter 7).

In addition, planning permission is not required for development on Crown or any other land which is undertaken by the Crown (Chapter 9).

Deemed Planning Permission (Permitted Development Rights)

In certain circumstances planning permission is deemed to have been granted and no application for permission is therefore necessary. The main source of deemed planning permission (sometimes referred to as permitted development rights) is the Permitted Development Order (below).

Deemed planning permission for the display of an advertisement in accordance with the Control of Advertisement Regulations,[49] development in Enterprise Zones and Simplified Planning Zones and development by a planning authority is discussed in Chapter 9.

Permitted Development Order

From March 13, 1992 the Permitted Development Order (the P.D.O.) has replaced the General Development Order (or G.D.O.) as the main source of deemed planning permission/permitted development rights.[50] The layout of the P.D.O. is different, but the majority of the permitted development rights remain the same, although exercise of these rights in conservation areas and within the curtilage of listed buildings is more restricted than before, and there is a reduction in the

[49] s. 62. See Chap. 9.

[50] s. 21, as amended; Town and Country Planning (General Permitted Development) (Scotland) Order 1992 (S.I. 1992 No. 223), as amended by Amendment Order 1992 (S.I. 1992 No. 1078), Amendment No. 2 Order 1992 (S.I. 1992 No. 2084) and Amendment Order 1993 (S.I. 1993 No. 1036).

scope of the deemed permission for agricultural development.[51]

Planning permission is deemed to be granted for developments within the descriptions printed in **bold** type in Schedule 1 of the P.D.O. The sub-paragraphs below each description specify the circumstances in which there is no deemed planning permission granted (although planning permission will only be required if the proposed work falls within the definition of development). Important terms are defined in article 2(1) or the appropriate part of Schedule 1.

For example, class 9 is in the following form:

> "(1) **The stone cleaning or painting of the exterior or any building or works.**
>
> (2) Development is not permitted by this class—
>
> (a) for the purposes of advertisement, announcement or direction;
>
> (b) where the building or works are in a conservation area;
>
> (c) where the building is a listed building."

The effect of class 9 is that planning permission is deemed to be granted for stone cleaning or painting of the exterior of a building. If the circumstances fall within one of the exceptions, an application for planning permission will be required only if the stone cleaning or painting falls within the definition of development. For example, there is no deemed planning permission for stone cleaning a building in a conservation area, but planning permission will only be required if the cleaning will materially affect the exterior of the building (see Building operations, above).

The P.D.O. cannot permit development:

(a) in breach of any condition attached to a grant of planning permission or deemed permission granted in terms of another order;

[51] Compensation claims had to be submitted by March 13, 1993 for loss suffered as a result of this removal of permitted development rights and a subsequent refusal of an application for planning permission: TCPSA s. 154, as amended.

(b) involving the formation, laying out or material widening of a means of access to a trunk or classified road, or which creates an obstruction to the view of persons using any road used by vehicular traffic, so as to be likely to cause danger to such persons (with some exceptions);
(c) entailing the laying or construction of a notifiable pipeline other than by a public gas supplier.

Permitted development rights conferred by the P.D.O. may be removed for any particular development or class of development within a specified geographical area (frequently a conservation area), by an article 4 direction.[52] If an article 4 direction removes permitted development rights for work and a subsequent application for planning permission for that work made within 12 months of the direction is refused, a claim for compensation may arise.[53] It is also competent to restrict future exercise of permitted development rights by imposing a condition upon a grant of planning permission (Chapter 6).

The P.D.O. specifies 69 classes of permitted development listed in Schedule 1, Parts 1–22, ranging from development within the curtilage of a dwelling-house to development at amusement parks. As many of the classes are of specialised interest only, the following discussion concentrates on the provisions which are likely to have a wider effect.

Part 1 Development Within the Curtilage of a Dwelling-house

It is important to note that the definition of "dwelling-house" for the purposes of the P.D.O. does not include a building containing one or more flats, or a flat contained within such a building. The permitted development rights specified in Part 1 therefore do not extend to a flat, which is defined as a separate and self-contained set of premises, whether or not on the same floor, forming part of a building from some other part of which it is divided horizontally.

[52] Art. 4.
[53] TCPSA, s. 154, as amended.

Neither the P.D.O. nor the T.C.P.S.A. define "curtilage." Broadly, the curtilage of a building includes any land or building used for its comfortable enjoyment or serving the purpose of the building in some necessary or reasonably useful way, although not marked off or enclosed in any way.[54] The curtilage of a typical dwelling-house is its garden. The extent of the curtilage is a question of fact and circumstances. The geographical relationship and the use made of the land and buildings will be important. Current ownership may be irrelevant, for example, the large grounds which often form the curtilage of listed buildings can be in the hands of several different owners.

Class 1 The enlargement, improvement or other alteration of a dwelling-house.

This class includes the erection of any building with a floor area greater than four square metres and within five metres of any part of the dwelling-house, but excludes the erection of a building within the curtilage of a listed building. There are restrictions on the increase in floor area and the total area of ground covered by buildings within the curtilage. In addition, there must be no increase in height beyond the height of the highest part of the roof of the original dwelling-house. Development near either the boundary of the curtilage of the dwelling-house or any road bounding the curtilage is limited. This class does not permit the cladding of any part of the exterior of a dwelling-house in a conservation area.

Class 2 Any alteration to the roof of a dwelling-house including the enlargement of a dwelling-house by way of an addition or alteration to its roof.

Planning permission is deemed to be granted for any alteration to the roof of a dwelling-house, other than a

[54] *Sinclair-Lockhart's Trustees* v. *Central Land Board*, 1951 S.L.T. 121, *per* Lord Mackintosh at p. 123. See Watchman and Young, "The Meaning of Curtilage" 1990 S.L.T. 77; Mynors, "The Extent of Listing" [1993] J.P.L. 99.

dwelling-house within a conservation area. The alterations cannot increase the height of any part of the dwelling-house beyond the highest part of the existing roof. There are also limits on the extension beyond the plane of any existing roof slope (which will restrict the installation of dormer windows without planning permission) and the increase in roof area. An application for planning permission will be required if any roofing material used materially affects the external appearance of the dwelling-house.

Class 3 The provision within the curtilage of a dwelling-house of any building or enclosure, swimming or other pool required for a purpose incidental to the enjoyment of the dwelling-house, or the maintenance, improvement or other alteration of such a building or enclosure.

The erection of buildings such as garages and garden sheds, walls or fences, and swimming pools, and any subsequent maintenance, improvement or alteration, will not require planning permission.

The building, enclosure or pool must be required for a purpose incidental to the enjoyment of the dwelling-house, which includes the keeping of poultry, bees, pet animals, birds or other livestock. However, permitted development rights under this class do not extend to the erection, maintenance or alteration of beehives, chicken sheds and similar structures if the livestock are kept for commercial purposes and not for the domestic needs or personal enjoyment of the occupants of the dwelling-house. Keeping up to 44 dogs in a cottage was held to be not a use incidental to the enjoyment of a dwelling-house, notwithstanding that the dogs were kept as a hobby.[55]

Development is not permitted by this class if it consists of a dwelling. There are also limits on the distance of the building or enclosure from any road which bounds the curtilage and from the dwelling-house, its floor area and height, and the

[55] *Wallington* (n. 26).

total area of ground covered by buildings or enclosures within the curtilage. If the land is within a conservation area or the curtilage of a listed building, permitted development rights under this class do not extend to the provision, alteration or improvement of a building with a floor area greater than four square metres.

Class 4 The provision within the curtilage of a dwelling-house of a hard surface for any purpose incidental to the enjoyment of the dwelling-house.

Planning permission is deemed to be granted for provision of hard surfaces such as areas of tarmac for car parking and paved patio areas, other than within a conservation area or the curtilage of a listed building. The hard surface must also be for a purpose incidental to the enjoyment of the dwelling-house (see class 3 above).

Class 5 The erection or provision within the curtilage of a dwelling-house of a container for the storage of oil.

This permitted development right does not apply within a conservation area or the curtilage of a listed building. In addition, there are restrictions on the capacity of the container, its height and its distance from any road bounding the curtilage. Deemed permission extends only to the provision of one container within the curtilage of a dwelling-house.

Class 6 The installation, alteration or replacement of a satellite antenna on a dwelling-house or within the curtilage of a dwelling-house.

The antenna must be sited so far as practicable to minimise its effect on the external appearance of the building or structure on which it is installed. There are also restrictions on the size and height of the antenna. Development is not permitted by this class if it would result in either more than one satellite antenna on the dwelling-house or within its curtilage, or the antenna is installed in a conservation area or national scenic area on any part of a dwelling-house which faces on to a road.

Part 2 Sundry Minor Operations

Class 7 ***The erection, construction, maintenance, improvement or alteration of a gate, fence, wall or other means of enclosure.***

The height of any new enclosure must not exceed two metres above ground level, or one metre if within 20 metres of a road. The height of an existing enclosure cannot be increased beyond these limits. Development is not permitted by this class if it would involve an enclosure surrounding a listed building or development within its curtilage. Permitted development rights under this class are not restricted to development within the curtilage of a dwelling-house.

Class 9 ***The stone cleaning or painting of the exterior of any building or works.***

This permitted development right does not include stone cleaning or painting for purposes of advertisement, announcement or direction, to which the control of advertisement regulations will apply (Chapter 9). Although the stone cleaning or painting of a listed building or building within a conservation area is also excluded, planning permission for these activities is required only if the external appearance of the building will be materially affected.[56] Painting includes the application of colour.

Part 3 Changes of Use

The Use Classes Order (U.C.O.) provides that changes of use within defined classes do not require planning permission (below). A material change of use from one class to another

[56] s. 19(2)(a).

will require permission. Part 3 of the P.D.O. permits certain changes of use between classes without permission (Figure 4.2).

Class 10

Permits a change of use from a use within class 2 (financial, professional and other services), class 3 (food and drink), or the sale or display for sale of motor vehicles to a use within class 1 (shops).

Class 11

Permits a change of use from class 3 (food and drink) to class 2 (financial, professional and other services).

Class 12

Permits a change of use from class 5 (general industrial) or class 11 (storage or distribution) to class 4 (business).

Class 13

Permits a change of use from class 4 (business) or class 5 (general industrial) to class 11 (storage or distribution), provided the change of use relates to no more than 235 square metres of the floor area in the building.

Part 4 Temporary Buildings and Uses

Class 14 ***The provision on land of buildings, moveable structures, works, plant or machinery required temporarily in connection with and for the duration of operations being or to be carried out on, in, under or over that land or on land adjoining that land.***

Any planning permission required for the operations must have been obtained. When the operations have been carried out, all buildings, structures, works, plant and machinery must be removed and the land on which these items were situated reinstated to its previous condition as soon as is

Fig. 4.2 Changes of Use Without Planning Permission

From class	*To class*
2 (Financial, professional and other services	1 (shops)
3 (Food and Drink)	1 (shops) or 2 (Financial, professional and other services)
4 (Business)	11 (Storage of Distribution), unless the floor area involved exceeds 235 sq.m.
5 (General Industrial)	4 (Business) or 11 (Storage of Distribution), subject to 235 sq.m. limit
11 (Storage or Distribution)	4 (Business)
Sale and display for sale of motor vehicles	1 (shops)

reasonably practicable. Development is not permitted by this class in connection with mining operations.

Class 15 ***The use of land (other than a building or land within the curtilage of a building) for any purpose, except as a caravan site or an open air market, on not more than 28 days in total in any calendar year, and the erection or placing of moveable structures on the land for the purposes of that use.***

This class permits temporary uses such as rock concerts and the erection of moveable structures such as tents in connection with these uses. The use of any site for such purposes must not exceed 28 days in a calendar year.

Part 6 Agricultural Buildings and Operations

Part 7 Forestry Buildings and Operations

Planning controls over agricultural and forestry development are examined in Chapter 9.

Part 8 Industrial and Warehouse Development

Class 23 ***The extension or alteration of an industrial building or a warehouse.***

The building as extended or altered must be used for the purposes of the undertaking concerned, and in the case of an industrial building, may only be used for the carrying out of an industrial process or the provision of employee facilities, or in the case of a warehouse, for storage or distribution or the provision of employee facilities. There are also restrictions on the size of the building as extended or altered, including a restriction on the increase in floor area to 25 per cent. or 1,000 square metres whichever is the greater. The planning authority can require an application for planning permission to be submitted if the external appearance of the premises would be materially affected by the extension or alteration.

Class 24 Development carried out on industrial land for the purposes of an industrial process consisting of

(a) the installation of additional or replacement plant or machinery;
(b) the provision, rearrangement or replacement of a sewer, main, pipe, cable or other apparatus; or
(c) the provision, rearrangement or replacement of a private way, private railway, siding or conveyor.

Development is not permitted if it would materially affect the external appearance of the premises or any plant or machinery would be higher than 15 metres above ground level or the height of anything replaced, whichever is the greater.

Part 12 Development by Local Authorities

Class 30 The erection or construction and the maintenance, improvement or other alteration by a local authority of:

(a) any building, works or equipment not exceeding four metres in height or 200 cubic metres in capacity on land belonging to or maintained by them, being building works or equipment required for the purposes of any function exercised by them on that land otherwise than as statutory undertakers;
(b) lamp standards, refuse bins, public shelters and similar structures or works required in connection with the operation of any public service administered by them.

Class 31 The carrying out by a roads authority on land outwith but adjoining the boundary of an existing road of works required for or incidental to the maintenance or improvement of the road.

Class 32 Any development relating to sewerage by a regional or islands council being development not above ground level required in connection with the provision, improvement, maintenance or repair of a sewer, outfall pipe or sludge main and associated apparatus.

Use Classes Order

The Use Classes Order (U.C.O.) specifies 15 classes of use. Within each class are listed uses of a broadly similar character. Provided both uses are in the same class, a change from one use to another use does not involve development and, therefore, no planning permission is required for the change.[57] For example, any change from use as a post office to use for the sale of tickets will not amount to development because both uses are within Class 1 (below). Primary use is the determining factor for the provisions of the U.C.O. and planning permission is not required where ancillary or incidental uses fall within a different class from the primary use.[58]

It should not be assumed that any change of use from one class to another therefore requires permission. There may be deemed planning permission for the change under the P.D.O. (above). In the absence of deemed permission, an application for planning permission is only necessary if the change of use is material.

The TCPSA declares that certain changes of use will always be material and, therefore, require planning permission (see Material change of use), such as subdivision of a dwelling-house into two or more dwelling-houses,[59] which would otherwise be a change of use within class 14 (Houses). In addition, a condition imposed upon a grant of planning permission can restrict changes of use notwithstanding that the change of use does not constitute development in terms of the U.C.O. (Chapter 6).

The following uses are excluded from the provisions of the U.C.O. and planning permission will, therefore, be required for any change to or from these uses (the character of these uses is such that the change is likely to be material):

(a) as a theatre;
(b) as an amusement arcade or centre, or funfair;

[57] s. 19(2)(f), as amended; Town and Country Planning (Use Classes) (Scotland) Order 1989 (S.I. 1989 No. 147), as amended by Amendment Order 1993 (S.I. 1993, No. 1038), art. 3.
[58] art. 3(3).
[59] s. 19(3)(a).

(c) for the sale of fuel for motor vehicles;
(d) for the sale or display for sale of motor vehicles[60];
(e) for a taxi business or for the hire of motor vehicles;
(f) as a scrap-yard or a yard for the breaking of motor vehicles;
(g) for the storage or distribution of minerals;
(h) as a public house; or
(i) for any works registrable under the Alkali, etc. Works Regulation Act 1906.

Where a single undertaking occupies land on a single site or on adjacent sites which is used for purposes within any two or more of classes 4 to 10 (business and industrial groups), those uses may be treated as if they were in a single class in considering the use of that land, provided this will not result in a substantial increase in the area used for a purpose falling either within class 5 (general industrial) or within classes 7–10 (special industrial groups).[61]

The 15 use classes are:

Class 1 Shops

(a) the retail sale of goods other than hot food;
(b) as a post office;
(c) for the sale of tickets;
(d) as a travel agency;
(e) for the sale of cold food for consumption off the premises;
(f) for hairdressing;
(g) for the direction of funerals;
(h) for the display of goods for sale;
(i) for the hiring out of domestic or personal goods or articles;
(j) as a launderette or dry cleaners; or

[60] A change of use from sale and display for sale of motor vehicles to class 1 (Shops) does not require planning permission — P.D.O., class 10.
[61] U.C.O. art. 3(4).

(k) for the reception of goods to be washed, cleaned or repaired;

where the sale, display or service is principally to visiting members of the public.

The P.D.O. permits change of use of motor vehicle showrooms and premises falling within class 2 (financial, professional and other services) or class 3 (food and drink) to a class 1 use without planning permission.

Class 2 Financial, professional and other services

Use for the provision of

(a) financial services;
(b) professional services; or
(c) any other services (including use as a betting office);

which it is appropriate to provide in a shopping area and where the services are provided principally to visiting members of the public.

Thus a change of use from an estate agency to a solicitors' office will not require planning permission, as both uses fall within class 2. Office uses which do not serve the public directly fall within class 4 (Business), to avoid loss of shop-front property.

In terms of the P.D.O., where the established use of a property falls within class 2, no planning permission is required for a change to a use within class 1 (Shops). However, in consequence of the perceived desirability of preserving shop units, planning permission will be required for a change of use from class 1 to class 2. The P.D.O. also provides that no permission is required for a change of use from class 3 (Food and drink) to class 2.

Class 3 Food and drink

Use for the sale of food and drink for consumption on the premises or of hot food for consumption off the premises.

This class includes hot food shops, restaurants and snack bars. For example, planning permission is not required for a change of use from a cafe to a hot food takeaway, notwithstanding the traffic generation, noise and litter, and later opening hours often associated with such a change. However, planning permission will be required if the cafe is to become a public house (unlike the equivalent position in England and Wales).[62]

A newsagent's shop selling hot pies at lunchtime involves uses within classes 1 and 3. If the sale of hot pies cannot be described as ancillary or incidental to the shop use, a material change of use may have occurred and planning permission be required.[63]

In terms of the P.D.O., a change of use from class 3 to either class 1 (Shops) or class 2 (Financial, professional and other services) does not require planning permission.

Class 4 Business

(a) as an office, other than a use within class 2 (financial, professional and other services);
(b) for research and development of products or processes;
(c) for any industrial process;

being a use which can be carried on in any residential area without detriment to the amenity of that area by reason of noise, vibration, smell, fumes, smoke, soot, ash, dust or grit.

This combines some of the uses within the office and light industrial classes of the previous U.C.O. The wording of class 4 allows a business park to become an office campus without planning permission. Planning authorities are concerned that this may lead to displacement of manufacturing activities and spread of office developments outwith city centres.[64] It may also force traditional industries out of town centres in favour of higher rental office use.

[62] art. 3(5).
[63] See n. 37.
[64] For example, Glasgow District Council's Policy Report on Office and Business Class Development in Glasgow (June 1990).

The flexibility of this class is increased by the permitted changes of use under the P.D.O. from classes 5 (General industrial) and 11 (Storage or distribution) to class 4. In addition, no permission is required for a change of use from class 4 to class 11 (Storage or distribution) provided the floor area involved does not exceed 235 square metres.

Class 5 General industrial

Use for the carrying on of an industrial process other than one falling within class 4 (Business) or within classes 6–10 (Special Industrial Groups).

The P.D.O. permits a change of use from class 5 to class 4 (Business). A change to class 11 (Storage and distribution) is also competent without permission provided the floor area involved does not exceed 235 square metres.

Classes 7–10 Special Industrial Groups.[65]

Class 11 Storage or distribution

Use for storage or as a distribution centre.

An established class 11 use holds the potential of a change without permission to the flexible class 4 (Business).

Class 12 Hotels and hostels

Use as a hotel, boarding house, guest house, or hostel where no significant element of care is provided, other than premises licensed for the sale of alcoholic liquor to persons other than residents or to persons other than persons consuming meals on the premises.

[65] Class 6 was deleted by the Town and Country Planning (Use Classes) (Scotland) Amendment Order 1993 (S.I. 1993 No. 1038).

No planning permission is required to change a nurses' home to a hotel use, despite such planning consequences as increased traffic, especially buses and taxis, with resultant parking difficulties, and increased cooking smells. The reference to the sale of alcoholic liquor excludes public house uses from class 12 (public houses are completely excluded from the U.C.O.).

Class 13 Residential institutions

Class 14 Houses

Use as a house, other than a flat, whether or not as a sole or main residence,

(a) by a single person or by people living together as a family, or
(b) not more than five residents living together including a household where care is provided for residents.

Working at home may involve a change of use of part of the dwelling-house to use for business purposes. However, planning permission will not be required if the overall character of the use as a residence is unchanged. Factors such as increased visitors and deliveries will be relevant. A change of use to multiple occupancy involving more than five residents who are not members of a family will require planning permission.

Class 15 Non-residential institutions

Class 16 Assembly and leisure

Determination Whether Planning Permission Required: Certificates of Lawfulness of Use or Development

With the lack of a precise definition of "development," it is often unclear whether planning permission is necessary for an operation or change of use. Such difficulties can be resolved by obtaining a formal determination from the planning authority, either in advance of the development or following its completion.

Previously an application would be made to the planning authority for a section 51 determination or an established use certificate. A section 51 determination indicated whether planning permission was required for proposed operations or change of use. Although the section 51 determination was described as good as a grant of planning permission, there had been some uncertainty surrounding its legal status. An established use certificate was conclusive evidence that the use was immune from enforcement action, but did not render the use lawful. Section 51 determinations and established use certificates granted prior to September 25, 1992 remain valid.

From that date, determinations will be given in the form of Certificates of Lawfulness of Use or Development.[66] The applicant for a certificate must provide the planning authority with the information to reach its decision. The procedure cannot be used as a "fishing expedition" to obtain information from the planning authority on existing lawful uses or development, or an indication of what classes of use or development would be lawful.

This new procedure would seem to remove the possibility of arguing that a written statement by an officer is a formal determination even although no formal application had been made for such a determination. It is a well-established principle that statements by planning officers cannot bind the planning authority. Notwithstanding a statement by a planning officer that planning permission is not required for proposed work, the planning authority may take enforcement action against the work on the grounds that permission was required (Chapter 7). Under the new procedure the only way to prevent such enforcement action is to apply for a certificate.

A Certificate of Lawfulness of Proposed Use or Development (CLOPUD) will be issued if the planning authority is satisfied that the use or operations would be lawful

[66] TCPSA ss. 90–90C, as substituted by 1991 Act, s. 42, and Town and Country Planning (General Development Procedure) (Scotland) Order 1992, arts. 26–29, as substituted by 1992 Amendment Order (S.I. 1992 No. 2083).

(presumably by reference to statute, the P.D.O. or U.C.O., and case law) if begun at the time of the application. There is an irrefutable presumption that the use or operations specified in the certificate are lawful, unless the law changes before the use or operations are begun.

The Certificate of Lawfulness of Existing Use or Development (CLEUD) is a determination of the lawfulness of either any existing use of land or buildings, or any operations which have been carried out, or any failure to comply with a condition or limitation attached to a grant of planning permission. The lawfulness of any use or development specified in the certificate is conclusively presumed. For the first time this enables a statutory document to be obtained certifying the lawfulness of existing operational development or use as a single dwelling-house.

A use or operation is lawful if it is immune from enforcement action (Chapter 7) and is not in contravention of the requirements of any enforcement notice or breach of condition notice which is in force (this removes the concept of established or immune development). Once the lawfulness of a use or operation has been certified, that use or operation enjoys the permitted development rights conferred by the P.D.O.[67]

Any person (not just the owner of the land) may apply to the planning authority for a Certificate of Lawfulness of Proposed/Existing Use or Development. A completed form similar to that for an application for planning permission is submitted, together with full supporting information. There is no requirement to give notice to persons with an interest in the land which is the subject of the application, or neighbours. The planning authority is not obliged to publicise the application. Owners/tenants/neighbours/other interested parties will therefore not be alerted to the application unless they routinely inspect the planning register in which details of the application will be entered. Although the planning authority is not required to consult interested parties, it may choose to do so.

[67] Following revocation of art. 2(3) of the P.D.O. by Amendment No. 2 Order (S.I. 1992 No. 2084).

The fee payable is set by reference to the fees for an application for planning permission for the operation or change of use in respect of which a certificate is sought: in the case of a CLOPUD, 50 per cent. of that fee; and for a CLEUD, the full fee, or £58 for an application relating to a failure to comply with a condition. If an application for a CLOPUD is refused, there is no exemption from payment of the full fee for any application for planning permission which is lodged in consequence of that refusal.

The onus is on the applicant to provide sufficient information of the lawfulness to satisfy the planning authority, but not to prove the lawfulness beyond reasonable doubt. Corroboration of the applicant's evidence does not appear to be required. If there is no evidence to contradict or cast doubt upon the applicant's evidence, the Scottish Office advises that the application should not be refused, provided the evidence is sufficiently precise and unambiguous to justify the grant of a certificate on the balance of probability.[68] This leaves open the question of whether it is ever competent for the planning authority to adopt an active role to seek out information to rebut the applicant's evidence.

The origin and identity of the applicant, and the planning merits of the use or development have no relevance to the legal issues involved in the determination of the application. As a result, it may be appropriate for determination of such applications to be delegated to planning officers rather than left in the hands of the councillors sitting on the planning committee.

As the effect of a certificate is similar to a grant of planning permission, the authority will require to specify precisely the description of the use or development and the boundaries of the site, to avoid giving permission for more than is intended. The authority may modify the description of the use, operation or other matter specified in the application, presumably to avoid refusing the application.

If sufficient information is provided, the authority will issue a certificate which shall conclusively presume the lawfulness

[68] Scottish Office Environment Department Circular 36/1992, "Planning and Compensation Act 1991 — Lawful Development and Enforcement," para. 69.

of any use, operations or other matters specified in the certificate. For the purposes of certain statutes, the certificate will have effect as if it were a grant of permission. A refusal is not conclusive evidence that the use or development is unlawful and will not preclude a further application based on new evidence.

It is an offence either knowingly or recklessly to make a statement which is false or misleading in a material particular or, with intent to deceive, to use any document which is false or misleading in a material particular, or to withhold material information. The planning authority may revoke a certificate without compensation if a statement was made or a document used which was false in a material particular or any material information was withheld. The possibility of revocation without compensation will limit the value of a certificate to any subsequent owner of the land.

The applicant has a right of appeal to the Secretary of State against a refusal or part refusal to issue a certificate. There is no right of appeal against a failure to determine an application within the two-month time limit. The normal appeal procedures apply, with a choice of written submissions procedure or a public local inquiry (Chapter 8).

The decision of the Secretary of State on appeal may be challenged in the Court of Session (Chapter 8). However, such a challenge is limited to allegations that he acted illegally and his decision on the facts is final.

Chapter 5

DEVELOPMENT CONTROL II — APPLYING FOR PLANNING PERMISSION

If planning permission is required for a proposed development, an application for that permission must be made to the planning authority for the district in which the development site is located. When applying for planning permission it is easy to fall into the trap of treating the planning authority as the "enemy" to whom information should only be given as a last resort. In reality they fulfil a valuable consultative role. All but the simplest of applications for planning permission should be discussed in advance with the planning officer responsible for the area in which the development site lies. Although any indications given by the officer cannot dictate the decision eventually reached by the planning committee on the application, careful consideration should be given to his comments regarding relevant policies and possible alterations to the proposals to make the application more likely to be awarded permission. No fee can be charged for this service.[1]

The general rules governing the procedure for applying for planning permission, formerly part of the General Development Order (G.D.O.) are now contained in the Development Procedure Order (D.P.O.).[2] In addition to these rules, each planning authority has its own internal procedures for handling planning applications.

Types of Application

Before applying for planning permission, a decision has to be made on the type of permission to be sought, as this must be

[1] *R.* v. *Richmond upon Thames Borough Council, ex p. McCarthy & Stone (Developments) Limited* [1991] 3 W.L.R. 941; 1992 S.P.L.P. 35:22.

[2] Town and Country Planning (General Development Procedure) (Scotland) Order 1992 (S.I. 1992 No. 224), as amended by Amendment Order 1992 (S.I. 1992 No. 2083) and Amendment Order 1993 (S.I. 1993 No. 1039).

indicated on the application form. This decision will be influenced by the nature of the proposed development, the planning history of the site and, to some extent, the attitude of the planning authority as indicated in pre-application consultations (above).

(a) Full or Detailed Planning Permission

The terms "full" or "detailed" planning permission do not appear in the TCPSA, but are used interchangeably in practice to highlight the difference between what the Act refers to as "planning permission" and "outline planning permission." An application for full or detailed planning permission is appropriate where the applicant has decided all the details of the proposed development and these details can be submitted to the planning authority for its approval. If that approval is given, the development can proceed and be completed without further applications to the authority, unless permission is needed to change some of the details of the development or the permission is subject to a condition requiring the approval of the authority for some further matter.

(b) Outline Planning Permission

It is competent for outline planning permission to be granted for the carrying out of any development except a material change of use (Chapter 4).

Outline permission is sought when the applicant wishes to obtain consent to the outlines or principle of the development before drawing up a detailed scheme, thereby saving the expense of that work if outline permission is not granted. Following a grant of outline permission, a further application must be made to the authority for its approval of the detailed scheme, in compliance with the condition imposed upon every grant of outline permission requiring subsequent approval to be obtained from the planning authority for specified areas of detail, known as reserved matters (below).

Where it is intended to sell land with the benefit of permission (the grant of permission will normally increase the value of the land and therefore its sale price), it is often advisable to obtain outline rather than detailed planning permission. A grant of outline planning permission provides a guarantee that the broad outlines of the development have been approved, leaving the purchaser free to draw up detailed proposals to his own requirements and obtain approval by submitting an application for approval of reserved matters.

An application for outline planning permission necessarily contains less detail than an application for detailed permission, but is similar in other respects. Further details and information can be requested from the applicant if the planning authority consider that in the circumstances of the case the application ought not to be considered separately from the siting, design or external appearance of the building, or the means of access thereto or the landscaping of the site.[3]

(c) Approval of Reserved Matters

Every outline planning permission is granted subject to a condition preventing commencement of development until approval of specified reserved matters is obtained from the planning authority. If no such condition is specified, the permission is deemed to have been granted subject to such a condition.[4]

Reserved matters can be any matters concerning the siting, design or external appearance of a building, or its means of access, or the landscaping of the application site, in respect of which details were not given in the application for outline planning permission.[5] Density, drainage and disposal of sewage, and treatment of boundary walls and fences, are matters which may be reserved for future approval within these categories.[6] The design of a building includes its shape and size, and its floor space. However, a reserved matters

[3] D.P.O., art. 4(2).
[4] TCPSA, s. 39, as amended.
[5] D.P.O., art. 2(1).
[6] *Inverclyde District Council* v. *Inverkip Building Co.*, 1983 S.L.T. 563.

application could not be refused on the grounds that the design provided more office floor space than was needed to make the class 4 development viable.[7]

Application for approval of reserved matters is made in a broadly similar form to an application for full or detailed permission, with the same requirement to notify owners, agricultural tenants and neighbours (below). The application must give particulars sufficient to identify the outline planning permission in relation to which it is made. The details submitted, and the reserved matters approval granted, cannot depart from the ambit of the outline planning permission.

The application must be submitted (but need not be granted) within three years from the date outline permission was granted, or six months from the date any earlier application for approval was refused, or six months from the date of the dismissal of an appeal against such a refusal, whichever is the latest. Moreover, only one application may be made after three years from the date outline permission was granted. The planning authority may attach a condition to the outline planning permission substituting longer or shorter periods, or specify separate periods for separate parts or phases of the development.[8] Approval may be sought in a single or separate applications. However, submission of an application in respect of some, but not all of the reserved matters, or for part only of the site, within the time limit does not prevent the remainder of the outline permission from expiring.[9] An application for approval of reserved matters which is submitted outside the time limit is treated as not made in accordance with the terms of the permission.[10]

(d) Consent, Agreement or Approval

Planning permission is often granted subject to conditions requiring aspects of the development to meet a standard

[7] *Camden L.B.C.* v. *Secretary of State for the Environment* [1993] J.P.L. 466.
[8] TCPSA, s. 39.
[9] *Hunterston Development Company Ltd.* v. *Secretary of State for Scotland*, 1992 S.L.T. 1097.
[10] s. 40(7)(b).

acceptable to the planning authority. The wording of such conditions will require the developer to apply to the planning authority for its approval. Such applications should identify the planning permission and the condition in terms of which approval is sought, and describe the matter to be approved. These applications appear to fall outwith the scope of the D.P.O. and the normal requirements, such as notification, therefore do not apply.

(e) Variation of Planning Permission

An applicant may request the planning authority to vary the grant of planning permission. Such variation is competent provided it appears to the authority that the change sought is not material.[11] This allows minor changes to be made to the details of a development without the submission of a fresh application for planning permission. As the change is not material, the normal requirements for an application, such as notification of parties, do not apply.

(f) Retrospective Planning Permission

As a result of the complex rules governing when planning permission is required (Chapter 4), as well as public ignorance, it is inevitable that development is sometimes carried out without planning permission. Often the omission only comes to light during the sale of land or buildings, or when the planning authority takes enforcement action (Chapter 7). In these circumstances an application may be made for permission for development already carried out, more commonly known as retrospective planning permission.[12] The procedure for submitting such an application is similar to that for an application for full planning permission. If permission is granted, it will have retrospective effect from the date on which the work or use began. This procedure may also be used where development has been carried out in breach of a condition attached to a planning permission, or

[11] s. 31A, as inserted.
[12] s. 29.

has not been ceased on the expiry of a temporary planning permission (below).

(g) Renewal of Permission

Every grant of planning permission is subject to a condition requiring development to commence or an application for approval of reserved matters to be submitted within a specified time. Provided the development has not commenced and the time limit has not expired, it is possible to apply for the permission to be renewed.[13]

The legal status of an application to renew a permission is uncertain. Arguably it should be determined as if it were a fresh application, and permission could be refused if the material considerations (below) had changed since the previous decision. In these circumstances, it would be open to the applicant to implement the previous permission by commencing the development prior to the expiry of the time limit specified in the condition attached to the permission.

Unlike most other applications, there is no form to complete and neighbour notification (below) is not required. The only requirements are that the application be made in writing and indentify the previous grant of planning permission. An application fee may be payable, calculated as if it were a fresh application for permission.[14] It may, therefore, be cheaper for the applicant to implement the permission thereby saving it from expiry. The methods of implementing a permission by commencing development are discussed later in this chapter (see Duration, below at p. 166.)

(h) Duplicate Applications: Twin Tracking

Where problems in obtaining permission are anticipated, many applicants submit two applications in exactly the same terms. The submission of duplicate applications allows an appeal to be lodged against the deemed refusal (below) of one application while negotiations continue with the planning

[13] D.P.O., art. 5.

[14] Circular 10/1990, "Town and Country Planning (Fees for Applications and Deemed Applications) (Scotland) Regulations 1990", Annex, para. 7(f).

authority with a view to permission being granted for the other application. If submitted within 28 days of the first application, the fee for the second application is 25 per cent. of the fee paid for the first.

A similar practice involves the submission of a fresh application for the same development when an appeal is lodged in respect of the original application. In most such cases, no fee is payable in respect of the duplicate application provided it is submitted within 12 months. The appeal decision may be a material consideration which the authority must take into account when deciding the application (see below). One option available to the planning authority is to refuse the application as premature until the appeal has been decided.

Submission of Application

An application for planning permission should be lodged with the planning authority for the area in which development is proposed. This will be the district council, the regional councils in the case of developments in the regions of Borders, Dumfries and Galloway and Highland, or the islands councils for developments in Orkney, Shetland or the Western Isles.

The application is made by completing and submitting an application form (form D1), obtained from the planning authority. The completed application form should be accompanied by a plan sufficient to identify the location of the site of the proposed development and such other plans and drawings as are necessary to describe the proposed development. The application form usually specifies the number of copies of the form and associated plans and drawings required by the planning authority. Copies are requested to enable at least one copy of the application and supporting plans to be made available for public inspection. The planning authority may require the applicant to provide further information or evidence in respect of information accompanying the application including plans or drawings.[15]

[15] D.P.O., art. 13.

In addition to lodging the completed application form and supporting plans, the applicant must also submit signed certificates relating to notification of owners, agricultural tenants and neighbours, and enclose any fee payable for the application. These matters are discussed below.

Description of Proposed Development

The description of the proposed development given on the application form is important because it governs the extent of the permission sought. Ancillary documents such as plans cannot extend the description. The description is also significant because it is used in both the notices served by the applicant upon notifiable persons and newspaper advertisements, which alert parties to their opportunity to inspect the application and lodge representations.

The description must be accurate, convey the substance of what is applied for and give full and fair notice to possible objectors. A grant of planning permission for petrol stations, restaurants, car parks and a 40-bed lodge was challenged successfully by a third party on the grounds that the application, neighbour notification notices and newspaper advertisements had merely described the proposed development as a roadside petrol station, notwithstanding that the full extent of the development had been shown in the accompanying plans.[16]

Notification of Owners and Agricultural Tenants

Although the applicant seeking permission is not required to own or control the site of the proposed development nor obtain the consent of the owner of the land to the application, the benefit of any grant of planning permission attaches to the land rather than to the applicant, who will be unable to commence the development without the agreement of the landowner.

The applicant must notify the owner that an application for planning permission is being submitted for a proposed

[16] *Cumming* v. *Secretary of State for Scotland*, 1993 S.L.T. 228.

development on his land.[17] This avoids the possibility of an owner selling land without knowing its true value following a grant of planning permission. The applicant must also notify any tenant of an agricultural holding on the site, whose security of tenure may be affected by a grant of permission. Special rules apply for developments consisting of the working and winning of minerals (Chapter 9).

For these purposes the expression "owner" includes a tenant with a lease which still has more than seven years to run.[18] The identity of the owner or tenant may be ascertained from the valuation roll kept by the regional council, or from a search of the Register of Sasines or the Land Register.[19] The applicant must utilise all steps reasonably open to him for tracing the owner, but there is provision for advertisement of applications if the owner cannot be traced (below).

Agricultural holdings are defined by the Agricultural Holdings (Scotland) Act 1949 as land used for the purposes of agriculture as a trade or business. There is no conclusive method for identifying agricultural tenants, other than requesting this information from the landowner or making inquiries in the locality. It is therefore surprising that there is no provision for the possibility of an agricultural tenant being untraceable (below).

The application form obtained from the planning authority will contain a copy of the prescribed form of notice to be served upon owners and tenants of agricultural holdings. The notice is intended to alert these parties to the submission of the application and their right to make representations regarding the application to the planning authority within 21 days of the date of service of the notice (an extended period may be available if the application is advertised, and many authorities will accept representations outwith specified time limits). The notice also states that the grant of permission

[17] TCPSA, s. 24, as amended. The new s. 24 to be substituted by the PCA provides for these matters to be dealt with in regulations, but no substantive change is anticipated, other than the introduction of an increased fine for the offence and a two-year time limit for prosecution.

[18] s. 24(7). The general definition of "owner" is contained in s. 275(1).

[19] Members of the public can carry out searches in person at the Registers of Scotland in Edinburgh (tel: 031 659 6111) or a professional searcher can be instructed.

does not affect owners' rights to retain or dispose of their property unless there is an agreement to the contrary, but that it may affect the security of tenure of a tenant of an agricultural holding.

The applicant completes the notice by filling in details of the application, including the description of the proposed development (above). The notice is normally sent by recorded delivery post or delivered (methods of serving notices are examined in Chapter 7).

Together with the completed application form, the applicant must submit a signed certificate stating that in the period of 21 days ending with the submission of the application, either:

(a) the applicant was the owner of all the land to which the application relates; or

(b) has given the requisite notice of the application to all other persons who within that period were owners of any of that land, specifying their names, the addresses at which notice was served, and the date of service of each notice; or

(c) is unable to notify all the owners, but has notified those specified in the certificate (setting out their names, and the addresses and date of service as above), and has taken such steps as are reasonably open to him (specifying them) to ascertain the names and addresses of the remainder; or

(d) is unable to notify any of the owners, but has taken such steps as are reasonably open to him (specifying them) to ascertain their names and addresses.

If any owners cannot be identified, the applicant must publish an advertisement giving requisite notice of the application in a local newspaper circulating in the locality of the site of the proposed development.[20] The advertisement must be published at least 21 days before submission of the application. The certificate submitted with the application

[20] Prescribed form: D.P.O., Sched. 3.

must give details of the advertisement, including the date of publication and name of the newspaper.

In relation to agricultural tenants, the applicant is required to certify either that none of the land to which the application relates constitutes or forms part of an agricultural holding, or that the requisite notice has been given to any person (other than the applicant) who was a tenant of such an agricultural holding within the period of 21 days ending with submission of the application, setting out the name, address and date of notice.

Unless the applicant has certified that he owns the whole of the site of the proposed development, and that it is not part of an agricultural holding, the planning authority cannot determine the application until 21 days after the last date of service of notice or date of publication of an advertisement, whichever is later.

A failure to notify an owner or agricultural tenant may leave a subsequent grant of permission open to challenge in judicial review proceedings (below). In addition, it is an offence to issue knowingly or recklessly a certificate which contains a statement which is false or misleading in a material particular, with liability on summary conviction to a fine not exceeding level 3 on the standard scale (appendix 1).

Notification of Neighbours

The applicant for planning permission is also required to serve notice of submission of the application upon the owners and occupiers of land neighbouring the site of the proposed development.[21] The equivalent procedure in England and Wales is discretionary and carried out by the planning authority. The purpose of neighbour notification is to alert those who will be most affected by the proposed development of their opportunity to make representations to the planning authority regarding the application.

Neighbour notification is one of the most problematic parts of the procedure for submission of planning applications. It generates many (unjustified) complaints from members of the

[21] TCPSA, s. 23, as amended, and D.P.O., arts. 2 and 9.

public mainly because of widespread public overestimation of the extent of notification required. Broadly, only those neighbours within four metres of the site, excluding the width of any road, must be notified. In urban tenement property areas this may result in identification of over 100 notifiable neighbours, but in the majority of cases only 10–20 persons will require to be notified. The complexity of the procedure makes it unpopular with applicants, not least because of the wide opportunity for errors to be made. Despite this unpopularity, the requirement for neighbour notification is an important aspect of planning applications and is unlikely to be removed.

While notification of owners and agricultural tenants is required for "any application for planning permission," the requirement for neighbour notification only extends to applications for full or detailed permission, outline permission, and for approval of reserved matters. The applicant must serve notice upon those persons holding a "notifiable interest" in "neighbouring land" who have not been notified of the application as an owner or agricultural tenant of the site of the proposed development.

The term "neighbouring land" is defined as land which is conterminous with or within four metres of the boundary of land for which the development is proposed. In most cases the boundary will be clear, but on large sites it may seem more appropriate to identify a boundary within the site. To some extent this is dealt with by the provision that part of such neighbouring land must lie within 90 metres of any part of the development in question. Where the proposed location of the development is more than 90 metres from the boundary, neighbours should suffer minimal impact as a result of the development and there is no justification for requiring them to be notified. However, this leaves open the question of where the boundaries of a site can be drawn (and there have been instances of boundaries being redrawn to avoid notifying neighbours). The boundaries of the planning unit may be a useful guide (Chapter 4).

The best method to identify neighbouring land is by measuring the distances from a large scale Ordnance Survey map for the area (1:1250 for urban areas), as illustrated in Figure 5.1. In calculating the four-metres distance, the width of any road up to a limit of 20 metres is disregarded, unless the planning authority dispense with the requirement of notification in such circumstances, either as a matter of policy or on request for an individual application. Although there are rules for identifying neighbouring land which consists of buildings divided into separate units such as tenements, the safest course must always be to notify all persons within such buildings.

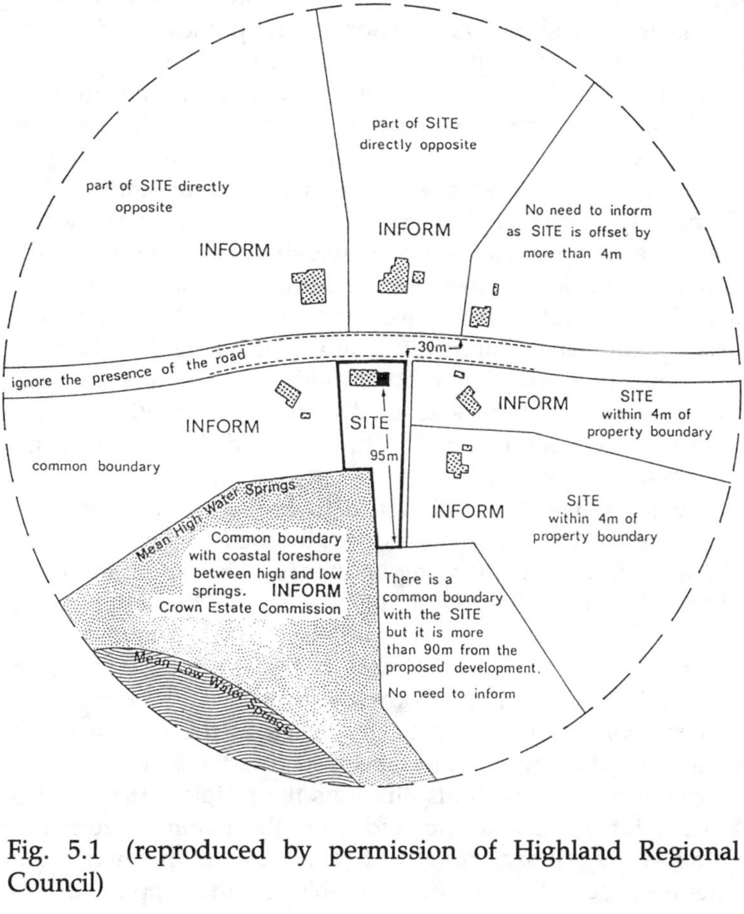

Fig. 5.1 (reproduced by permission of Highland Regional Council)

Once neighbouring land has been identified, the next step is to identify the persons holding a "notifiable interest" in the land. If the neighbouring land is entered on the valuation roll as consisting mainly of commercial premises, separate notification should be sent to each of the named owners, lessees and occupiers at the addresses given on the roll. Where the valuation roll fails to provide this information, notification should be sent to the premises of the neighbouring land individually addressed to "the Owner," "the Occupier" and "the Lessee" respectively (this procedure may also be adopted as a safety measure even where the parties are identified on the roll). In addition, it would seem advisable to send also notification to any parties or addresses known to the applicant, but not specified on the roll.

For any land not entered on the valuation roll, including all residential property, separate notification should be sent addressed to "the Owner" and "the Occupier" respectively at the address of the premises on the neighbouring land.

There is provision for the application to be advertised if there are no premises on the neighbouring land to which notice can be sent. However, it may be possible to persuade the planning authority to dispense with an advertisement if the applicant can demonstrate that the notice has been sent to the notifiable party at another address. Alternatively, the authority may be requested to dispense with notification if a road runs between the site of the proposed development and the neighbouring land.

The prescribed form of notice to be served on notifiable neighbours will be included with the application form obtained from the planning authority. The applicant completes the form by specifying details of the application, including the location of the proposed development and its description (normally in the same terms as the description on the application form). The form also states that the application and supporting plans can be inspected at the offices of the planning authority or other specified locations, such as post offices in rural areas. It also informs the recipient that written representations may be lodged with the planning authority within 14 days beginning with the date of the notice (an extended period may be available if the application is advertised, and many authorities will accept representations outwith specified time limits). The completed notice, together with a location plan showing the site of the proposed development, is normally served upon the notifiable neighbours by recorded delivery letter or delivered by hand (methods of service are examined in Chapter 7).

Together with the completed application form, the applicant must submit a plan showing the location of the neighbouring land in respect of which notification has been carried out, and complete one of the certificates included with the application form which states either that[22]:

(a) notification has been carried out, giving the names and addresses of the persons to which notification has been sent and their interest ("owner," "lessees" or "occupier"), with land entered on the valuation roll and other land listed separately; or
(b) no notification is necessary because there are no notifiable neighbours; or
(c) it is not possible to carry out notification because there are no premises situated on the neighbouring land to which the notification can be sent.

As the applicant is no longer required to notify persons by name and provision is made for advertising applications if there are no premises to which a notice can be addressed, the applicant no longer has the opportunity to certify that he has taken all the steps reasonably open to him to ascertain the names and addresses of all the notifiable neighbours, but is unable to ascertain some or all of their names and addresses.

If the applicant certifies that there are no premises on the neighouring land to which notification can be sent, or if the planning authority dispenses with neighbour notification in respect of land separated from the development site by a road and the applicant has not signed a neighbour notification certificate, the authority is required to publish notice of the application in a local newspaper.

The planning authority must not determine the application until 14 days after the date of its receipt or the date of publishing of an advertisement, whichever is the later.[23] This

[22] D.P.O., arts. 3(c)(iv), 4(c)(iv) and 6(c)(ii) refer to art. 9(4) when the context indicates that what is meant is art. 9(5).
[23] art. 14, as amended.

gives neighbours 14 days in which to lodge representations. In practice most authorities will accept representations received outwith this 14 day period.

Failure to notify a neighbour may leave a subsequent grant of permission open to challenge in judicial review proceedings (below). In addition, it is an offence to issue knowingly or recklessly a notification, make an advertisement other than a newspaper advertisement, or supply a certificate, which purports to comply with these provisions, but which contains a statement which is false or misleading in a material particular.[24] The penalty on summary conviction is a fine not exceeding level 3 on the standard scale (appendix 1). Proceedings for such an offence may be brought within two years of commission of the offence rather than the normal six-month period.

Error in Notification Certificates

The planning authority cannot entertain a planning application unless it is accompanied by the appropriate notification certificates. In relation to notification of neighbours, it cannot entertain an application if any statutory requirement relating to notification has not been satisfied.[25] In most cases the authority will simply check that the appropriate certificates have been completed correctly. It seems unlikely that this statutory duty extends to checking the accuracy of the notification process, but this point is uncertain.

Once possible deficiencies in the notification process are drawn to its attention, the planning authority should investigate and require the applicant to correct any errors. There seems no reason why an application should be rejected as invalid due to errors in the notification procedure,[26] unless the errors are so major that the whole procedure is better repeated. The objective of notification is to alert those persons

[24] TCPSA, ss. 23(3) and (5), as amended.

[25] ss. 23(4) and 24(1), as amended. The new s. 24(4) to be inserted by the Planning and Compensation Act 1991, s. 46 will impose a similar restriction in relation to notification of owners and agricultural tenants.

[26] But see, *Lochore* v. *Moray District Council*, 1992 S.L.T. 16, *per* Lord Cullen at p. 20 K-L; *Pollock* v. *Secretary of State for Scotland*, 1993 S.L.T. 1173, 1993 S.P.L.P. 38:19 (both cases were decided on other grounds).

whom the law perceives to have a special interest to the submission of the application and their opportunity to object to the application. The present practice of most planning authorities is to suspend consideration of the application and request the applicant to remedy defects by serving notification on overlooked persons. At the end of the further period which must be allowed for representations to be received from those persons, the application is then considered in the normal way. This practice fulfils the objective of the notification requirements and therefore seems acceptable. The alternative is for the authority to reject the application as invalid, leaving the applicant to make good the deficiency in notification and resubmit the application.

Errors in the notification process, particularly those pointed out to the planning authority prior to its decision, but not remedied, may leave a grant of permission open to challenge in the courts by a person with a notifiable interest who received no notification of the application. The extent of the error required before the permission may be challenged successfully is not clear. A factual error in a certificate could be regarded as a mere irregularity which would not justify the court in striking down the planning decision. The exercise of the court's discretion may be influenced by the length of time since the grant of permission and the knowledge or otherwise of the application for permission of the person seeking to challenge that permission.[27]

Application Fees

A fee is payable for submission of most applications for planning permission.[28] This is intended to cover the administrative costs incurred by the planning authority in processing and determining applications, although fees are charged on a general scale rather than by reference to the time spent on individual applications. Most authorities

[27] *Main* v. *Swansea City Council* [1985] J.P.L. 558.

[28] Town and Country Planning (Fees for Applications and Deemed Applications) (Scotland) Regulations 1990 (S.I. 1990 No. 563), as amended by S.I. 1990 No. 2474, S.I. 1991 No. 2765, S.I. 1992 No. 1951 and S.I. 1993 No. 3211.

provide a list of fees when dispensing application forms; not every application requires payment of a fee. A telephone call to the authority prior to submission of the application should confirm the correct fee. Failure to pay the correct fee will delay processing of the application.

Processing of Application

In the majority of cases the planning authority will decide straightforward applications in two-three months. Some authorities have a better record than others and much will depend on the development pressures in the district at the time. In complex cases a decision may not be received for many months or even years. The applicant has the opportunity to appeal against a deemed refusal after two months, but if the details of the proposed devlopment are still being negotiated with the authority such an appeal is unlikely to succeed and is not an option worth pursuing, leaving the applicant with no alternative but to persevere with the application.

Each authority has its own internal procedures for processing applications, but the general outline of the procedure is similar, as illustrated in Figure 5.2.

(a) Registration

On receipt of the application and any fee required, the planning authority must send to the applicant a letter of acknowledgement in the prescribed form. This letter acknowledges receipt of the application, but states that examination of it has not been completed and a further communication will be sent if it is discovered to be invalid because statutory or other requirements have not been met. It also advises the applicant of the statutory right to appeal to the Secretary of State if the application has not been determined within two months of the date of receipt of the application as specified in the letter.

The application must comply with the statutory requirements. The correct fee must be included with the application, together with the cost of any advertisement which the applicant is required to pay (below). The application form is

Fig. 5.2 Processing planning application

Application submitted

↓

Acknowledged and compliance with statutory requirements checked

↓

Registration

↓ (branches to: Advertisement (if required) → and → Decline to determine application if Secretary of State refused similar application within previous 2 years)

Advertisement (if required)

Decline to determine application if Secretary of State refused similar application within previous 2 years

↓

Consultation with statutory and other bodies

↓

Planning officer visits site and forms view on proposed development

↓

Negotiations with applicant regarding possible alterations

↓

Officer prepares report with recommendation to grant or refuse application

↓ (branches to both)

Decision by Director of Planning under delegated powers

Decision by Planning Committee

checked to ensure that the appropriate certificates have been signed in connection with notification of owners, agricultural tenants and neighbours. The required number of copies of the application form and associated drawings and plans must be submitted. If the application does not meet any of these requirements, the authority must as soon as possible advise the applicant that the application is invalid. Usually, it will also advise the applicant of the steps necessary to validate the application. For the purposes of a deemed refusal appeal, the date of receipt becomes the date on which the applicant lodges a valid application.[29]

Once the planning authority is satisfied that a valid application has been submitted the application is registered. The applicant is informed in writing of the registration date and the right to lodge an appeal to the Secretary of State if the planning authority does not decide the application within two months of that date (a deemed refusal appeal). Authorities are required to keep a register of applications for planning permission made to them and to make this register available for inspection by the public at all reasonable hours.[30] This register, commonly referred to as the planning register, must contain copies of every application not finally disposed of, together with copies of any plans and drawings submitted along with the application. Another part of the register details the progress of applications, specifying such matters as the date of receipt, the decision (if any) of the authority on that application and the date of that decision, and the date of any subsequent approval given in relation to the application. Entries in the register must be made within seven days.[31] The register allows members of the public to monitor the submission and determination of applications.

Following registration, the application is allotted to a planning officer who is often named in the registration letter.

(b) Power to Decline to Determine Application

Since September 25, 1991 planning authorities have had power to decline to determine an application prior to

[29] D.P.O., arts. 12(6) and 14 (3).
[30] TCPSA, ss. 31(2) and (4), as amended.
[31] D.P.O., art. 10 and Sched. 5, as amended, and art. 11.

considering its merits.[32] This power is exercisable if, within the two years prior to submission of the application, the Secretary of State has refused a similar application either on appeal or under a reference to him, and in the opinion of the authority there has been no significant change in the development plan or in any other material considerations since his decision. This is a two-stage process: firstly, the authority has to decide whether as a matter of fact the application is "similar," and, secondly, whether as a matter of discretion to decline to consider it on its own merits.[33]

Applications are considered "similar" if the proposed development and the site to which the applications relate are the same or substantially similar. If the application has been revised in what appears to be a genuine attempt to take account of objections to an earlier proposal, the Scottish Office guidance states that it should not be regarded as similar. The power should be used only where the authority believes the applicant is intending to exert pressure by submitting repeated similar applications. In doubtful cases the authority should proceed to determine the application.[34]

There is no right of appeal to the Secretary of State against the decision of the planning authority to decline to determine the application in this way. Judicial review of the decision of the authority will be competent, but requires the applicant to show that the exercise of this discretionary power was illegal rather than merely wrong (Chapter 8). Provided all relevant considerations are taken into account, the courts will be unwilling to interfere with the decision made by the authority on what is essentially a factual matter. For example, where the first application concerned an "amusement centre and ancillary retail sales" and the second a reduced area for an "amusement centre/snack bar (with exclusive retail area)," the authority were entitled to have regard to the fact that the second application raised substantially the same planning considerations as the first, including being contrary to the

[32] TCPSA, s. 26A.

[33] *The Noble Organisation* v. *Falkirk D.C.*, 1994 S.L.T. 100.

[34] Scottish Office Environment Department Circular 22/1991, "Planning and Compensation Act 1991", Annex 2.

development plan, and to refuse the second application as similar.[35]

(c) Advertisement

There are several situations in which an application must be advertised in a local newspaper. If the applicant certifies that he has been unable to serve notice on some or all of the owners of the site of the proposed development, he is required to publish an advertisement before submitting the application. Where, in the opinion of the planning authority, the proposed development would affect the character or appearance of a conservation area, or affect the setting of a listed building, the application must be advertised by the planning authority and a site notice displayed for at least seven days.[36]

An application must be advertised in a local newspaper by the planning authority, but at the expense of the applicant where[37]:

> (i) the planning authority has dispensed with the neighbour notification requirement in respect of land separated from the development site by a road up to 20 metres wide, and the applicant has not completed a neighbour notification certificate (as the D.P.O. provides for the applicant to certify that no notification is required, this provision for advertisement if no certificate is completed seems redundant);
>
> (ii) the applicant seeks permission for one of the specified classes of development known as "bad neighbour development," which are considered to have such a potentially adverse effect on amenity that applications for those developments must be advertised. Bad neighbour developments include public conveniences, sewage works, theatres, fun fairs, licensed premises, hot food shops and other specified leisure-related premises[38];

[35] *The Noble Organisation* v. *Falkirk D.C.* (n. 33).
[36] TCPSA, s. 25, as amended.
[37] s. 23, as amended, and D.P.O., arts. 12(5) and (8).
[38] Appendix 2 gives the full list.

(iii) the applicant certifies that there are no premises situated on neighbouring land to which neighbour notification can be sent; or

(iv) an environmental statement is submitted in connection with a planning application (below).

The applicant is required to pay the cost of this advertisement when submitting the application. The planning authority must publish the advertisement as soon as practicable after receipt of the application.

A single advertisement is sufficient to satisfy the requirements of all or any of the above provisions.[39] Advertisements in relation to ownership notification and conservation areas or listed buildings must state that representations may be made to the planning authority within 21 days.[40] In the other cases, a 14-day period is allowed for representations to be submitted.[41] The planning authority cannot decide the application until the expiry of the appropriate period. Where a site notice is displayed, the application cannot be determined until 21 days after the first date of display.[42]

If the local authority itself is applying for planning permission, it is required to give notice of its intention in a local newspaper and allow for representations to be made to the authority (Chapter 9).

Before granting planning permission for a development which does not accord with the provisions of the development plan, the planning authority must advertise the application in a local newspaper and allow 21 days for representations.

(d) Consultation

Before making its decision on the application, the planning authority is required to consult various bodies requesting their views on the proposed development.[43] In addition to these

[39] D.P.O., art. 12(7); Prescribed form: Sched. 8.
[40] TCPSA, s. 24(4), as amended, and s. 25(2) and (3), as amended.
[41] D.P.O., art. 14(1).
[42] TCPSA, s. 25(3)(b), as amended.
[43] D.P.O., art. 15 specifies the bodies.

statutory consultees, it is open to the planning authority to consult with any body regarding the application, and many authorities have informal consultation processes involving community council and civic amenity groups. Such informal practices may give rise to a legitimate expectation of future consultation (Chapter 8).

The bodies to be consulted vary depending upon the circumstances of each development. A typical development would require consultation with the roads authority on access and traffic issues, the environmental health department on issues such as smells or dust, and the water and drainage department on drainage and sewerage provision. Developments in rural areas may require consultation with Scottish Natural Heritage (Chapter 9), and the local river purification board.

Statutory consultees must be given at least 14 days to comment and the application cannot be determined until the expiry of that period. Any representations from such a body must be taken into account in deciding the application. There is an opt-out provision whereby bodies that require to be consulted can inform the planning authority in writing that consultation will not be required in respect of any case or class of case or in respect of development within a specified area.

(e) Environmental Assessment

Unless the application includes an environmental statement, the planning authority must consider whether assessment of the environmental effects of the proposed development is required.[44] Environmental assessment (EA) is the term used to describe the process of gathering information and reporting on the environmental effects of the proposed development. The result of the process is the submission of an environmental statement which reports on the environmental impact of the proposed development (for this reason it is often referred to as an environmental impact assessment).

[44] The Environmental Assessment (Scotland) Regulations 1988 (S.I. 1988 No. 1221) and Circular 13/1988, "Environmental Assessment."

There is no prescribed form of environmental statement, but it must include specified information such as a description of the proposed development, comprising information about the site and the design and size or scale of the proposed development. It should report on the likely significant effects of the proposed development, direct and indirect, on human beings, flora, fauna, soil, water, air, climate, the landscape, the interaction between these effects, material assets, and the cultural heritage. Where significant adverse effects are identified, a description must be given of the measures envisaged in order to avoid, reduce or remedy those effects. Consideration may also have to be given to the use of natural resources, the emission of pollutants, the creation of nuisances, and elimination of waste. A non-technical summary must be given.

Environmental assessment is required for every Annex I project, including crude-oil refineries, major chemical and steel works, aerodromes with runway lengths over 2,100 metres, and the permanent storage or final disposal of radioactive and other toxic waste.

Annex II projects only require EA if the authority considers that the proposed development is likely to give rise to *significant environmental effects*, having taken into account:

(i) whether the project is a major one of more than local importance, especially in terms of size;
(ii) whether the location of the site of the proposed development is sensitive and for that reason may have significant effects on the environment even though the development is on a smaller scale;
(This falls short of creating an automatic presumption in favour of EA for projects in designated areas such as National Scenic Areas, conservation areas and SSSIs (Chapter 9). The determining factor is whether the project is likely to give rise to significant effects on the environment of the area.)
(iii) whether the project is thought likely to give rise to particularly complex or adverse effects, for example, in the discharge of pollutants.

The Scottish Office guidance suggests indicative criteria and thresholds for Annex II projects, but reminds authorities that the fundamental test remains the likelihood of significant environmental effects. There is no presumption that EA is not required for a development which falls below the threshold, or where there is no threshold. Examples of Annex II projects include large pig- and poultry-rearing units, ore extraction, metal processing, chemical, food, textile or rubber industry, waste disposal sites and urban development projects.

It is always open to the authority to suggest that EA be carried out in connection with a project which falls outwith Annexes I and II.

An applicant for planning permission has the option of requesting an advance ruling from the planning authority on whether EA is likely to be required. The authority has four weeks to reach a decision, although this period may be extended with the agreement of the developer. If no opinion is given within this time, the applicant is entitled to assume at that stage the opinion of the planning authority is that EA is not required. If the authority concludes (timeously) that EA will be required, but the applicant disagrees, the applicant may apply to the Secretary of State for a direction on whether it is required. This is effectively a right of appeal.

Where an application is submitted with no environmental statement, the planning authority has four weeks to notify the applicant that such a statement is required. If the information accompanying the application differs materially from that available when its opinion was given, the authority can require a statement even although it previously indicated that no EA would be required. The applicant has four weeks to indicate his intention to supply an environmental statement or apply to the Secretary of State for a direction that no statement is required, failing which the application is deemed to have been refused four weeks from the date of notification from the planning authority. There is no right of appeal in these circumstances. If the applicant agrees to submit an environmental statement, there is no time limit for submitting the statement and the time limit for a deemed refusal appeal runs from when the statement is supplied.

Where the planning authority has determined that EA is required or the Secretary of State has so directed, various public bodies are obliged to make available information to the applicant, including Scottish Natural Heritage, the Health and

Safety Executive, and the River Purification Boards. These bodies are notified by the planning authority and a list of their names and addresses given to the applicant. The bodies are only obliged to provide information which is in their possession and are not required to carry out research. Confidential information may be withheld. A reasonable charge may be made for providing the information. A copy of the environmental statement must be sent free of charge to each body.

Where an application includes an environmental statement, there are additional publicity requirements. The applicant must serve notice on all notifiable neighbours prior to submitting the environmental statement. If the statement is submitted with the application, this may be combined with notification of submission of the application. In addition, the planning authority must advertise submission of the environmental statement in a local newspaper and the Edinburgh Gazette, at the expense of the applicant. Both the advertisement and the notice served upon neighbours must state that a copy of the environmental statement is available for public inspection and purchase at a specified address in the locality, specifying the charge (if any), and that there is a four week period for making representations to the authority in connection with the statement.

Two copies of the environmental statement must be submitted to the authority and one copy placed on the planning register. The planning authority is given 16 weeks to determine the application rather than the usual eight weeks. It is obliged to consult various bodies including Scottish Natural Heritage, the Health and Safety Executive, the River Purification Authority, and the Secretary of State, allowing them four weeks to lodge representations. It is always open to the authority to request further information from the applicant. The decision on the application must be intimated to the applicant, the Secretary of State, all consultees, and the notifiable neighbours.

As the EA process is carried out by the applicant, many objectors to proposed developments cast doubt on the reliability of the information contained in the environmental statement. At least one planning authority in England and Wales has persuaded the applicant to pay for the services of an environmental consultant to comment on the environmental statement lodged with the application.

If an appeal is lodged in connection with a planning application which does not include an environmental statement, the Secretary of State may require such a statement to be lodged. The reporter hearing the appeal may apply to the Secretary of State for a direction on the matter.

Deciding the Application

Once the application has been processed, the planning officer normally visits the site and then prepares a report which gives details of the proposed development and its site. It also summarises the representations received, the consultation responses, the relevant provisions of the structure and local plans, and any relevant Scottish Office advice. The report ends with a recommendation of how the application should be decided. Copies of this report must be made available to members of the public, generally three clear days before the relevant committee meeting takes place.[45] The function of the report is to brief the person or persons determining the application and ensure that they are in possession of all the relevant considerations before making a decision. While the report recommends a decision, the decision-maker is not bound to follow the recommendation.

Once the report has been prepared, the application can be decided. The decision-making process varies between authorities. The Director of Planning may have delegated power to decide classes of application which are considered non-contentious, with all other applications being decided by the councillors who sit on the planning committee of the authority. There are variations on this theme, and for highly contentious applications, the decision may be referred to a meeting of the full authority. Increasingly, authorities are adopting a system of circulating reports to its members in advance of the committee meeting with the direction that unless a member indicates otherwise, the application will not be discussed at the meeting and will be determined in accordance with the recommendation in the report.

[45] Local Government (Scotland) Act 1973 ss. 50B and E.

It is important to identify which body within the authority will actually determine the application. If the application will be decided by the councillors, it must be considered whether the development proposals are presented in a clear and attractive fashion. The applicant may wish to brief in advance the councillors who will make the decision (not all councillors are receptive to lobbying). If the Director of Planning will make the decision, less care need be taken to avoid the use of technical terms.

What are the factors behind the decision on the application? In making a decision on the application, the authority must not fetter its discretion and each application must be individually decided on its merits. There is a presumption in favour of granting planning permission: unless there are sound planning reasons for refusing permission, it must be granted. When making its decision the authority must take into account the provisions of the development plan, all material considerations and all representations received. Once the relevant provisions of the Planning and Compensation Act 1991 are brought into force on 7 March 1994, the application will require to be determined in accordance with the provisions of the development plan unless material considerations indicate otherwise (commonly referred to as "the plan-led" system). The authority may refuse planning permission, or grant permission unconditionally or subject to conditions. It may also grant permission for a development in different terms to that proposed by the application.

The decision on the application is an exercise in balancing the competing considerations. The planning authority must take into account all considerations which are both material and relevant to the application and ignore any other matters. A failure to fulfil this duty may result in an illegal decision, unless the same decision would have been reached on other valid reasons.[46] The consideration challenged need not have been the dominant reason for reaching the decision, and provided it was not insubstantial or insignificant there is no requirement to prove that a different conclusion would have been reached had it not been taken into account.[47] The courts

[46] *R.* v. *Broadcasting Complaints Commission, ex p. Owen* [1985] Q.B. 1153.
[47] *Simplex* v. *Secretary of State for the Environment* [1988] 3 P.L.R. 25.

will not interfere with the decision of the planning authority on the weight to be given to each consideration.[48]

Where there is a material change in circumstances in the course of the determination of the application, the authority must take that change into account. This highlights the risk of so-called "minded to grant" decisions, which involve the authority resolving to grant permission once certain outstanding matters, normally execution of a section 50 agreement (Chapter 6), have been resolved. Such a decision gives the applicant no guarantee that permission will be granted. For example, where an authority resolved to grant permission once a section 50 agreement was concluded, it was open to that authority to refuse to enter into the agreement and not grant permission if there was a change of circumstances in the intervening period.[49]

Presumption in Favour of Development

There has always been a presumption in favour of development, deriving from government policy. In other words, the applicant for permission is under no onus to show that permission should be granted. The Scottish Office guidance states that permission should only be refused where there are sound and clear-cut reasons for such a refusal.[50] In England and Wales, the equivalent guidance indicates that permission should only be refused where the proposed development would cause demonstrable harm to interests of acknowledged importance. Except in the case of inappropriate development in the green belt (Chapter 9), the applicant is not required to prove the case for the proposed development, and the onus is on the planning authority to demonstrate clearly why the development cannot be permitted.[51]

This presumption arises from the historical background to the planning system. When the requirement for planning

[48] *Seddon Properties* v. *Secretary of State for the Environment* [1978] J.P.L. 835.
[49] *John G. Russell (Transport) Ltd.* v. *Strathkelvin D.C.*, 1992 S.L.T. 1001.
[50] Circular 17/1985 "Development Control — Priorities and Procedures," para. 3; NPPG 1 "The Planning System," para. 44.
[51] Department of Environment PPG1, "General Policies and Principles," para. 15.

permission was introduced nationally in 1947, it removed the rights of landowners to do as they pleased on their land and forced them to apply to the State for permission to develop their land. It would have been draconian to require them further to demonstrate why they should be allowed to develop their land in a particular way. As a result, it has always been government policy that the State's control over development should only be exercised to prevent development where it can show good planning reasons for refusing permission.

To some extent this presumption will be modified by the introduction of the "plan-led" system (below), becoming a presumption in favour of development which accords with the provisions of the development plan. However, the force of the presumption will still apply.

Development Plan

When determining a planning application the planning authority must have regard to the provisions of the development plan (Chapter 3). Following the shift to the "plan-led" system on 7 March 1994 when the relevant provisions of the Planning and Compensation Act 1991 were brought into force the determination will require to be made in accordance with the provisions of the development plan unless material considerations indicate otherwise.[52] This creates a presumption in favour of development proposals which are in accordance with the provisions of the development plan.

This does not amount to a requirement that the planning authority decide all applications according to the terms of the development plan. Instead, any relevant policies in the development plan should be noted first. Attention then turns to other material considerations. These considerations may dictate that the application be decided contrary to the terms of the plan. A material consideration does not require any special weight to overcome the presumption in favour of the development plan.[53] One relevant factor will be the age of the

[52] TCPSA, s. 18A and s. 26(1), as amended.

[53] *St. Albans D.C.* v. *Secretary of State for the Environment* [1993] J.P.L. 370.

plan: to carry its full weight it needs to be up-to-date and consistent with prevailing national and regional policies as well as relevant to the proposal in question.

The presumption in favour of the development plan highlights the importance of making representations during the process of replacement or renewal of development plans (Chapter 3) in an attempt to ensure that the new or revised plan contains provisions favourable to envisaged development proposals or does not promote development detrimental to the interest of a landowner or developer. Once a provision is enshrined in an adopted development plan it will be difficult to overcome.

The importance of development plans to the determination of planning applications is underlined by the requirement for notification and advertisement of applications contrary to provisions of development plans for which planning authorities propose to grant permission, and the power of regional planning authorities to call-in applications contrary to the provisions of the structure plan (below).

Other Material Considerations

In addition to the terms of the development plan, the planning authority must also take into account all other material considerations when determining an application. These considerations provide the grounds for both the reasons for granting/refusing to grant planning permission and for objecting to planning applications. It is, therefore, not suprising that what amounts to a material consideration is one of the most debated topics in planning law.

No definition of "material considerations" is provided by the legislation. As the power to determine an application for planning permission is vested in the planning authority by the TCPSA, to be material a consideration must be a planning consideration. There are many theories of planning (Chapter 1) and therefore many different answers to the question: What is "planning"? Case law is continually identifying new examples of planning considerations. Although this leads to uncertainty, it gives planning authorities a necessary degree of flexibility in the matters which they may take into account when deciding an application.

Broadly, any consideration which relates to the use and development of land is capable of being a material planning consideration.[54] The courts have provided more specific guidance, but only on a case-by-case basis. Court decisions make it possible to state whether or not certain matters are planning considerations, but do not give a general indication of what may account to a material planning consideration.

Specific examples of material considerations are now considered. The list is not exhaustive.

(a) Suitability of Site

The suitability of the site for the proposed development is one of the main material considerations. Instability as a result of mineworkings (British Coal is a statutory consultee in areas of coal working), tipping, or liability to flooding, may make sites unsuitable for certain types of development. Any potential contamination of the site is relevant and authorities will require investigation of likely contaminated sites prior to development.[55]

(b) Appearance of the Proposed Development and its Relationship to its Surroundings

The decision on the application necessarily involves consideration of the appearance of the proposed development and its relationship to its surroundings. Relevant matters include the materials to be used; the height, scale, massing, layout and density, in comparison to buildings in the surrounding area; landscaping; privacy, both for surrounding properties and the occupiers or users of the proposed development; overshadowing; lack of natural light; noise, smell and fumes, and glare from floodlights or headlights of vehicles.

A controversial issue is the extent to which planning authorities can consider the design of a proposed building, which is a highly subjective matter. The external appearance

[54] *Per* Cooke J. in *Stringer* v. *Minister for Housing* [1971] All E.R. 65.
[55] S.D.D. PAN 33, "Development of Contaminated Land."

of a building can have a significant effect on the character of an area, but architects complain that too often planning authorities take a restrictive, conservative view towards innovative design.

(c) Impact

The impact of the proposed development upon the surrounding area must be evaluated. Regard must be had to the desirability of preserving the setting of a listed building, and of preserving or enhancing the character and appearance of a conservation area or national scenic area (Chapter 9). Any general loss of amenity or privacy, increases in noise level and volume of traffic, questions of safety and other potential social costs must be considered.[56] The impact of the development on private individuals must also be considered. For example, there may be a resultant loss of privacy, sunlight or amenity suffered by neighbouring proprietors, whether or not these proprietors are notifiable neighbours. Thus material considerations may be either the public or private interests of both the applicant and objectors.[57]

In dismissing an appeal for a major toxic-waste plant in England, the Secretary of State took into account the deleterious effect on local employment, investment and industry, and public fears of long-term effects on health, although the major determining factor was potential pollution of the underground acquifer.[58]

(d) Compatibility with Existing Uses

In addition to its general impact on the surrounding area, the compatibility of the proposed development with existing uses is a material consideration.[59] In one case, the effect of dust created by a proposed concrete plant on neighbouring

[56] *per* Lord Denning in *Esdell Caravan Park* v. *Hemel Hempstead Rural District Council* [1965] 3 All E.R. 737 at p. 743F.

[57] *City of Glasgow D.C.* v. *Secretary of State for Scotland and Bank of Scotland*, 1993 S.L.T. 1332, 1993 S.P.L.P.38: 21.

[58] APP/F4410/A/89/126733 (Doncaster Incineration Appeal).

[59] *Collis Radio* v. *Secretary of State for the Environment* (1975) 29 P. & C.R. 390.

factories manufacturing precision products and requiring clean air was a relevant factor.[60] Alternatively, existing uses may be incompatible with proposed developments such as a proposed housing development on land neighbouring an explosives factory. However, it may be proper for a planning authority to wish to encourage residential development in an area of existing industrial users.[61] While planning powers should not be used to protect commercial interests, it may be relevant to consider the degree to which the opening of a shopping centre might lead to the decay of existing centres.[62] The desirability of preserving a balance of uses may also be a material consideration.

(e) Desirability of Retaining the Existing Use

The existing use of the site is a material consideration, such as the continuation of industrial uses which are important to the character and functioning of a city.[63] It may be desirable to continue an existing residential use in an area where there is a shortage of housing.[64] This ground would require evidence of a reasonable probability that a refusal of permission would result in the continuance of the existing use. Alternative permitted uses of the site must also be considered. The planning authority is not bound to apply a competing needs test of desirability of preserving the existing use versus the merits of the proposed new use, as this would override the presumption in favour of planning permision (above).[65]

(f) Existence of a Better Alternative Site

The existence of a better site for the proposed development may be a material consideration either as a result of characteristics of the proposed development or its site,

[60] *R.M.C. Management Services* v. *Secretary of State for the Environment* (1972) 222 E.G. 1593.
[61] *R.* v. *Exeter C.C., ex p. Thomas* [1990] J.P.L. 129.
[62] *R.* v. *Doncaster Metropolitan District, ex p. British Railways Board* [1987] J.P.L. 444.
[63] *Westminster C.C.* v. *Great Portland Estates* [1985] A.C. 661.
[64] *Clyde & Co.* v. *Secretary of State for the Environment* [1977] 1 W.L.R. 926.
[65] *London Residuary Body* v. *Lambeth L.B.C.* [1990] 2 All E.R. 309.

including whether the adverse effects of the proposed development might have a reduced impact on a specified alternative site.[66] The existence of alternative sites is likely to be relevant only where the proposed development is major or has significant planning effects. The planning authority is not required to determine which site is better, but only to consider the other site as an alternative.[67] Where the development on the proposed site is acceptable, planning permission should not be refused on the grounds that it would be more acceptable on an alternative site, with the possible exception of competing applications for the same development, but on different sites, in circumstances where permission can be granted for one development only.[68] If the site of the proposed development is unsuitable, the applicant may be required to demonstrate the need for the proposed development on that site.

(g) Financial Viability

The cost of the proposed development is not a material consideration in itself.[69] Assessment of the financial viability of the proposed development is best carried out by the developer and most planning authorities do not have the expertise to make such an assessment. However, the planning consequences of the financial viability of the proposal can be considered.[70] Lack of financial viability results in some developments being abandoned before completion, sterilising the site against future development and leaving the authority with the problem of how the site should be managed.

There may be assertions by the applicant that no other form of development is financially viable on the site and that as a

[66] *Ynystawe, Ynforgan & Glair Gipsy Site Action Group* v. *Secretary of State for Wales* [1981] J.P.L. 874.

[67] *R.* v. *Royal County of Berkshire, ex p. Mangnall* [1985] J.P.L. 258.

[68] *Trusthouse Forte* v. *Secretary of State for the Environment* (1986) 53 P. & C.R. 293; [1986] 2 E.G.L.R. 185; *G.L.C.* v. *Secretary of State for the Environment* [1986] J.P.L. 193.

[69] *J. Murphy & Sons* v. *Secretary of State for the Environment* [1973] 1 W.L.R. 560; 2 All E.R. 26.

[70] *Per* Woolf J. in *Sosmo Trust* v. *Secretary of State for the Environment* [1983] J.P.L. 806.

result, permission should be granted for the proposed development. Securing the retention and use of existing buildings, especially listed buildings (Chapter 9), may require the authority to permit economically viable development notwithstanding that the proposed development is not wholly appropriate.

(h) Planning Benefits

The law regarding the extent to which planning benefits are permissable, and therefore become material considerations, is still evolving and reference must be made to the latest court decisions for the current approach.

Planning benefits are used by applicants to "sweeten the pill" by off-setting the planning disadvantages of the proposed development. Such benefits may arise from the terms of the application or provisions of a planning agreement entered into between the applicant and the authority (Chapter 6). If the benefits do not amount to material considerations, the authority must ignore them when determining the application. A planning benefit is not a material consideration solely because it is included in the planning application.[71] The materiality of the benefits is a matter for the judgment of the authority in light of all the facts and circumstances, including its policy on community benefits.[72]

To form a material consideration, the benefits must be required for a planning and not for any ulterior motive, and fairly and reasonably relate to the proposed development. It is not necessary for the benefits to be required to overcome, remedy or alleviate planning objections to the proposed development.[73] There must be a clear and direct nexus or a recognised and real relationship between the benefit and the proposed development. This nexus or relationship may be geographic, functional or financial.[74] A reasonable prospect of the benefit arising is sufficient and there is no requirement

[71] *Barber* v. *Secretary of State for the Environment* [1991] J.P.L. 559.

[72] *R.* v. *Plymouth C.C. ex p. Plymouth and South Devon Co-operative Society Ltd.* [1993] J.P.L. 538 and (on appeal) [1993] E.G.C.S. 113.

[73] *Ibid., Tesco* v. *Secretary of State for the Environment* [1993] E.G.C.S. 133.

[74] *Northumberland C.C.* v. *Secretary of State for the Environment* [1989] J.P.L. 700.

that the benefit be guaranteed, for example, through a planning agreement.[75] In determining an application for a sports facility at one site, it was a material consideration that the grant of permission would enable redevelopment of another site. The consequent benefits to the conservation area of this redevelopment outweighed the harm to important conservation interests at the site of the new sports facility.[76] In contrast, traffic management measures to be financed by the applicant were not a material consideration because there was no direct nexus between the proposed superstore and the improvements where these measures were aimed at problems already in existence.[77] Offers of community benefits such as provision of a tourist information centre, a bird-watching hide and a static art feature were upheld as a material consideration in the determination of an application for a superstore development.[78]

Policies contained in development plans seeking community benefits from applicants do not automatically render the offer (or lack of an offer) of such benefits material considerations. Benefits sought by the authority in planning conditions or agreements must be imposed for a planning purpose, be fairly and reasonably related to the proposed development, and not so unreasonable that no reasonable authority could have imposed them (Chapter 6).

The proposed development may be presented as enabling other more worthy development to proceed. The profits of the substantial office development included in the scheme for the redevelopment of the Royal Opera House, London were to be applied to improve the Opera House and it was competent for the planning authority to take this consideration into account when granting permission contrary to the provisions of the development plan.[79] This concept of enabling development is still evolving and it is uncertain what degree, if any, of functional, geographical or physical relationship is required.

[75] *Crawley B.C.* v. *Secretary of State for the Environment* [1993] J.P.L. 148.
[76] *Wansdyke D.C.* v. *Secretary of State for the Environment* [1992] J.P.L. 1168.
[77] *Safeway* v. *Secretary of State for the Environment* [1990] J.P.L. 759, but see *Tesco* v. *Secretary of State for the Environment* (n. 73, *supra*).
[78] *R.* v. *Plymouth C.C., ex p. Plymouth and South Devon Co-operative Society Ltd., supra.*
[79] *R.* v. *Westminster C.C., ex p. Monahan* [1989] J.P.L. 107.

Applications for housing or other highly profitable development frequently include proposals attractive to planning authorities such as renovation of listed buildings or relocation of football grounds to modern purpose-built stadia, with the applicant stating that the more attractive element of the proposed development cannot proceed without the funds generated from the housing development.[80] If this economic or planning benefit is a material consideration, the authority must consider whether the benefit is sufficient to justify granting permission. In most cases, the applicant will require to demonstrate that there is no source for securing these benefits other than the enabling development.

(i) Economic Benefits

Economic benefits arising from the proposed development can be a material consideration.[81] It is common for applicants to point to the number of jobs which will be created if the development goes ahead.

(j) Social Considerations

There is a social dimension to planning (Chapter 1) and some of the material considerations identified above have social elements. In so far as social considerations can be subsumed into planning considerations, these considerations will be material. In one case, the need for a period of social stability and consolidation was a good reason for refusing permission.[82] Many development plans contain policies on low-cost or affordable housing. The provision of low-cost rented accommodation is not a material consideration, as it does not serve a planning purpose which relates to the character or the use of the land. It is therefore not permissible for a planning authority to seek to ensure or require provision of low-cost rented accommodation.[83] Planning conditions requiring

[80] *Brighton B.C.* v. *Secretary of State for the Environment* [1979] J.P.L. 173.

[81] *Northumberland C.C.* v. *Secretary of State for the Environment* (n. 74, *supra*).

[82] *Severn Trent Water Authority* v. *Secretary of State for the Environment* [1989] J.P.L. 21.

[83] *Mitchell* v *Secretary of State for the Environment*, Court of Appeal, November 1, 1993, Unreported. The Secretary of State has given notice of appeal.

proportions of housing developments to be allocated to meet local authority housing needs were held to be illegal.[84]

(k) *Provision of Suitable Access and Traffic*

The traffic aspects of the proposed development must be taken into account. If the development involves forming or altering an access to a road, or is likely to cause a material increase in the volume of traffic entering or leaving the road, the planning authority must consult the roads authority about the proposed development and take their comments into account when the application is determined (the Secretary of State is consulted if the road is a trunk road).[85] The roads authority may advise that the access from the development to the road is unsatisfactory or unsuitable, perhaps due to the dangers of turning traffic; or insufficient visibility and no possibility of visibility splays being provided to preserve visibility for vehicles using the access; or the unsuitability of the road for the traffic generated by the development; or insufficient parking provision.

The planning authority is not bound to follow the advice offered by the roads authority. In many cases, the roads authority response is dictated by adopted policies and the planning authority may consider that the policy is not appropriate in the circumstances of the particular development.

(l) *Sewerage, Drainage and Water*

There must be provision for proper disposal of surface water and sewerage, and an adequate supply of water for the development. Permission can be refused because of inadequacies of the existing public sewers.[86] Overcapacity in the drainage system is sometimes cited as a reason for refusing

[84] *R.* v. *Hillingdon Borough Council, ex p. Royco Homes* [1974] 2 All E.R. 643; *David Lowe & Sons* v. *Musselburgh Town Council,* 1973 S.C. 130.

[85] D.P.O., art. 15.

[86] *George Wimpey & Co. Ltd.*v. *Secretary of State for the Environment* [1978] J.P.L. 773.

planning permission. The planning authority cannot allow a policy of the sewerage authority, imposing a total embargo on further sea discharges, to dictate its decision on a planning application, although this would be a relevant factor to be taken into account when determining the application.[87]

(m) Pollution and Contamination

The likelihood of pollution as a result of the proposed development appears to be a material consideration, irrespective of the existence of other statutory powers such as integrated pollution control (IPC) under the Environmental Protection Act 1990.[88] Noise and odour have always been important planning issues, but it seems that planning authorities should now be taking into account pollution of any type. The environmental impact of emissions to the atmosphere is a material consideration as is the existence of the statutory pollution control regime. There will come a point when the authority is entitled to be satisfied that, having had regard to the existence of EPA controls, residual concerns over pollution matters should not constitute a reason for refusal of planning permission.[89]

Contamination or the potential for it, is a material consideration.[90] Contamination may give rise to hazards, for example putting at risk people working on, or in the immediate vicinity of, the site, or affecting structural durability. It may be possible to use the planning benefit of cleaning up contaminated land to justify the grant of permission for development which would not otherwise be permitted (see Planning benefit above).

The contents of any environmental statement submitted in association with the application must be taken into account (below).

[87] *Ynys Mon B.C.* v. *Secretary of State for Wales* [1993] J.P.L. 225.

[88] Draft PPG, "Planning and Pollution Control", published by Department of the Environment in June 1992 for consultation.

[89] *Gateshead M.B.C.* v. *Secretary of State for the Environment*, Queen's Bench Division, September 29, 1993, Unreported; see also Kitson & Harris, "A Burning Issue. Planning Controls, Pollution Controls and Waste Incineration" [1994] J.P.L. 3.

[90] S.D.D. PAN 33, "Development of Contaminated Land".

(n) Archaeology

The effects of the proposed development on archaeological remains and their setting is a material consideration. Where the physical preservation *in situ* of the remains is not justified in the circumstances, and the development will result in the destruction of the remains, the planning authority should satisfy itself before granting permission that the developer has made appropriate and satisfactory provision for the excavation and recording of the remains.[91]

(o) Nature Conservation

In determining an application for planning permission, the authority must have regard to the desirability of conserving Scotland's flora and fauna, geological and physiographic features, and its natural beauty and amenity. The authority also has a duty to ensure that adequate provision is made for the preservation or planting of trees (Chapter 9).

(p) Need

To require the landowner to show the need for a proposed development is excessive interference with rights of ownership. This is the basis for the presumption in favour of granting planning permission, now modified by the presumption in favour of development in accordance with the terms of the development plan. The need for the development only requires to be demonstrated if its detrimental effects are such that an overriding need must be shown. Thus an overriding need may require to be demonstrated for particular types of development or development in particular locations, such as in the Green Belt (Chapter 9), or where there is a better alternative site (above).

In the same way, lack of need is not a valid reason in itself for refusing permission, unless the lack of need is relevant because of the detrimental effects of the development.

[91] Scottish Office Environment Department NPPG 5 "Archaeology and Planning" and PAN 42 "Archaeology — The Planning Process".

(q) *Creation of an Undesirable Precedent*

Planning authorities are not obliged to follow their previous decisions on similar applications. However, consistency in decision-making is desirable and it is a material consideration that granting permission for the proposed development might set a precedent making it difficult for similar applications to be refused in the future.[92] A generalised concern is insufficient and there must be some evidence for this view.[93]

(r) *Planning History of the Site*

It is relevant to consider what development can be carried out on the site in terms of existing permissions or by exercising permitted development rights under the P.D.O. or U.C.O. (Chapter 4). Grants of planning permission for similar developments on the same site may be used to show that the authority have conceded the principle of development of the site. Previous planning decisions in respect of the site cannot be followed slavishly[94] and each application must be decided upon its merits. As a result, there may be several grants of permission for one site which are mutually inconsistent and conflicting.[95] Multiple implementation of permissions in such circumstances may be problematic (below).

(s) *Duplicate Applications*

The outcome of an appeal may be a material consideration for the planning authority in determining a duplicate application for the same, or a similar development. Depending upon the stage reached in the appeal proceedings, the authority may be obliged either to delay deciding the application until the appeal decision has been received and can be taken into account, or to reject the application as premature. For

[92] *Collis Radio* v. *Secretary of State for the Environment* (n. 59, *supra*).

[93] *Poundstretcher* v. *Secretary of State for the Environment* [1988] 3 P.L.R. 69.

[94] *North Wiltshire D.C.* v. *Secretary of State for the Environment* [1992] J.P.L. 955; *Standard Securities Estates* v. *Secretary of State for the Environment* [1992] E.G.C.S. 129.

[95] *Pilkington* v. *Secretary of State for the Environment* [1973] 1 W.L.R. 1527 *per* Widgery C.J. at p. 1531.

example, where a public local inquiry had been held and the reporter's decision was awaited, it was unreasonable for the planning authority to grant permission for a duplicate application as the outcome of the appeal had become a material consideration to which the authority had to have regard when it considered the application.[96] The stage reached in the appeal proceedings is not conclusive.[97]

(t) Decisions on Similar Proposals in respect of other sites

There is no concept of binding precedents in the planning system whereby an authority might be obliged to follow the same approach taken in a previous decision. Each application must be decided upon its individual merits. However, previous decisions by the same authority relating to other sites might be used to show a consistent pattern in the application of its policies. Decisions by other authorities are unlikely to be of assistance in this manner.

Appeal decisions are not binding precedents, but show how the policy of the Secretary of State has been applied. If appeal decisions showing that planning permission is likely to be granted on appeal can be exhibited to the planning authority, this can be a factor in its determination of the application. The desirability of avoiding losing an appeal should not be a material consideration in itself, but is an important administrative consideration for all authorities.

(u) Statements of Policy in Circulars

It had been thought that statements of the policy of the Secretary of State contained in circulars and other policy instruments were a material consideration.[98] However, a recent decision of the Court of Session has cast a doubt on whether the planning authority are bound to have regard to comments and observations by a civil servant in circular.[99]

[96] *Trusthouse Forte* v. *Perth & Kinross District Council*, 1990 S.L.T. 737.
[97] *Pickering* v. *Kyle & Carrick D.C.*, 1991 G.W.D. 7–361.
[98] *J.A. Pye (Oxford) Estates* v. *Wychavon D.C.* [1982] J.P.L. 575; *Gransden* v. *Secretary of State for the Environment* [1986] J.P.L. 519 and [1987] J.P.L. 365.
[99] *The Noble Organisation Ltd.* v. *Falkirk D.C.*, 1994 S.L.T 100.

Although the advice in a circular has no binding or legal force, in practice there is pressure on planning authorities to follow the provisions of circulars as these represent the policy which will be applied by the Secretary of State or his reporter when deciding an appeal. Thus ignoring the advice within the circular carries with it a considerable risk of losing any subsequent appeal.

Guidance issued by the Department of the Environment and the Welsh Office may be a material consideration, and is frequently used, in the absence of Scottish Office guidance.[1]

(v) Draft Development Plan

The provisions of draft development plans can be a material consideration.[2] However, taking into account the policies of a draft plan which have not been adopted by the planning authority may pre-empt the outcome of the plan-making process. An application may properly be refused on the ground that the development will be likely to prejudice the outcome of the draft development plan, but all that is required is that the effect of the proposed development on the policies and proposals of the draft plan should be considered before the application is decided.[3]

(w) Applicant's Personal Circumstances

Planning relates to the use of land rather than to the user.[4] The general rule is that the personal circumstances or attributes of the applicant should be ignored by the authority. For example, it is not relevant that the applicant has lived in the area for many years. However, personal circumstances may be taken into account in exceptional cases where refusal of permission would cause an applicant great hardship.[5]

[1] 1983 S.P.L.P. 10:90 and 1984 S.P.L.P. 11:8.

[2] *R.* v. *City of London Corporation, ex p. Allan* (1980) 79 L.G.R. 223.

[3] Young and Rowan-Robinson *op. cit.*, p. 211.

[4] *East Barnet Urban District Council* v. *B.T.C.* [1962] 2 Q.B. 484, *per* Parker C.J. at p. 498; *David Lowe* v. *Musselburgh Town Council*, 1973 S.C. 130, *per* Lord President Emslie at p. 142.

[5] *Westminster C.C.* v. *Great Portland Estates* [1985] A.C. 661, *per* Lord Scarman.

The private interests of the applicant are a material consideration and it was, therefore, held to be relevant to take into account improvements in efficiency, service and staff accommodation which would result from the proposed development.[6]

(x) Prematurity

Planning permission may be refused on grounds of prematurity where the development plan is in preparation or under review. This would be competent only in respect of development proposals which are individually so substantial or likely to be so significant cumulatively, as to predetermine decisions about the scale, location or phasing of new development which ought properly to be taken in the development plan context.[7] An application may also be premature where an appeal decision for the same proposed development is awaited (Duplicate applications, above).

Non-Material Considerations

In general, the following considerations are not material and should be ignored:

(a) the personal circumstances of the applicant (but not always, above);
(b) the identity of the occupier, user or developer;
(c) private interests such as a landowner losing a desirable view from his property. However, it is relevant for the planning authority to take into account any loss of visual amenity (which in some respects includes loss of a view), daylight or privacy which will be caused to properties neighbouring the site of the proposed development;
(d) moral considerations arising from developments such as sex shops, or religious objections to Sunday working;
(e) political considerations or ideological dislike of projects such as private hospitals;

[6] *City of Glasgow D.C.* v. *Secretary of State for Scotland and Bank of Scotland*, 1993 S.L.T. 1322; 1993 S.P.L.P. 38:21.
[7] *Arlington* v. *Secretary of State for the Environment* [1989] J.P.L. 166.

(f) the cost of the development (contrast financial viability, above);
(g) title restrictions which may prevent the development from going ahead as the restrictions may be varied or discharged by the Lands Tribunal for Scotland.[8]
(h) the applicant's lack of ownership of part of the application site.[9] The planning authority's function is to decide whether or not the proposed development is desirable in the public interest. The answer to that question should not be affected by the consideration that the land-owner is determined not to allow the development. However, where there are competing sites for a desirable development, difficulties of bringing about implementation on one site which are not present in relation to the other might affect the choice of site to receive permission. All other things being equal it is possible that an assembled site package would be preferable to one with unresolved ownership problems.

Overlap with Other Statutory Powers

It may be thought that planning powers should not be used to regulate matters more properly dealt with under other specific statutory powers. Indeed, Scottish Office policy strongly favours this view.[10] However, as a matter of law, it is competent for planning powers to be exercised in such circumstances provided a planning purpose is being served.

For example, the likely creation of litter as a result of a proposed development may be a relevant planning consideration because it could affect residential amenity.[11] A refusal of permission on the ground that the land would be required for future road widening was valid despite the result that the authority avoided paying the compensation which would have been due if other statutory powers had been exercised.[12]

[8] See Paisley, "Feudal Conditions and Statutory Planning Powers" 1990 S.P.L.P. 31:74.
[9] *British Railways Board* v. *Secretary of State for the Environment* [1994] J.P.L. 32.
[10] For example, S.D.D. Circular 18/1986, "The use of conditions in planning permission", para. 21.
[11] *City of Aberdeen D.C.* v. *Secretary of State for Scotland*, 1993 S.L.T. 1325; [1992] 1 P.L.R. 1.
[12] *Westminster Bank* v. *Minister of Housing* [1971] A.C. 508.

Planning powers can be used to restrict opening hours notwithstanding that the same power is available under the gaming legislation.[13] The overlap between planning and integrated pollution control powers conferred by the Environmental Protection Act 1990 may also cause difficulties. There will come a point when the existence of EPA controls results in residual concerns over pollution matters not forming a valid reason for refusing planning permission (see Pollution and Contamination, above).

Representations Received and Consultation Responses

When deciding an application for planning permission, the authority must also take into consideration representations received timeously under the provisions regarding notification of owners, agricultural tenants and neighbours, bad neighbour development, and the advertisement and display of notice under the provisions applicable to development within conservation areas (above).[14]

Although the wording of the statute fails to qualify this requirement by limiting the relevance of such representations to planning considerations, this qualification is implicit in the general legal requirement that the planning authority ignores all irrelevant considerations. As a result, the authority should only take into account representations which raise planning considerations. Objections from neighbouring proprietors on the grounds that the proposed development will reduce the value of their property should therefore be ignored. However, some of the factors giving rise to the reduction in value may be relevant planning considerations.

It must also take into account responses timeously received from the bodies which it was required to consult. Although there is no requirement to consider representations by other interested parties, such representations may raise material considerations which the authority is obliged to consider.

The authority would be acting illegally if it ignored material considerations on the grounds that these considerations were submitted late.

[13] *Ladbroke* v. *Secretary of State for the Environment* [1981] J.P.L. 427.
[14] TCPSA, ss. 26(2)–(4), as amended.

Environmental Statement

The authority must also take into account the contents of any environmental statement submitted with the application, but these contents can only influence its decision insofar as they amount to planning considerations.

Fettering of Discretion

The power to grant planning permission is discretionary. Improper exercise of this discretion may render the decision illegal (Chapter 8). The planning authority must always exercise its discretion freely and each case must be considered on its merits.

Proper exercise of the discretionary power requires the decision to be made by the planning authority. Unless authorised by statute, it is not competent for the authority to delegate this power. Planning authorities are permitted by statute to delegate the power to determine a planning application to a committee or sub-committee of the authority, an officer of the authority such as the Director of Planning, or another local authority in Scotland.[15] The authority remains responsible for the decision made under delegated powers and retains the power to revoke the delegation of power.

The views of other bodies on the application may be taken into account, but the authority cannot allow these views to dictate the decision on the application as the authority would be effectively delegating its power to that body. A decision to refuse permission on the grounds of a policy of another statutory body placing an embargo on future development was therefore illegal.[16]

Each application must be decided on its merits. This principle does not prevent the authority from formulating policies applicable to certain types of development (indeed, policies encourage consistent decision-making). However, the policy cannot dictate the decision, otherwise the policy has fettered the exercise of discretion.[17] The authority can apply

[15] Local Government (Scotland) Act 1973 s. 56, as amended.
[16] *Ynys Mon B.C.* v. *Secretary of State for Wales* (n. 87, *supra*).
[17] *Lavender* v. *Minister of Housing* [1970] 3 All E.R. 871; *Stringer* v. *Minister of Housing* [1970] 1 W.L.R. 1281, *per* Cooke J. at p. 1298.

its policy in deciding the application but the possibility of making an exception to that policy must be considered in each case.

The Decision

The report by the planning officer summarises the provisions of the development plan, other material considerations, and other matters to be taken into account. It recommends how the application should be determined, but the final decision rests with the decision-making body, which is normally the planning committee. Written notice is given of the decision, stating the reasons for a refusal of permission or imposition of conditions upon a grant of planning permission. This notice must be accompanied by a form notifying the applicant of his rights of appeal. For the purposes of time limits for lodging an appeal, the date of the decision by the authority is the date on which the notice bears to have been signed on behalf of the authority.[18] Details of the decision must be entered into the Planning Register.

The authority may refuse the application, or grant it unconditionally, or subject to such conditions as it thinks fit.[19] If the application is not determined within two months, the applicant may choose to lodge an appeal on the grounds that the authority is deemed to have refused planning permission. In addition, there is some scope for its decision to change the terms of the application. The various types of decision will now be explored.

(a) Deemed Refusal

If the authority fails to determine the application within two months of the date of its receipt, the applicant has the option of lodging an appeal on the grounds that the authority is deemed to have refused the application.[20] Such an appeal

[18] TCPSA, s. 30A.
[19] s. 26(1).
[20] It is interesting to note that in the Republic of Ireland planning permission is deemed to have been granted if no decision is made within two months.

must be lodged within six months of the expiry of the two-month period. Where the authority obtains the written agreement of the applicant to an extension of the two-month period, no appeal against a deemed refusal can be lodged until the agreed extension has expired.[21]

The decision to appeal will be influenced by the costs involved in pursuing the appeal, the prospects of further delay when the authority may be close to a favourable decision, and the chances of the appeal being successful. It will be important to consider whether significant unresolved issues exist in connection with the application to render an appeal worthless. Deemed refusal appeals are sometimes used as a tactical device to pressurise authorities into granting permission on a duplicate application (above).

(b) Refusal

If the planning authority decides to refuse the application, the notice of its decision must specify its reasons for that decision. The application can only be refused on planning grounds and these reasons will be drawn from the material considerations relevant to the application. The applicant has six months from the date of the notice to appeal to the Secretary of State (Chapter 8).

(c) Resolution to Grant Permission

In the case of complex developments, it is not unusual for the planning authority to resolve to grant permission once certain matters have been resolved, most typically the execution of a section 50 agreement. The resolution, normally followed up with a "minded to grant" letter which states that the authority is minded to grant permission, does not amount to a grant of planning permission. Nor does it oblige the authority to grant permission, as any change in circumstances must be taken into account and could lead to a refusal of permission.[22] However, it may provide sufficient comfort to

[21] TCPSA, s. 34, as amended and D.P.O., arts. 14(2) and 23(2).
[22] *John G. Russell (Transport) Ltd.* v. *Strathkelvin D.C.*, 1992 S.L.T. 1001.

the applicant that permission will be granted to persuade him to resolve the outstanding matters.

(d) Conditional Grant of Permission

Strictly speaking, a grant of planning permission can never be unconditional as the conditions relating to the duration of planning permission apply to every grant of permission (below). However, the authority may decide to grant planning permission without any other conditions attached.

The planning authority has a wide discretionary power to grant planning permission "subject to such conditions as it thinks fit" (Chapter 6). Permissions for large or complex developments may be subject to over 50 conditions. The reasons for imposing each condition must be specified in the decision letter. There are various means by which the applicant can attempt to challenge the imposition of conditions (Chapter 6). Implementation of a permission (below) implies acceptance of the conditions. The lack of any right of appeal against a breach of condition notice (Chapter 7) emphasises the importance of ensuring that conditions are acceptable prior to implementation.

(e) Temporary and Personal Permissions

The planning authority may grant permission subject to a condition requiring the removal of any buildings or works or discontinuance of any use of land authorised by the permission at the end of a specified period.[23] Such a temporary permission may be justified where a trial period is necessary to assess the effect of the development of the area. On expiry of the specified period, planning permission is not required for resumption of the previous use provided that use is lawful (Lawful Development, Chapter 7).[24]

Planning permission normally enures for the benefit of the land rather than the applicant (below). Personal permissions are grants of permission subject to conditions restricting the benefit of the permission to specified persons, often the

[23] s. 27(1)(b).
[24] s. 20(5).

applicant alone. It is seldom desirable to grant a personal permission but there may be exceptional circumstances where it is proposed to grant permission for use of a building for some purpose which would normally be allowed, for some compassionate or other personal grounds.[25]

(f) Outline Permission

Outline planning permision is always granted subject to a condition requiring subsequent approval of reserved matters to be obtained from the authority. The reserved matters are any matters of detail not specified in the application concerning the siting, design or external appearance of any building to which the planning permission or the application relates, or the means of access to such building, or the landscaping of the application site.[26] These reserved matters may extend to density, drainage and disposal of sewage, and treatment of boundary fences.[27] Other conditions may also be imposed on the grant of outline permission, possibly requiring submission of further details for the approval of the authority.

(g) Approval of Reserved Matters

There is a time limit specified for submission of the application for approval of reserved matters following on a grant of outline permission (below). The reserved matters application concerns details of the development and may be refused only on grounds arising out of the reserved matters. It cannot be used by the authority as an opportunity to reconsider the principle of development which it approved by granting outline permission.

(h) Grant of Planning Permission for Revised Development

In the negotiations prior to determination of the application for planning permission, it is common for the applicant to

[25] S.D.D. Circular 18/1986, para. 79.
[26] D.P.O., art. 2(1).
[27] *Inverclyde District Council* v. *Inverkip Building Company*, 1983 S.L.T. 563.

make changes to the proposals, often following suggestions by the planning officer dealing with the application. Unless these changes are material, most authorities will not suggest that the application be renotified/readvertised. However, this may deprive those persons whose views must be taken into account by the authority of an opportunity to give their views on what would be a different proposal, with the possible result that the permission is illegal. If there is any doubt, the safest course must always be to renotify all parties and give fresh notice by advertisement.

It is competent for the authority to grant planning permission for a development different from that proposed in the application.[28] A grant of planning permission which reduced the size of the proposed development from 35 acres and 420 dwellings to 25 acres and 250 dwellings was upheld on the basis that the result did not differ substantially from the development proposed in the original application.[29] This suggests a test of character: does the permitted development have a substantially different character from the development proposed in the original application? For example, an amendment was material where it increased the site area by 50 per cent, brought the proposed gypsy camp significantly closer to three nearby residences and increased the number of pitches which might be accommodated.[30]

The authority may also regulate matters ancillary or incidental to the proposed development, but which do not form part of the application, such as the provision of children's play areas and public open spaces for a large housing development.[31]

(i) Development Contrary to the Development Plan

Provided that the authority have regard to the provisions of the development plan, it is competent for planning permission to be granted for a development which is contary to the

[28] *Kent County Council* v. *Secretary of State for the Environment* (1976) 33 P. & C.R. 70.

[29] *Bernard Wheatcroft* v. *Secretary of State for the Environment* [1982] J.P.L. 37.

[30] *Breckland* v. *Secretary of State for the Environment* [1992] 3 P.L.R. 89.

[31] *Britannia (Cheltenham) Ltd.* v. *Secretary of State for the Environment* [1978] J.P.L. 554.

terms of the plan. However, the authority must first have followed certain procedures, unless the notification requirements apply (below).[32]

Notice must be given by advertisement in a local newspaper and any representations received in the 21 days following publication considered. In two-tier areas, the authority must send to the other authority (i.e. district council sends to regional council, or vice versa) a statement of their reasons for proposing to grant permission. Where the statement is sent from district to regional council, a copy of the application, the plans, and any environmental statement relating to the proposed development must also be sent. This gives the regional planning authority an opportunity to exercise its call-in powers (below). The authority must consider any observations received from the other authority within 21 days of receipt of the statement.

Planning authorities are no longer required to submit to the Secretary of State details of individual grants of planning permission contrary to an approved local or structure plan, and report departures from development plans in their statistical return.

Notification and Call-in

(a) Notification

If the planning authority proposes to grant planning permission for certain types of development, they must first notify the Secretary of State and, in the case of a district planning authority, the regional planning authority (previously, notification was required upon receipt of the application).[33] This notification procedure alerts the Secretary of State and the regional planning authority to applications which it may be appropriate for them to call-in for determination. Where the regional planning authority proposes to grant permission

[32] Town and Country Planning (Development Contrary to Development Plans) (Scotland) Direction 1994, attached to Circular 3/1994, "National Planning Policy Guideline 'The Planning System', etc."

[33] Town and Country Planning (Notification of Applications) (Scotland) Direction 1988, attached to S.D.D. Circular 29/1988.

for a development contrary to a structure plan approved by the Secretary of State, it shall in addition notify the district planning authority.

The types of development to which this requirement applies include changes of use of 2 hectares or more of agricultural land within Macaulay classes 1, 2 or 3.1; industrial development requiring more than 100 hectares of land; retail shopping developments comprising gross retail floor space of 40,000 square feet; significant departures from structure or local plan policies; and certain developments in National Scenic Areas or affecting SSSIs (Chapter 9).

Together with the notification, copies must be sent of the application and plans, any environmental statement, observations by consultees, representations received, and the authority's reasons for proposing to grant permission. The Secretary of State confirms the date of receipt of notification and the planning authority cannot decide the application until 28 days after that date. If no response is forthcoming within the 28-day period, the authority may grant permission.

There is a separate requirement to notify the Secretary of State before granting permission for any development which includes or involves alteration or extension of a listed building unless listed building consent is required.[34]

In addition to the notification requirements, the district planning authority is also required to furnish to the regional planning authority weekly lists of all applications it has received.[35]

(b) Call-in

Both the Secretary of State and the regional planning authorities have the power to direct that an application be referred to them for decision, instead of being determined by the planning authority. This process is commonly known as calling-in an application. Exercise of this call-in power is not restricted to applications notified to them by the planning authority.

[34] D.P.O., art. 20.

[35] Town and Country Planning (Planning Applications — Weekly Lists) (Scotland) Direction 1984, issued with S.D.D. Cicular 6/1984.

The Secretary of State's call-in power is exercised by giving a direction to a particular planning authority or authorities generally (including regional planning authorities) that any application or type of application be referred to him for decision.[36] After an application is called-in for decision by the Secretary of State, either the applicant or the authority may request as of right a hearing (normally a public local inquiry) before a reporter, who will prepare a report for the Secretary of State. The non-delegated appeal procedure rules apply (see Chapter 8), with some slight differences in pre-inquiry procedure. The Secretary of State serves a written statement of the reasons for the call-in 28 days before the inquiry, and the planning authority lodges its statement of observations 14 days in advance of the inquiry. The decision of the Secretary of State on the called-in application is final, but may be challenged by application to the Court of Session on legal grounds only within six weeks (Chapter 8).[37]

Regional planning authorities may call-in an application if the proposed development does not conform to a structure plan approved by the Secretary of State, or raises a major planning issue of general significance to the region.[38] The planning authority (but not the applicant) have a right of appeal to the Secretary of State against such a call-in.[39] The applicant has a right of appeal to the Secretary of State against the decision of the regional planning authority on the application or against a deemed refusal after three months (four months if the application includes an environmental statement).

Following the call-in of an application, the planning authority must notify the applicant of the terms of the call-in direction and of any reasons given for issuing that direction. If the application has been called-in by the Secretary of State, the notice must inform the applicant of his right to request a hearing and that the decision on the application will be final.[40]

[36] TCPSA s. 32, as amended.
[37] ss. 32(6), 231 and 233.
[38] Local Government (Scotland) Act 1973, s. 179(2), as amended.
[39] *Ibid*, s. 179(4).
[40] D.P.O., art. 21.

Where an application has been called-in for decision by the regional planning authority or the Secretary of State, other than the points mentioned above, the procedure for determining that application is the same as that applicable to determinations by planning authorities.

Effect of Planning Permission

Many consequences arise from the grant of planning permission. The important legal consequences are examined below. An important practical consequence is that the permission generally increases the value of the land over which it has been granted. Once planning permission has been granted, other statutory consents, such as building warrants, may still be required before development can commence.

(a) Enures for the Benefit of the Land

With the exception of personal permissions (above), the grant of planning permission is not personal to the applicant or the owner of the application site, but enures for the benefit of the land on which development is permitted and is transferred with the ownership of the land.[41]

(b) Does not Prevent Future Applications

There is no obligation to commence the development permitted by a grant of planning permission. While the grant of planning permission remains unimplemented it is competent for any person including the original applicant to make further applications for planning permission in respect of the same site. A further application may seek a more favourable grant of permission for a similar development, or propose an entirely different development. The planning authority is required to consider each application on its merits, ignoring any previous grants of permission and pending applications for the same site.[42] There is no limit on the number of grants

[41] TCPSA, s. 30(1).
[42] *Pilkington* v. *Secretary of State for the Environment* [1973] 1 W.L.R. 1527.

of planning permission in respect of an individual site, and the owner can select which permitted development should proceed. This can lead to problems with multiple implementation of permissions (below).

(c) Interpretation

The wording of the decision letter granting planning permission will be given its ordinary and natural meaning.[43] It will not be construed against the interests of the authority in favour of the applicant (*contra proferentem*).[44] In general, only the document granting planning permission, and any reasons stated thereon, can be considered.[45] Other documents, such as the application form or plans, cannot be used to help interpret the permission, unless the permission refers to those documents. Similarly, it will not be competent to refer to the resolution of the authority to grant permission, except where the issue is whether planning permission was granted.

(d) Duration

Every grant of planning permission is subject to conditions requiring the commencement of the development authorised by the permission within a specified period.[46] Outline permissions are also subject to conditions requiring submission of applications for approval of reserved matters within a specified period. There are separate provisions applicable to the limit of duration of planning permission for winning and working minerals (Chapter 9). Failure to adhere to these time limits will cause the permission to expire.

In the absence of an express condition, a condition is deemed to have been imposed requiring commencement of development within five years of the date of the grant of permission. For outline permissions, the development must

[43] *Wyre Forest District Council* v. *Secretary of State for the Environment* [1989] J.P.L. 362.

[44] *Crisp from the Fens* v. *Rutland County Council*, 1950 L.G.R. 210.

[45] *Miller-Mead* v. *Minister of Housing* [1963] 2 Q.B. 196; but see *Wivenhoe Port Ltd.* v. *Colchester B.C.* [1985] J.P.L. 396.

[46] TCPSA, ss. 38 and 39 (as amended).

begin either within five years of the grant of outline permission, or within two years of the final approval of the reserved matters (or the final approval of the last reserved matter), whichever is later. In both cases, the authority may impose an express condition specifying a longer or shorter period which they consider appropriate having regard to the provisions of the development plan and to any other material considerations.

In a similar way, every grant of outline planning permission is subject to an express or implied condition requiring an application for approval of reserved matters to be made within either three years of the grant of outline planning permission, or six months of refusal of an earlier application for approval, or six months from dismissal of an appeal against such a refusal, whichever is latest. If three years from the grant of outline permission have elapsed only one application for approval may be made. This gives the applicant a last chance to submit an acceptable application. When granting permission the authority may substitute a longer or shorter period for the three-year period as it considers appropriate. Submission of an application in respect of some but not all of the reserved matters, or for part only of the development site, within the time limit will not preserve the remainder of the outline permission from expiry.[47]

When a development is split into distinct parts or phases, it is competent for the authority to specify separate periods for the submission of applications for approval of reserved matters for each part or phase. The requirement for commencement of development should be framed correspondingly by reference to those parts rather than to the development as a whole. In imposing such conditions, the authority must have regard to the provisions of the development plan and to any other material considerations.

For these purposes, development commences on the earliest date on which any of the following specified operations begins to be carried out[48]:

[47] *Hunterston Development Company Limited* v. *Secretary of State for Scotland*, 1992 S.L.T. 1097.

[48] s. 40, as amended.

(i) construction work in connection with the erection of a building;

(ii) any work of demolition of a building;

(iii) digging of a trench for the foundations of a building, even although the trenches are immediately back-filled[49];

(iv) laying any underground main or pipe to the foundations of a building or to a trench for the foundations;

(v) any operation in the course of laying out or constructing part of a road, including marking out the route of a road with pegs[50];

(vi) specified changes of use which constitute material development.

Any of these specified operations in respect of part of a development scheme will be sufficient for implementation of the entire scheme.[51]

Any development commenced after the grant of permission has expired in terms of these express/implied conditions will be treated as not authorised by the permission and, therefore, as a breach of planning control (Chapter 7). Similarly, application for approval of reserved matters submitted after expiry of outline permission will be treated as not made in accordance with the terms of the permission.[52] To avoid expiry of the permission, an application for renewal of the permission may be made before its expiry (above).

(e) Abandonment

It cannot be implied that a valid planning permission capable of being implemented has been abandoned or lost through the actions of the holder of the benefit of the permission.[53]

[49] *High Peak Borough Council* v. *Secretary of State for the Environment* [1981] J.P.L. 366.

[50] *Malvern Hills District Council* v. *Secretary of State for the Environment* (1983) 46 P. & C.R. 58.

[51] *City of Glasgow D.C.* v. *Secretary of State for Scotland*, 1993 S.L.T. 268.

[52] TCPSA, s. 40(7).

[53] *Pioneer Aggregates* v. *Secretary of State for the Environment* [1985] A.C. 132. Contrast with existing use rights (Chapter 4).

(f) Revocation or Modification

The planning authority has power to revoke or modify any grant of permission to such extent as it considers expedient at any time before the change of use has taken place or prior to completion of building or other operations.[54] However, instances of the exercise of this power are limited in consequence of the liability to pay compensation as a result.[55]

Once the revocation/modification order has been confirmed by the Secretary of State, only those building or other operations carried out prior to the date of confirmation are authorised by the permission. The only procedure for challenging the validity of a confirmed order is an application to the Court of Session (Chapter 8).[56]

(g) Variation

The planning authority may vary any permission at the request of the applicant if it appears to it that the variation sought is not material.[57] This obviates the need for a fresh application and renotification/readvertisement, but will necessarily be limited to minor variations.

Consequences of Implementation of Planning Permission

The grant of planning permission is implemented on commencement of any of the specified operations (see Duration, above). Implementation prevents expiry of the permission which then endures in perpetuity, with important implications for the completion of the development and the competence of implementing other permissions for the same site.

(a) Completion of Development: Completion Notice

There is no duty or obligation to complete a development which has been commenced. As a result, sites may be

[54] TCPSA, s. 42, as amended; *Caledonian Terminal Investments* v. *Edinburgh Corporation*, 1970 S.C. 271.
[55] s. 153, as amended.
[56] s. 231, as amended.
[57] s. 31A.

sterilised from future development. The possibility that the remainder of the permission may be implemented in due course would seem to be a material consideration in the determination of any fresh application. The planning authority should consider imposing a condition or suggesting a planning agreement to prevent further implementation of the permission, prior to granting a fresh permission.

The planning authority may serve a completion notice where it is of the opinion that the development has been commenced, but will not be completed within a reasonable time.[58] The notice will only take effect if confirmed by the Secretary of State. On the expiry of the period specified in the notice no further development in terms of the permission will be competent and only the development carried out by that date will be authorised by the planning permission. The effectiveness of completion notices is therefore limited to situations in which the developer has some intention of proceeding with the development. Use of completion notices is unusual.

(b) Multiple Implementation of Permissions

Difficult questions arise where a permission has been partially or fully implemented and work commences in implementation of another permission applicable to the same site.[59] The central question is whether it is possible to carry out the development authorised by the permission, having regard to what was done or authorised to be done under the permission which has been implemented.[60] If the position is uncertain, an application could be made to the planning authority for a Certificate of Lawfulness of Proposed Use or Development (Chapter 4).

This test is one of physical possibility, not just of construction but also provision of the curtilage (Chapter 4) for the building identified in the application. Where two permissions authorised erection of a farmhouse, but in different locations within the same 50-acre site, their effect

[58] s. 41(2), as amended.

[59] Cullar, "Multiple Implementation of Planning Permissions" [1993] J.P.L. 627.

[60] *Pilkington* v. *Secretary of State for the Environment* [1973] 1 W.L.R. 1527.

was that the landowner was entitled to build a farmhouse in either location for use as a farmhouse in connection with farming the 50 acres. Having built one, he could not build on the other so long as there was a farmhouse standing and used for farming the 50 acres.[61] Mere incompatibility with the other permission already implemented is insufficient.[62] The intention of the planning authority in granting permission may be thought relevant, but in interpreting planning permissions reference may only be had to the decision letter (above).

A permission which is mutually inconsistent with an implemented permission remains in suspense (subject to time limits for implementation), until its implementation becomes physically possible.

(c) Challenge of Conditions

Implementation of the planning permission seems to prevent an appeal being lodged against conditions attached to the permission (there appears to be no statutory provision to this effect). By implementing the permission, the developer has accepted the conditions which are a part of that permission and cannot later seek to challenge those conditions. However, in such circumstances it is still competent to apply permission to develop the land without compliance with the conditions (Chapter 6).

Consequences of Refusal of Application

(a) Challenging the Refusal

Chapter 8 examines the procedures for challenging decisions on planning applications.

(b) Purchase Notice

Following a refusal of planning permission, or a grant subject to conditions, the owner or lessee of land which is incapable

[61] *Ellis* v. *Worcestershire C.C.* (1961) 12 P & C.R. 178.
[62] *Prestige Homes* v. *Secretary of State for the Environment* [1992] J.P.L. 842.

of reasonably beneficial use may serve a purchase notice on the planning authority.[63] There is no requirement to demonstrate a causal connection between the decision on the planning application and the fact that the land is incapable of reasonably beneficial use.[64] If the planning authority is willing to comply with the notice, it is deemed to acquire the land compulsorily. Compensation is assessed as for compulsory purchase. If the authority refuses to comply, the notice is referred to the Secretary of State for decision. He may either confirm the notice, grant planning permission, revoke or amend conditions, or direct that planning permission be granted for an alternative development if the appropriate application is made.

[63] TCPSA, s. 169, as amended.
[64] *Purbeck D.C.* v. *Secretary of State for the Environment* (1982) 80 L.G.R. 545.

Chapter 6

DEVELOPMENT CONTROL III — PLANNING CONDITIONS AND PLANNING AGREEMENTS

Planning permission is a crude device for controlling development: either the proposed development is acceptable or it is not. The power to impose conditions upon the grant of permission enables the planning authority to go beyond the adjudicative "yes-no" role by using conditions to control the detailed aspects of developments. Therefore, the imposition of conditions can be identified as a powerful tool for promoting flexibility within development control. However, the use of conditions is limited by legal restrictions.

As if to emphasise the weakness of the requirement to obtain planning permission as a development control tool, planning authorities have further statutory powers enabling them to enter into agreements with applicants. Controversially, these powers are often used to achieve "planning gain." Use of these powers has increased in the past decade, partly as a result of the restrictions placed on the use of conditions by the requirements for legal validity.

Planning Conditions

Planning conditions may be used to provide greater control and flexibility within the development control process by virtue of their dual role:

(a) making an otherwise unacceptable development acceptable, thereby furthering the presumption in favour of development,[1] always subject to the limits to

[1] S.D.D. Circular 18/1986, "The Use of Conditions in Planning Permissions," Annex, paras. 1 and 4.

which conditions can modify the proposed development (below); or

(b) controlling the details of an otherwise acceptable application, allowing the development to be "fine-tuned" making it more satisfactory. In this way, a development which is generally acceptable can be tailored to meet the needs of the surrounding locality and details such as landscaping and design settled.

There is no duty upon the planning authority to draw up and use a condition in the first role, but if the application is acceptable it has a duty to consider whether conditions can be imposed to make it more acceptable.[2] Standard lists of conditions may be used to achieve parity of treatment between applications and to promote consistency of decisions, although the decision to impose conditions must be considered for each application on its merits.

One investigation found that many planning officers believed that conditions were imposed for their psychological impact.[3] This provides an example of what has been described as a game of bluff.[4] Applicants are willing to accept conditions which may be invalid, or at least may never be enforced, because this persuades the authority to accept the application. The authority may similarly doubt the possibility of enforcing the obligation in practice, but impose the condition in the hope that the applicant will accept and implement it. Research has suggested that enforcement of conditions may be minimal.[5] The introduction of the power to serve breach of condition notices (Chapter 7) may result in a higher level of enforcement.

Conditions attached to planning permissions must be scrutinised and their effect considered before the permission

[2] *Mason* v. *Secretary of State for the Environment* [1984] J.P.L. 332; *Garbutt* v. *Secretary of State for the Environment* (1989) 57 P. & C.R. 284.

[3] Booth, "Development Control and Design Quality Part 1 — Conditions: A Useful Way of Controlling Design?" (1983) 54 T.P. Rev. 265.

[4] McAuslan *Land, Law and Planning* (1974).

[5] Loughlin *Local Needs Policy* (1984): 49 per cent of developments in one council area had failed to comply with agricultural occupancy conditions. See also Booth (above) and Peart and Rutherford, "Opencast Guidance — Opportunities for Green Policies" [1989] J.P.L. 406.

is implemented (Chapter 5). Once the development has commenced it will be too late to appeal against the conditions imposed.

Power to Impose Conditions

In determining an application for planning permission, planning authorities "may grant planning permission, either unconditionally, or subject to such conditions as they think fit."[6] This power only extends to the imposition of conditions upon land which forms part of the site of the proposed development as identified in the application.

Without prejudice to this general power to impose conditions, there is an additional power to attach conditions regulating the development or use of any land under the control of the applicant (whether or not it forms part of the application site), or requiring the carrying out of any works on any such land, so far as appears expedient for the purposes of or in connection with the authorised development.[7] The consequence of this additional power is that only land which is neither within the terms of the application for planning permission nor under the control of the applicant is not potentially subject to a planning condition.[8] It is a question of fact and degree whether the applicant has sufficient control to ensure compliance with the conditions.[9]

There are also statutory powers to impose specific types of conditions. Every permission is subject to an express or implied condition providing for the expiry of the permission if the development authorised by the permission is not commenced within a specified period of time (Chapter 5). A condition may be attached to a grant of temporary permission requiring removal of buildings or works authorised by the permission, or discontinuance of any authorised use of land, and reinstatement of the land on the expiry of that permission.[10] Conditions may also limit the benefit of a

[6] TCPSA, 26(1), as amended.
[7] s. 27(1)(a), as amended.
[8] *Birnie* v. *Banff* C.C., 1954 S.L.T. (Sh.Ct.) 90.
[9] *George Wimpey* v. *New Forest D.C.* [1979] J.P.L. 314.
[10] TCPSA, s. 27(1)(b), as amended. See also Chap. 5.

planning permission to a named person (a personal permission), or specify the use of a proposed building.[11] The planning authority has a duty to ensure that, where appropriate, conditions are imposed upon a grant of planning permission to secure adequate provision for the preservation and planting of trees.[12]

Scope of Planning Conditions: Legal

Planning authorities have the power to impose such conditions as they think fit. The width of this discretionary power is limited by the requirements for the legal validity of a planning condition which have been formulated by the courts through a process of statutory interpretation. A planning condition must have a planning purpose, fairly and reasonably relate to the permitted development, and not be so unreasonable that no reasonable planning authority could have imposed it.[13]

(a) Planning Purpose

The power to impose conditions is conferred by the planning legislation and must therefore be used to achieve a planning purpose and not an ulterior object.[14] As a result of the vagueness of the objectives of planning (Chapter 1), it is difficult to draw the line between a "planning" and an "ulterior" object. The TCPSA provides no guidance on the objects of planning powers, and the courts can only provide assistance on a case-by-case basis. As a result, there can be no precise guidelines on the requirement for a planning purpose. However, as the examination of material considerations has shown (Chapter 5), the scope of potential planning

[11] s. 30(1) and (2).
[12] s. 57(a), as amended.
[13] *Newbury D.C.* v. *Secretary of State for the Environment* [1981] A.C. 578 at p. 607; [1980] J.P.L. 325.
[14] *Pyx Granite* v. *Minister of Housing* [1958] Q.B. 554, *per* Lord Denning at p. 572.

matters is wide-ranging and the need for a planning purpose should not be an onerous requirement.

Planning has been held to relate to the use of land rather than to the user.[15] However, if the purpose of the condition relates to the use of the land, it is valid notwithstanding that it limits categories of users.[16] Thus, a condition limiting occupation of a dwelling house to agricultural workers was valid because it was imposed to further the policy of protecting the Green Belt.[17] Other decisions on "planning purpose" also involve conditions imposed to further planning policies. Inclusion of a policy within the development plan may give it the badge of "planning purpose," although this will not always be the case.[18] For example, many structure plans state that the area has been declared a "nuclear-free zone."

It was held that a condition restricting the extension or connection of water and sewerage service pipes to serve any other residential development had the valid planning purpose of prohibiting an arrangement between landowners which would lead to excessive provision of housing.[19] In contrast, a condition amounting to a requirement that a road be constructed and dedicated to the public was invalid because it had the ulterior purpose of requiring the developer to take on the duty of the highway authority.[20] Similarly, conditions imposed on a housing development requiring that the houses should first be occupied by persons on the local authority's housing waiting list were invalid because they required the developer to assume the duty of the local authority as a housing authority as his own expense.[21] Provision of small, low-cost rented accommodation was not a material consideration, as it did not serve a planning purpose which related to the character or the use of the land.[22]

[15] *Westminster C.C.* v. *Great Portland Estates* [1985] A.C. 661.
[16] *cf. David Lowe & Sons* v. *Musselburgh Town Council*, 1973 S.C. 130.
[17] *Fawcett Properties* v. *Buckingham C.C.* [1961] A.C. 636.
[18] *Westminster Renslade* v. *Secretary of State for the Environment* [1983] J.P.L. 454.
[19] *North-East Fife D.C.* v. *Secretary of State for Scotland*, 1992 S.L.T. 373.
[20] *Hall* v. *Shoreham-By-Sea Urban District Council* [1964] 1 W.L.R. 240.
[21] *R.* v. *Hillingdon L.B.C., ex p. Royco Homes* [1974] 2 All E.R. 643.
[22] *Mitchell* v. *Secretary of State for the Environment*, Court of Appeal, November 1, 1993, Unreported. The Secretary of State has given notice of appeal.

Other guidance on possible planning purposes may be found in the court decisions interpreting the scope of "material considerations" (Chapter 5).

The authority may have many purposes in mind when imposing a condition. A condition might have other purposes, but must not be imposed solely to serve some other purpose or purposes.[23] This suggests that the mere presence of a planning purpose is enough. There must, however, come a point at which the planning purpose becomes subordinated to the other purposes to such an extent that it has negligible influence on the decision. Another view suggests that the purpose must be solely or primarily to achieve a planning objective.[24] Once the planning purpose becomes secondary to the other purposes then the condition is invalid. This seems the preferable view. In practice, however, planning authorities are unlikely to mention any non-planning purposes in their written reasons for imposing the condition, in an attempt to avoid any appeal against their decisions.

(b) Fairly and Reasonably Relates

The condition must fairly and reasonably relate to the development authorised by the permission.[25] This is the result of the wording of the statutory power to impose conditions which links inextricably, and subordinates, this power to the decision to grant permission. Since permission is given for a specified development, any condition must also relate to that development.

What is the meaning of "fairly and reasonably relates"? It has been suggested that a "recognised and real relationship" is required, which is a question of fact and judgment, rather than requiring the condition to be imposed to remedy some direct adverse consequence ("mischief") caused by the development. It would be enough that the condition was imposed because of matters "merely consequential" to the development. Any test is open to subjective application, and

[23] *Newbury D.C.* v. *Secretary of State for the Environment* [1981] A.C. 578, *per* Lord Fraser at p. 618.
[24] Grant, *Urban Planning Law* (1981), p. 337.
[25] *Pyx Granite* v. *M.H.L.G.* [1958] 1 Q.B. 554, *per* Lord Denning at p. 572.

while the test of directness is capable of narrow application, the "merely consequential" test may achieve the same result as a test of directness applied broadly. Each case is determined on its facts and it is difficult to identify a consistent approach in the court decisions.

By including land within the application, the developer may be taken to admit the connection between that land and the proposed development. A more contentious issue arises where conditions are imposed on land under the control of the applicant which is not contained within the terms of the application. The statutory power to impose such conditions (above) requires the condition to be "expedient for the purposes of or in connection with the development authorised by the permission." This wording would appear to achieve a similar result to the "fairly and reasonably relates" test. Court decisions relating to this statutory power may therefore be used to help interpret the "fairly and reasonably relates" requirement.

Doubt has been expressed whether conditions attached to land under the control of the applicant a mile away rather than immediately adjacent to the development would be valid.[26] Geographical separation cannot be conclusive, but the directness of the relationship between condition and development must deteriorate with physical distance.[27]

Cases have affirmed conditions relating to land or buildings on the same site as the development, to the purpose of the development, and to its possible effects. Where machinery was used to process quarried stone, there was a direct relationship between the use of the machinery and the quarry development, with the result that a condition relating to the use of that machinery sufficiently related to the development.[28] As a factory extension allowed an existing building to be used more effectively, conditions controlling the use of machinery in the existing factory were valid as connected to the purpose of the permitted development.[29] A condition designed to control noise caused by air traffic fairly and

[26] *Ibid.*
[27] *Peak Park J.P.B.* v. *Secretary of State for the Environment* [1980] J.P.L. 114.
[28] *Pyx Granite* v. *M.H.L.G., op cit.*
[29] *Penwith D.C.* v. *Secretary of State for the Environment* (1977) 34 P. & C.R. 269.

reasonably related to the construction of a new terminal building required because of increased air traffic.[30]

Conditions have been struck down for failing to fairly and reasonably relate to the proposed development. A condition intended to restrict residential development elsewhere was held invalid because it did not reasonably relate to the proposed residential development.[31] A condition requiring demolition of buildings had nothing to do with the change of use for which planning permission was sought.[32] However, there was arguably an indirect connection because the continued use of the building affected the amenity of the neighbourhood. A condition regulating the killing of foxes could have been validly imposed on a grant of permission for construction of fox pens, but a condition preventing the slaughter of any animals on the premises was too remotely connected to the permitted development to be valid.[33] Similarly, a condition requiring installation of frosted glass in windows imposed when an occupancy condition was altered to allow a change of occupier was held to be unrelated to the development and therefore invalid, since the requirement for the glass was not brought about by the proposed occupation, but dated back to the first occupation of the building.[34] However, it could be argued that the change of use did not cause the need for the condition, but continued that need.

(c) Reasonableness

The imposition of a condition must be reasonable, but in the special legal sense (referred to as Wednesbury reasonableness). A condition will be invalid on the ground of unreasonableness only if it is so unreasonable that no reasonable planning authority would have imposed that condition.

Unfortunately the term "reasonableness" has come to be used as an umbrella term for other legal requirements which

[30] *B.A.A.* v. *Secretary of State for Scotland*, 1979 S.C. 200.
[31] *North-East Fife D.C.* v. *Secretary of State for Scotland* (n. 19, *supra*).
[32] *Newbury D.C.* v. *Secretary of State for the Environment* [1981] A.C. 578.
[33] *Gill* v. *Secretary of State for Environment* [1985] J.P.L. 710.
[34] *Elmsbridge B.C.* v. *Secretary of State for the Environment* [1989] J.P.L. 277.

have developed, such as certainty and necessity (below). It should be used as a residual category, for use only where a condition meets all other requirements, but demonstrates such a perverse or irrational exercise of the statutory discretion that it is illegal. The danger is that the concept of reasonableness may be stretched to the stage that it is used to interfere with the merits of the decision, enabling the court to reject a condition of which is disapproves without having to show that the condition is defective in any more specific way.

This problem may be resolved by adopting the reformulation of the grounds for judicial review (Chapter 8) to restate the requirements for the legal validity of a condition as follows:

1. planning purpose;
2. fairly and reasonably relates to the permitted development;
3. the condition must be otherwise legal; and
4. that it is otherwise rational, and not "so outrageous in its defiance of logic or of accepted moral standards that no sensible person who had applied his mind to the question to be decided could have arrived at it."

Matters often discussed under the heading of reasonableness, which could be relocated under the heading of legality, include contributions from the applicant, derogation from the benefit of permission, certainty, enforceability and necessity.

(d) Contributions from the Applicant

A condition cannot require payment of a monetary contribution by the applicant.[35] It would also be invalid for a condition to require the applicant to provide another form of contribution, such as relinquishing land for use by the public as open space[36] or parking.[37] For these purposes it is irrelevant that

[35] *R.* v. *Bowman* [1898] 1 Q.B. 663; *Attorney General* v. *Wilts United Dairies* (1922) 91 L.J. (K.B.) 89.

[36] *M.J. Shanley* v. *Secretary of State for the Environment* [1982] J.P.L. 380.

[37] *Westminster Renslade* v. *Secretary of State for the Environment* (n. 18, *supra*).

the applicant has agreed: validity cannot be conferred by consent.[38]

(e) Derogation from the Benefit of Permission

Although imposition of a condition necessarily alters the development proposed by the application, there must be a limit to such alteration. Conditions cannot be used to derogate from the benefit of the permission, with the result that the nature of the development permitted is significantly different to that proposed in the application for planning permission. In other words, the planning authority cannot seek to take away with one hand what it has granted with the other. This requirement derives from the statutory wording which subordinates the power to impose conditions to the power to grant permission. Use of conditions to alter radically the proposed development would leave no opportunity for the public to give their views on what would be a substantially different proposal.

It must always be a question of fact and degree whether a particular condition takes away the substance of the permission.[39] It is competent to impose conditions scaling down an application, but not to the extent of altering the substance of the development. A condition reducing the size of the proposed development from 35 acres and 420 dwellings to 25 acres and 250 dwellings was upheld on the basis that the result did not differ substantially from the development proposed in the original application.[40] This suggests a test of character: does the permitted development have a substantially different character from the development proposed in the original application? Conditions requiring "ancillary or incidental" development, such as the provision of children's play areas and open space in a housing development, have also been upheld.[41]

[38] *Birnie* v. *Banff C.C.* (n. 8, *supra*).
[39] *Kent C.C.* v. *Secretary of State for the Environment* (1976) 33 P. & C.R. 70.
[40] *Bernard Wheatcroft* v. *Secretary of State for the Environment* [1982] J.P.L. 37.
[41] *Britannia (Cheltenham) Ltd.* v. *Secretary of State for the Environment* [1978] J.P.L. 554.

A grant of permission on appeal seeking to restrict the benefit of a permission previously granted for development of adjacent ground was held invalid.[42]

(f) Certainty

A condition must be capable of being understood so that the owner of the burdened property can comply with it. A planning condition is only void for uncertainty if it can be given no meaning or no sensible or ascertainable meaning, and not merely because it is ambiguous or leads to absurd results.[43] A Scottish judge has suggested that it would equally be invalid to impose a condition which produced an absurd result which was plainly not the one intended. This suggestion should be treated with caution, as it is not supported by previous decisions and was made in a case where the condition was void for uncertainty.[44]

The courts will take pains to find some meaning in the terms of a condition,[45] and have refused to construe the terms of a condition against the interest of the authority in favour of the applicant (*contra proferentem*).[46] Thus, mere ambiguity or doubtful instances will not render a condition invalid.[47] Even vagueness will probably not be sufficient to invalidate a condition. Terms such as "local"[48] have been upheld even though incapable of precise definition. It is enough that such terms can be understood and applied. It would appear that there is effectively a presumption that a condition is certain in its wording, and this is emphasised by the few instances of successful challenges.[49]

[42] *North-East Fife D.C.* v. *Secretary of State for Scotland* (n. 19, *supra*).

[43] *Fawcett Properties* v. *Buckingham* C.C. [1960] 3 All E.R. 503, *per* Lord Denning at p. 517; [1961] A.C. 636.

[44] *Eastwood D.C.* v. *Mactaggart & Mickel Ltd.*, 1994 S.L.T. 38; 1992 S.P.L.P. 37:76.

[45] *Kingsway Investments* v. *Kent C.C.* [1971] A.C. 72.

[46] *Crisp from the Fens* v. *Rutland C.C.*, 1950 L.G.R. 210, *per* Singleton J.

[47] *Inverclyde D.C.* v. *Inverkip Building Co.*, 1983 S.L.T. 563; *cf. David Lowe & Sons* v. *Musselburgh Town Council*, 1973 S.C. 130.

[48] *Alderson* v. *Secretary of State for the Environment* [1984] J.P.L. 429.

[49] *Eastwood D.C.* v. *Mactaggart & Mickel Ltd.* (see n. 44, *supra*); *David Lowe & Sons* v. *Musselburgh Town Council op. cit.* is a doubtful authority.

(g) *Enforceability*

There are two senses in which a condition may be unenforceable: if it requires action that is outwith the control of the applicant, and if it is too vague to form the subject of enforcement action.

A condition which requires any action that is outwith the control of the applicant is unenforceable and therefore invalid because there are no steps that the applicant can take to secure the required result. As control of air traffic was the statutory responsibility of another body, a condition specifying the direction of aircraft flights was unenforceable because the applicant was unable to meet the requirements of the condition.[50] A condition relating to land that is neither within the application nor under the control of the applicant must be unenforceable, because the applicant will have no power to ensure compliance with the condition.[51] A condition requiring access to be by way of a specified road was invalid because the road was neither within the application site nor under the control of the applicant and in consequence there were no steps which the applicant could take to secure or ensure that all vehicles used the prescribed route.[52] On similar reasoning, a condition may be unenforceable and invalid if it relates to land within the application site, but outwith the control of the applicant.

Where it would be invalid to impose a condition requiring action outwith the control of the applicant, the same result can be achieved legitimately by using a negatively worded (or suspensive) condition (see below). The effect of such a condition is that the development cannot commence until the action is achieved. The obligation to be enforced would not be the obligation to achieve the result, but rather the lack of permission to start the development until the result was achieved. The decision to commence the development is under the control of the applicant.

The other sense of enforceability relates to the need for the meaning of a condition to be precise enough for enforcement

[50] *B.A.A.* v. *Secretary of State for Scotland*, (n. 30, *supra*).
[51] *Birnie* v. *Banff C.C.* (n. 8, *supra*).
[52] *Mouchell Superannuation Trustees* v. *Oxfordshire* C.C. [1992] 1 P.L.R. 97.

action to be taken against any breach of its terms. Conditions that are so vague as to be incapable of definition, or physically incapable of performance, may be unenforceable. A condition requiring the first opportunity to buy houses to be given to local people was declared unenforceable because there was no indication of the method or terms upon which this opportunity was to be offered.[53] It is not enough that the condition is merely difficult to enforce.[54] Conditions may be valid even though breaches of the condition may be difficult to detect.[55]

If a condition can be certain enough for the applicant to understand the limits placed on his property rights, but open to challenge on the basis that it is unenforceable, it is difficult to resolve the requirements for certainty (above) and enforceability of conditions,[56] and it has been suggested that there is no independent head of challenge to the validity of a condition relating to its enforceability.[57]

(h) Necessity

The Court of Session has declared that an unnecessary condition is invalid, by applying an expediency test to the imposition of all conditions irrespective of their statutory source.[58] This aspect of the decision has been criticised. (The conditions were also found invalid on the ground that they related to activities that were outwith the power of the applicants or to land that was outwith the control of the applicants and were therefore unenforceable.)

This concept of necessity can be criticised for taking the courts beyond questions of legality into the merits of a decision. The review jurisdiction of the courts is limited to

[53] *M.J. Shanley* v. *Secretary of State for the Environment* (n. 36, *supra*).

[54] *Chichester D.C.* v. *Secretary of State for the Environment* [1992] 3 P.L.R. 49.

[55] *Kent C.C.* v. *Secretary of State for the Environment* (n. 39, *supra*).

[56] This can be seen from the discussion in *Bromsgrove District Council* v. *Secretary of State for Environment* [1988] J.P.L. 257 of the decisions in *M.J. Shanley* (n. 53, *supra*); *Penwith D.C.* v. *Secretary of State for the Environment* [1986] J.P.L. 432; *Bizony* v. *Secretary of State for the Environment* [1976] J.P.L. 306.

[57] *Chichester D.C.* v. *Secretary of State for the Environment* (n. 54, *supra*).

[58] *B.A.A.* v. *Secretary of State for Scotland*, 1979 S.C. 200. Only TCPSA, s. 27(1) refers to conditions being "expedient."

examining the legality of a decision (Chapter 8). It is difficult to imagine an unnecessary condition that would be reprehensible enough to be illegal. If a condition is unnecessary because the application did not require it, then it should be caught by the "fairly and reasonably relates" test. The close link between the condition and the mischief caused by the development required by the concept of necessity appears to go further than the "fairly and reasonably relates" test and renders it redundant. However, the concept of proportionality, which also requires a close link between the action taken and the mischief at which it is aimed, has been rejected by a British court as going beyond the notion of Wednesbury reasonableness into the question of the merits of a decision.[59]

The decision can also be criticised on its facts. One condition was found to have no practical need or effect because another body had already taken action to achieve the desired result. It could be argued that the condition was harmless and no burden to the applicant, and guarded against the possibility of the action being reversed in the future. Other conditions were held unnecessary on the ground that if they were validly imposed on one permission then there was no need to duplicate them on other permissions. Duplication gives the authority greater opportunity for enforcement and adds greater force to the requirement.

It is therefore suggested that the courts should not declare conditions invalid on the basis of lack of necessity. To do so would lead to judicial intervention in the merits of a planning decision. The question of necessity should be left to the planning authority and the Secretary of State, as they can examine the issue of necessity as part of the planning merits of the condition.

Scope of Planning Conditions: Policy

In considering whether to impose conditions upon a grant of planning permission the planning authority is bound by the legal requirements for the validity of a condition. The authority must also have regard to the policy laid down by

[59] *R.* v. *Secretary of State for the Home Department, ex p. Brind,* [1991] A.C. 696.

the Secretary of State. As this policy is used in the determination of any appeal, authorities anxious to avoid successful appeals against their decisions will give it careful consideration when applying conditions.

The Scottish Office policy is more restrictive than the legal requirements, stating that a condition must be necessary, relevant to planning, relevant to the development to be permitted, enforceable, precise and reasonable in all other respects.[60] The nature of the development permitted or its effect on the surroundings must call for the condition to be imposed. A greater burden is placed upon planning authorities to impose precise and clear conditions. The Secretary of State may find a condition unenforceable if breaches of the condition may be difficult to detect. The policy includes suggested models of acceptable conditions and indicates that conditions requiring the following results are not acceptable (the explanations in brackets have been added by the author):

(a) On policy grounds

1. completion of a development within a specified time limit;
2. delaying the commencement of development until a future date;
3. preventing the display of advertisements on the site (lack of planning purpose — there are separate statutory powers for control of advertisements — Chapter 9);
4. restricting occupation, for example, of flats, to a specified number of persons (difficult to enforce);
5. construction of an ancillary road by the applicant as and when required by the planning authority (vague);

(b) On legal grounds

1. that means of access shall be set back and splayed in agreement with the roads authority, when the latter is a third party (unenforceable — actions of third party);
2. that the land in front of the building shall be made available for future road widening (cession of land);

[60] *Circular 18/1986, Annex, para. 12.*

3. a lay-by, having been constructed, should thereafter be assigned to the roads authority (cession of land);
4. loading and unloading, and the parking of vehicles, shall not take place on the road in front of the premises (enforceability — road not under control of applicant);
5. the site shall be kept tidy at all times (certainty/enforceability — vague);
6. the applicant shall comply with the bye-laws and general statutory provisions in force in the district (lack of planning purpose);
7. furnishing shall be of a fireproof material (lack of planning purpose);
8. aircraft should only arrive or depart at an airfield on specified air traffic routes (lack of planning purpose — activity regulated by other statutory provisions; enforceability — outside control of applicant);
9. a shop window display to be maintained in an attractive condition (certainty/enforceability — no criterion by which it could be enforced);

The list of model conditions should be consulted for forms of condition which may achieve these results validly.

Challenge of Condition

There are several options available to the applicant for planning permission to challenge an unacceptable condition (fig 6.1), most of which are described in more detail in Chapter 8. The acceptability of the conditions must be considered before the permission is implemented (Chapter 5). With one exception, once development has commenced it will be too late to challenge any condition imposed.

(a) Negotiation

Formal procedures such as appeals are expensive and time-consuming for both the applicant and the planning authority, and negotiations must be in the interests of both parties. It may be possible to persuade the planning authority to dispense with the condition, with the result that permission is granted without the condition following a fresh application, or

Fig. 6.1 Challenging Planning Conditions

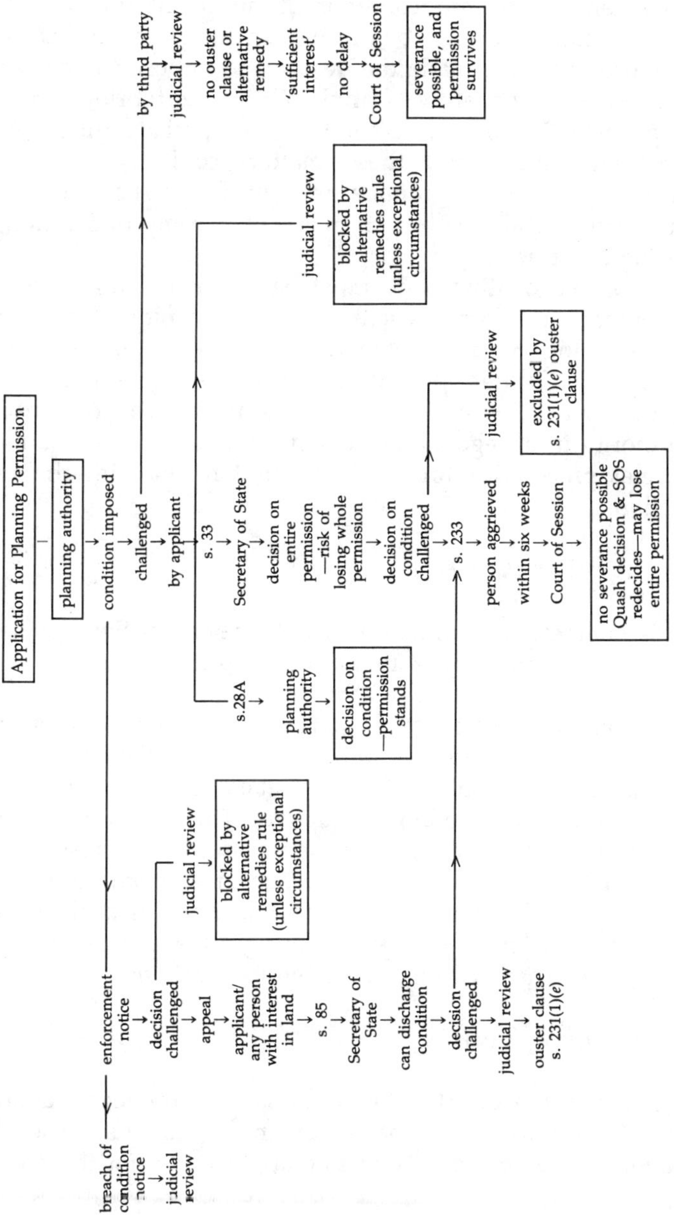

an application for permission to develop the land without compliance with the condition is approved (below). Additional information may be produced which was not before the authority when it made the decision to impose the condition. Developers frequently complain that authorities do not appreciate the impact of conditions, especially their adverse financial impact, and these matters could be put to the authority. If valid grounds of appeal can be shown, the authority may be willing to negotiate a compromise to avoid losing an appeal.

When negotiating, care must be taken that time limits for commencing a formal challenge do not expire. If time limits are looming, it is possible to lodge the challenge and sist (suspend) further procedure with the agreement of the authority to allow negotiations to continue. To pressurise the authority into negotiating, it may be necessary to commence formal procedures for challenge in tandem with the negotiations.

(b) Appeal to the Secretary of State

It is competent to appeal to the Secretary of State against a grant of permission with an unacceptable condition.[61] The appeal must be lodged within six months of the decision by the planning authority. As part of the appeal, the planning merits of the condition and the facts of the case will be considered. The policy of the Secretary of State on imposition of conditions will be applied (above). The appeal is dealt with as if it were an application for planning permission. The Secretary of State may, therefore, reverse or vary any part of the original decision, no matter what aspect is challenged. In consequence, there is a risk of losing the entire permission or being burdened with a more onerous condition.

(c) Review by Court of Session

Review by the Court of Session relates to the legal validity of the condition and not its planning merits. The legal requirements for validity will be applied and not the policy of

[61] TCPSA, s. 33, as amended.

the Secretary of State. A distinction must be drawn between statutory and common-law judicial review:

1. statutory review is only competent for challenge of a decision by the Secretary of State on a condition.[62] It is available to any person aggrieved, but it is subject to a strict six-week time limit. The court has no power to sever the invalid condition from the remainder of the permission.[63] A successful challenge will therefore result in the permission being quashed and the matter being returned to the Secretary of State for re-decision. He may decide that without the condition, permission should be refused.
2. an application for judicial review at common law may be used to challenge a decision to impose a condition by either the planning authority or the Secretary of State. It is available to any person with title and interest to sue. There is no prescribed time limit, but delay may bar any challenge. Unless there are exceptional circumstances, the existence of an alternative remedy will exclude an application for judicial review at common law. The applicant for permission therefore cannot utilise the common-law judicial review procedure because of his statutory rights of appeal to the Secretary of State against a decision by the planning authority, and review by the Court of Session of the Secretary of State's decision.

Unlike statutory review, in the exercise of its common-law judicial review jurisdiction the Court of Session has the power to sever an invalid condition with the result that the remainder of the permission stands shorn of the condition.

There is no statutory test to determine whether a condition is severable, but several approaches can be identified from the cases. It is important to decide whether severance is a practical proposition. If the invalid condition is "inextricably interconnected" with the rest of the permission, severance may be impossible.[64] However, there is no absolute requirement for textual severability and the court may redraft a permission to retain the valid part.[65]

[62] s. 233, as amended.
[63] *B.A.A.* v. *Secretary of State for Scotland* (n. 58, *supra*).
[64] *R.* v. *Secretary of State for Transport, ex p. G.L.C.* [1985] 3 All E.R. 300.
[65] *D.P.P.* v. *Hutchison* [1990] 2 All E.R. 836.

A distinction can be drawn between fundamental conditions which go to the root of the permission, and conditions that are unimportant or incidental, superimposed or collateral to the permission. Only conditions of the latter type can be severed. This test is essentially one of substance or character: can the condition be severed without changing the nature of the grant of permission? Another approach focuses on the intentions of the planning authority, asking whether it would have granted the permission without the offending condition. If not, the condition should not be severed and the whole permission be quashed. It may be thought that a condition which does not fairly and reasonably relate to the permitted development is likely to be severable, but even in these circumstances the courts remain reluctant to alter the permission granted by the authority and prefer to quash the entire permission.

In consequence of the need to speculate on the intention of the planning authority in imposing the condition, the courts rarely declare a condition severable. There are only three reported cases in which an invalid condition has been severed from the planning permission.[66] It is, therefore, unlikely that a successful application for judicial review at common law will result in anything other than invalidation of the whole permission.

(d) Application for Permission to Develop Land Without Compliance with Condition

An application can be made to the planning authority for permission to develop the application site without complying with the conditions subject to which the permission was granted.[67] In deciding the application, the authority can only consider the conditions and there is no risk of losing the permission. If it decides permission should be granted subject to the same conditions, the application will be refused. If the

[66] *Allnatt Properties* v. *Middlesex C.C.* (1964) 15 P. & C.R. 288, *R.* v. *St. Edmundsbury B.C., ex p. Investors in Industry* [1985] 3 All E.R. 234; *Elmsbridge B.C.* v. *Secretary of State for the Environment* [1989] J.P.L. 277.

[67] TCPSA, s. 28A.

application is successful permission will be granted subject to different conditions or unconditionally.

The disadvantage of this procedure is that the application is made to the same body that imposed the condition. Powerful arguments will be required to convince it that the condition should not have been imposed or should now be discharged. Using this procedure to challenge a condition may only be an option if circumstances have changed since the condition was imposed.

(e) Ignore the Condition

The applicant may choose to ignore the condition in the hope that the planning authority will not take enforcement action. A breach of condition becomes immune from enforcement action, and lawful, after 10 years (Chapter 7). In the event that the authority serves an enforcement notice, an appeal may be lodged with the Secretary of State on the grounds that the condition ought to be discharged,[68] or an application for retrospective permission lodged. However, authorities are more likely to use the new power to serve a breach of condition notice where there is non-compliance with a condition regulating the use of land. There is no right of appeal against such a notice although it may be possible to seek judicial review at common law on the grounds that the condition which is the subject of the notice is invalid. If attempts to challenge the enforcement or breach of condition notice are unsuccessful, failure to comply with its terms is a criminal offence.

(f) Application for Retrospective Permission

An application for retrospective permission may be made for development which was carried out without complying with a condition subject to which permission was granted.[69] As part

[68] s. 85(1)(a).
[69] s. 29, as amended.

of the application, it would be necessary to convince the authority that there was no need for the condition. If no such application is made, the breach of condition will only become immune from enforcement action after 10 years.

Types of Conditions

In addition to the two general statutory powers to impose planning conditions, there are several more particular statutory powers relating to expiry of permission, temporary and personal permissions, specification of use, and preservation and planting of trees (see above). Many other types of planning conditions have arisen in practice. Of these, four have been examined in particular detail by the courts: those relating to occupancy, restriction of use or development, avoidance of compensation payment, and the imposition of negative or suspensive conditions.

(a) Occupancy Conditions

As a basic proposition, conditions restricting the class of potential occupiers of property appear unduly restrictive of rights of private property. Indeed, the existence of an occupancy condition will restrict the opportunities to re-sell a property and therefore reduce its value for mortgage purposes. Planning relates to the use of the land rather than to the user.[70] However, personal circumstances can be taken into account in certain cases.[71] Conditions may, therefore, be imposed which restrict occupancy to a particular occupier or class of occupier, provided the condition relates to a legitimate planning purpose.

A condition limiting occupation of a dwelling to persons employed in agriculture (agricultural occupancy condition)

[70] *Westminster City Council* v. *British Waterways Board* [1985] A.C. 676; [1985] J.P.L. 102; *David Lowe & Sons* v. *Musselburgh Town Council*, 1973 S.C. 130, *per* Lord President Emslie at p. 142.

[71] *Westminster City Council* v. *Great Portland Estates* [1985] A.C. 661, *per* Lord Scarman at p. 669H (also [1985] J.P.L. 108).

was validly imposed where the reason for the condition was the protection of the Green Belt from residential development.[72] Similarly, a condition restricting occupation of commercial or industrial property to local firms was imposed to restrict the entry of new industry into the area.[73] In contrast, an occupancy condition imposed to relieve the authority of its statutory duty had no legitimate planning reason and was therefore invalid.[74]

The Scottish Office guidance states that occupancy conditions should only be used when the need for special planning grounds can be demonstrated, and permission would otherwise be refused. Conditions restricting the occupancy of commercial or industrial premises to local firms should not be imposed. Similarly, occupancy conditions should be imposed on housing developments only in the most exceptional cases where there are clear and specific circumstances that warrant allowing an individual house (or extension) on a site where development would not normally be permitted. Agricultural occupancy conditions should be imposed on residential development only where the proposed development would not otherwise be granted permission and there is a special need to provide accommodation on a farm unit for those employed in agriculture.[75]

(b) Restriction of Use/Development

It is competent to impose a condition restricting changes of use. This has the effect of restricting the freedom provided by the U.C.O. (Chapter 4), with the result that an application for planning permission may be required for any change from the permitted use. The condition may prohibit any change from the use permitted; alternatively, it may preclude specific alternative uses or restrict changes to specified classes of the U.C.O. For example, it may be valid to impose a condition

[72] *Fawcett Properties* v. *Buckingham City Council* [1961] A.C. 636.
[73] *Slough Industrial Estates* v. *Secretary of State for the Environment* [1987] J.P.L. 353.
[74] *R.* v. *London Borough of Hillingdon, ex p. Royco Homes* [1974] Q.B. 720.
[75] Circular 18/1986, Annex, paras. 78, 80, 82, 84 and 85.

preventing the change of use permitted by class 4 from light industrial to office use, provided the planning authority have valid planning reasons for imposing this restriction.[76]

It is similarly possible to restrict permitted development rights under the P.D.O.[77] For example, where permission is granted for erection of a dwelling-house in the grounds of an existing dwelling-house, it may be appropriate to restrict the permitted development rights which would otherwise be enjoyed by the new dwelling-house. This would have the effect of requiring an application for planning permission to be made which would provide the planning authority with an opportunity to consider the effects of fresh development on the existing dwelling.

The Scottish Office guidance states that there must be a general presumption against use of conditions to limit the provisions of the U.C.O. or P.D.O.[78] This type of condition requires to be carefully worded.[79]

(c) Liability to Pay Compensation

Where there is a choice of statutory powers, an authority can legitimately use the power that carries no liability to payment of compensation. It is therefore competent to impose a condition for planning reasons which has the effect of avoiding the payment of compensation,[80] although avoidance of the payment of compensation is not a planning consideration.[81] The Scottish Office policy is that conditions should not be imposed in order to avoid liability to pay compensation

[76] Compare *London Borough of Tower Hamlets* v. *Secretary of State for the Environment* [1990] J.P.L. 688 and *Camden London Borough Council* v. *Secretary of State for the Environment* [1989] J.P.L. 613.

[77] P.D.O., art. 3(4); *Gill* v. *Secretary of State for the Environment* [1985] J.P.L. 710.

[78] Circular 18/1986, Annex, para. 73.

[79] *Dunoon Developments* v. *Secretary of State for the Environment* [1992] J.P.L. 936.

[80] *R.* v. *Exeter City Council ex p. J.L. Thomas* [1991] 1 Q.B. 471; [1990] J.P.L. 129; *cf. Hall* v. *Shoreham-by-Sea Urban District Council* [1964] 1 W.L.R. 240; [1964] J.P.L. 316.

[81] *B.A.A.* v. *Secretary of State for Scotland*, 1979 S.C. 200, *per* L.P. Emslie at p. 218.

under other legislation, but that such conditions would not be illegal if justified on planning grounds.[82]

(d) Negative/Suspensive Conditions

Permission for a proposed development often hinges on an element outside the applicant's control, such as the provision of adequate sewerage facilities by the local authority. Since the result is outwith the applicant's control, any condition requiring him to achieve that result would be unenforceable (above). The solution is to word the condition negatively so that it provides that development will not commence until the result has been achieved. It is competent to impose such negative or suspensive conditions, often referred to as "Grampian" conditions.[83] Use of this type of condition may avoid the necessity of entering into a planning agreement (see below).

Until a recent decision of the House of Lords, it was trite law that it would be unreasonable and *ultra vires* to impose a negative condition on a grant of planning permission unless there was a reasonable prospect of the result being achieved.[84] In the absence of such a prospect, the authority would have granted a worthless permission. Scottish Office guidance links this reasonable prospect requirement to the likelihood of the precondition being fulfilled within such time as to enable the development to be commenced with the time limit imposed by the permission.[85]

In *British Railways Board*, the House of Lords overruled the reasonable prospect test.[86] If the negative condition is appropriate in light of sound planning principles, the fact that it appeared to have no reasonable prospects of being implemented did not mean that the grant of planning permission subject to it would be unlawful. What is appropriate depends on the circumstances and must be

[82] Circular 18/1986, Annex, paras. 22 and 24.
[83] *Grampian Regional Council* v. *Aberdeen District Council*, 1984 S.L.T. 197.
[84] *Norfolk House* v. *Secretary of State for the Environment* [1990] J.P.L. 490; *Jones* v. *Secretary of State for Wales* [1990] J.P.L. 907.
[85] Circular 18/1986, Annex, para. 39.
[86] *British Railways Board* v. *Secretary of State for the Environment* [1994] J.P.L. 32.

determined in the exercise of the discretion of the planning authority determining the application. The mere fact that a desirable condition appears to have no reasonable prospect of fulfilment does not mean that planning permission has to be refused.

The practical implications of this decision are uncertain. Authorities are likely to continue to regard the lack of a reasonable prospect of fulfilment as an important factor in their decision, albeit not a determining factor. Any fresh guidance from the Scottish Office in light of this decision will provide an important indication of any changes in practice. It should be noted that the case before their Lordships concerned the imposition of negative conditions to solve ownership difficulties, where it was clear that those difficulties had no relevance to the determination of the planning application. One can speculate that a different approach might be taken where the problems concern more important matters such as necessary infra-structure.

Negative conditions can also be used to control the separate phases of a large development. For example, a condition may require provision of specified infrastructure works (roads, drains, etc.) before the development or a further phase of the development commences. Such conditions ensure the provision of expensive works which the developer might be tempted to defer for many years.

Conclusion

The court decisions on the use of the particular types of conditions discussed above do not show the expected degree of judicial concern to protect private right of property against interference by way of conditions imposed on grants of planning permission.[87] Indeed, it seems that the courts generally favour the validity of conditions. Although the judges have developed a series of limitations on the exercise of the power to impose conditions, there are few instances

[87] *cf.* McAuslan's thesis that the courts favour individual rights of private property at the expense of the public interest, thereby upholding individual challenges to the actions of planning authorities — *Ideologies of Planning Law* (1980) and article of same name (1979) 2.U.L. & P.1.

where the courts have found conditions invalid. This may in part be due to the influence on the imposition of conditions of the Scottish Office/Department of the Environment guidance on the use of conditions which is often more restrictive than the legal requirements.

Planning Agreements

Planning agreements are contracts entered into between the landowner and planning authority (and often with other parties). Agreements can be entered into at any stage of the planning process, but most commonly arise in connection with applications for planning permission. There are several statutory powers which enable planning authorities to enter into agreements with developers. The widest and, therefore, most important is the power to enter into a section 50 agreement conferred by the TCPSA. Although many of the following points would apply to all forms of planning agreements, discussion will focus exclusively on section 50 agreements.[88]

It should be noted that the statutory power to enter into a section 106 obligation, which is the English equivalent of a section 50 agreement, is worded differently, partly as a consequence of differences between the land law of each legal system. Decisions of English courts relating to planning agreements must therefore be read with care.

The attraction for developers lies in the possibility of using a planning agreement to increase the likelihood of a grant of planning permission for a proposed development. This may be achieved by using an agreement to remove obstacles which would otherwise render the development unacceptable. Agreements can also be used to offer community benefits as a balance to offset the planning disadvantages of a proposed development. The development potential of a site can be unlocked through an agreement providing that the developer will undertake or pay for infrastructure improvements, such as roads and sewers, without which no development could be

[88] Other powers include Local Government (Scotland) Act 1973, ss. 69 and 85; Roads (Scotland) Act 1984, s. 48; Sewerage (Scotland) Act 1968, s. 8.

permitted on the site and which would otherwise be at the mercy of local government budgets. In the developer's eyes the agreement is a device to increase the likelihood of planning permission being granted. In consequence, it is essential to ensure that the planning authority may validly take into account the benefits promised in the agreement when determining the application for planning permission (see *Agreements as a Material Consideration*, below).

Although planning agreements are entered into voluntarily, it must be acknowledged that developers are often left with no alternative but to agree. If there are planning problems with the proposed development which can only be resolved through a planning agreement, planning permission cannot be obtained until the developer and the planning authority have negotiated the terms of the agreement. This places the planning authority in the position to dictate the terms, and possibly require the provision of planning gain. Without the agreement permission will be refused on appeal and the option of appealing to the Secretary of State against a deemed refusal of planning permission (Chapter 8) is, therefore, not available to the developer. The Secretary of State/reporter has no power to impose an agreement on the planning authority. The developer must agree terms with the authority or abandon the proposed development. However, the developer's negotiating position need not be inherently weak. Considerations such as the number of jobs which would be created by the proposed development may cause the planning authority to be anxious to avoid its abandonment.

For planning authorities, agreements are an alternative means of controlling developments, especially in light of the uncertainty regarding the validity of conditions (above), and their desire to avoid successful appeals against conditions. Agreements can also be used to control matters clearly beyond the scope of conditions. For example, conditions cannot validly require payment of money or provision of infrastructure such as roads and sewers on land outside the application site which is not under the control of the applicant for permission, even where the work is only necessary because of the proposed development. In addition, agreements can secure a degree of flexibility of control and management of development beyond the normal range of planning permission and conditions. Other attractions are the lack of any rights of appeal, and the availability of contractual remedies for enforcement without the procedural requirements of the planning enforcement regime (Chapter 7).

The use of planning agreements is not without criticism. It circumvents the formal procedures laid down for determining applications for planning permission and therefore avoids statutory protections and limitations. The lack of public scrutiny means that interests other than those of the negotiating parties may not receive proper protection. Most importantly, there is concern that the advantages (often referred to as "planning gain") accruing from the planning agreement may affect the objectivity of the authority in evaluating the planning merits of the scheme. In other words, that the process amounts to a sale of planning permission.[89] Above all, the objection is that it is precisely because conditions cannot be imposed that the applicant must "voluntarily" offer the benefit.[90] The legal restrictions placed on the use of conditions are circumvented by using planning agreements to achieve the desired objective. Criticism has focused on the use by planning authorities of agreements to secure planning gain or benefit for the community which does not form an essential part of the development.

A recent study of the use of section 50 agreements in Scotland found that on average considerably less than 1 per cent of planning applications are linked to agreements. It concluded that the negotiation of substantial unrelated gains seems to be uncommon, although several "relatively minor" cases were noted. At least half the authorities interviewed cited instances where the infrastructure requirement appeared to be in excess of what was strictly required for the development in question. The study concluded that there is an element of ill-considered use of agreements, especially when suspensive conditions would suffice. It recommended that planning authorities should review their use of agreements to see whether they are really required in all cases.[91]

[89] Loughlin, "Planning Gain — Law, Policy and Practice" (1981) 1 O.J.L.S. 61.
[90] Lichfield, "From Planning Gain to Community Benefit" [1989] J.P.L. 68.
[91] Rowan-Robinson and Durman "Section 50 Agreements" (1992) Scottish Office.

Developers have cited more specific objections to the practice of using agreements.[92] Negotiating the terms of agreements is time-consuming and delays the grant of planning permission. Agreements often include restrictions which are contrary to Scottish Office policy and would, therefore, be overturned in any appeal against refusal of planning permission. It is common for the first developer in an area to be left with no choice but to agree to pay for the provision of infrastructure and services which are then used by subsequent developers without any contribution to the cost. A frequent complaint is that restrictions proposed by planning authorities for inclusion in agreements exhibit a lack of understanding of the financial aspects of development.

It is clear that there is some distrust of the use of planning agreements. Indeed, it has been suggested that authorities should review their practices with a view to utilising suspensive conditions in place of planning agreements wherever possible. Nevertheless, it must be emphasised that the power to use agreements to achieve objectives other than planning gain (as distinct from benefits related to the development) provides planning authorities with a flexible development control power. Planning agreements have a useful role to play in the planning system for the interest of planning authority and developer alike.

Scope of Section 50 Agreements

Two issues arise in any discussion of the scope of section 50 agreements: firstly, the limits to the power of planning authorities to enter into such agreements; and, secondly, the circumstances in which it would be illegal for the planning authority to take into account the provision of planning gain in terms of the agreement when determining an application for planning permission. Only the first issue truly concerns the scope of section 50 agreements, the second forms more a practical limit beyond which developers will be unwilling to venture although it provides scope for a rival developer to seek to reduce a grant of planning permission. It must be

[92] *Ibid.* para. 10.0 *et seq.*

emphasised that it does not necessarily follow that where the provisions of an agreement cannot be validly considered when deciding an appliction, the planning authority must have exceeded its statutory power to enter into the planning agreement with the result that it is invalid.

(a) *Scope of the Statutory Power*

As the term suggests, the power to enter into a section 50 agreement is conferred by statute.[93] If a planning authority exceeds the power conferred by statute, it is acting outwith its power (*ultra vires*) and, thus, illegally. The limits of the statutory power of a planning authority to enter into a section 50 agreement are therefore important.

The wording of section 50 gives planning authorities power to enter into agreements "for the purpose of restricting or regulating the development or use of the land." It is difficult to identify what limits are placed on the scope of agreements by this wording. It has been suggested that "restrict" refers to the prohibition or limitation of what is done on land, while "regulate" is more concerned with ensuring that something is done in a particular way.[94] The wording of section 50 does not permit the agreement to restrict or regulate the development or use of land, other than the land described in the agreement. Thus agreements cannot restrict off-site uses such as routes used by vehicles after leaving the site.

This interpretation may suggest that section 50 agreements cannot require that some positive obligation be undertaken, in other words that the developer agrees to do something as opposed to not doing something. However, it has been argued that positive obligations can be included in section 50 agreements, provided that the sole or main purpose of the agreement is not to achieve the positive obligation. Thus planning authorities may require developers to pay all or part of the cost of providing sewers, roads, open spaces and so on, provided the purpose is to secure regulation of the development by ensuring that the development is adequately

[93] TCPSA, s. 50, as amended.
[94] Rowan-Robinson and Young *Planning by Agreement in Scotland* (1989), p. 22.

drained and served by roads.[95] Provision of a road was broadly interpreted as permently restricting use of the land on which the road was to be built, with the result that the restriction and not the provision of the road was the sole or main purpose of the agreement.[96]

The restrictions or regulations imposed by a section 50 agreement may be permanent or for a period prescribed by the agreement. The section 50 agreement may also contain "such incidental and consequential provisions (including provisions of a financial character) as appear to the planning authority to be necessary or expedient for the purposes of the agreement."

From this brief discussion it will be clear that the wording of the section 50 power is general and, therefore, open to interpretation. By way of comparison, the scope of the English equivalent of section 50 is more precise. A planning obligation may:

1. restrict the development or use of the land in any specified way;
2. require specified operations to be carried out in, on, under or over the land;
3. require the land to be used in any specified way; or
4. require a sum or sums to be paid to the planning authority on a specified date or dates or periodically.[97]

The first section of this chapter explored the limits on the power to impose planning conditions. Many of these limits have arisen from judicial interpretation of the statutory power. It has been suggested that if a condition would be invalid (*ultra vires*) then the same result cannot be achieved through the use of a section 50 agreement.[98] This implies that the same restrictions must apply to use of agreements under section 50 as apply to conditions. This statement is

[95] *Ibid.*, p. 24; S.D.D. Circular 22/1984, "Town and Country Planning (Scotland) Act 1972 Section 50 Agreements" para. 9.

[96] *R.* v. *Gillingham Borough Council, ex p. Parham* [1988] J.P.L. 336.

[97] Town and Country Planning Act 1990, s. 106.

[98] Most recently by Sir Graham Eyre Q.C. in *Eagle Star* v. *Secretary of State for the Environment* [1992] J.P.L. 434 at p. 440.

symptomatic of the judicial confusion over the scope of section 50 agreements, with conflicting statements and little in the way of clear guidance. It is interesting to compare the requirements for legal validity of conditions with judicial comments on the scope of section 50 agreements (reference should be made to the section on Conditions, above, for a full explanation of these requirements).

Both the powers to impose planning conditions and to enter into section 50 agreements are provided by the TCPSA, so there is a common requirement of a planning purpose.[99] As any consideration relating to the use and development of land can be a planning consideration,[1] this requirement should not unduly constrain the use of agreements.

Although most section 50 agreements are made in the context of applications for planning permission, agreements may be made in other situations. Unlike the power to impose conditions, the wording of section 50 does not connect the agreement to a grant of planning permission and the "fairly and reasonably relates" test therefore should not apply.[2] An agreement requiring provision of infrastructure beyond that required for the development has been upheld.[3]

While a fair and reasonable relation to the proposed development is not necessary for the agreement to be valid, some degree of a relationship is necessary before the authority can take into account the terms of the agreement when determining the application for planning permission (below).

The requirement of reasonableness or rationality is common to the exercise of all statutory discretionary powers by a public authority and applies both to conditions and agreements.[4] It may however be arguable that because a section 50 agreement is a contract this requirement should not apply.

From this brief examination, section 50 agreements appear to have greater scope than planning conditions because there

[99] *Good* v. *Epping Forest D.C.* [1993] J.P.L. 127.

[1] *Stringer* v. *M.H.L.G.* [1970] 1 W.L.R. 1281, *per* Cooke J.

[2] *Good* v. *Epping Forest D.C.; The Times*, November 11, 1993; [1993] E.G.C.S. 188.

[3] *R.* v. *Gillingham Borough Council, ex p. Parham* (n. 96, *supra*).

[4] *R.* v. *Wealden District Council, ex p. Charles Church* [1989] J.P.L. 837 but this element is only included in the Lexis transcript.

is no requirement that for an agreement to be valid its provisions must "fairly and reasonably relate" to the development. This conclusion necessarily implies that section 50 agreements may be used to achieve a result that could not be legally achieved through imposition of a planning condition.[5] Indeed, this is one of the attractions of section 50 agreements in the eyes of planning authorities.

(b) Agreements as a Material Consideration

In most cases a developer enters into a section 50 agreement because the terms of the agreement will increase the likelihood of planning permission being granted. This objective will not be attained unless the terms of the agreement form a material consideration in the determination of the application for planning permission (Chapter 5). If the terms are not a material consideration, it would be illegal for the planning authority to take account of them when deciding the application for planning permission. In such circumstances, the developer would still be bound by the terms of the agreement, but the authority would be bound to ignore these terms when reaching its decision on the application. Any failure to ignore the agreement when deciding the application would expose any grant of planning permission to the risk of challenge by a competing developer or concerned member of the public. Similar comments apply to the relevance of the agreement to an appeal to the Secretary of State.

Chapter 5 examines the circumstances in which the authority may take into account the agreement, which may give rise to planning benefits, when considering the application. The law in this area is still evolving, but for a planning benefit to be a material consideration it must have a planning purpose and fairly and reasonably relate to the development. The courts have rejected the contention that the benefit must be necessary to overcome, remedy or alleviate planning objections to the proposed development.[6]

[5] *Good* v. *Epping Forest D.C.*, n. 2, *supra*.

[6] *R.* v. *Plymouth C.C. ex. p. Plymouth and South Devon Co-operative Society Ltd.* [1993] J.P.L. 538 and (on appeal) [1993] E.G.C.S. 113; *Tesco* v. *Secretary of State for the Environment* [1993] E.G.C.S. 133.

For example, an agreement by a developer to pay for a new primary school in connection with a proposed housing development may be a material consideration as occupation of the new housing will increase the demand for school places. Much will depend upon the level of demand in comparison with the number of school places which the developer intends to fund. In contrast, the planning authority would be forced to ignore a similar agreement to pay for a school in connection with an office development when deciding the application for the office development, in consequence of the lack of connection between the need for the school and the proposed office.

A similar approach applies to other provisions of an agreement. It has been suggested that the agreement can only be a material consideration in the decision on the application in so far as it is relevant or material to the proposed development.[7] In other words, unless the need for the provisions contained in the agreement arises from the proposal in question, it must not influence the decision on the application. Traffic management measures to be financed by the applicant were held not to be a material consideration where there was no direct nexus between the proposed superstore and the improvements because these measures were aimed at problems already in existence.[8] However, offers of community benefits such as provision of a tourist information centre, a bird-watching hide and a static art feature were upheld as a material consideration in relation to another proposed superstore development.[9]

The conflict underlying the scope of section 50 agreements should now be apparent. The wording of section 50 and, therefore, the legal scope of planning agreements, does not require any connection between the provisions of the agreement and the proposed development, but this connection is required before the provisions may be taken into account by the planning authority in deciding the planning

[7] Rowan-Robinson and Young, *op. cit.*, p. 37.

[8] *Safeway* v. *Secretary of State for the Environment* [1990] J.P.L. 759.

[9] *R.* v. *Plymouth C.C. ex p. Plymouth and South Devon Co-operative Society Ltd.*, n. 6, *supra*.

application normally associated with the agreement. It is not necessarily outwith the powers of a planning authority to enter into a section 50 agreement which it would be forced to ignore as an irrelevant consideration when determining an application for planning permission. It is up to the developer to resist provisions which are not sufficiently connected to the development to form material considerations for the planning application.

The connection required between the benefits offered by the agreement and the proposed development before the agreement can be deemed a material consideration may seem similar to the "fairly and reasonably relates" requirement applicable to conditions. However, the potential scope of agreements must inevitably result in a wider degree of connection than that permitted under the "fairly and reasonably relates" test, as agreements can, for example, require either contributions from developers or control off-site works on land outside the control of the developer.

(c) *Scottish Office Guidance*

The Scottish Office has issued guidance on the use of planning agreements.[10] There is no right of appeal to the Secretary of State against the terms of a planning agreement. However, the guidance is an indication of the weight which will be given to the terms of a planning agreement in the course of determining an appeal to the Secretary of State against refusal of planning permission. It can, therefore, be used by developers in the course of negotiating the terms of section 50 agreement to resist excessive demands made by the planning authority.

The guidance reminds planning authorities that the question of requiring a developer to enter into an agreement should only arise where it would not be appropriate to grant planning permission without the agreement. Unacceptable development should never be permitted because of unrelated benefits offered by the developer, nor should an acceptable

[10] S.D.D. Circular 22/1984, "Town and Country Planning (Scotland) Act 1972 — Section 50 Agreements."

development be refused planning permission because the developer is unwilling to offer such benefits.

The requirements of the guidance emphasise the need for a connection between the terms of the agreement and the proposed development. As a result, any agreement which accords with the guidance is likely to be a material consideration in the determination of a planning application. The guidance states that agreements should only contain obligations to provide:

1. what is required to enable the development to go ahead, for example, provision of adequate access, water supply and sewerage and sewage disposal facilities; or
2. financial payments which will contribute to meeting the cost of providing such facilities in the near future; or
3. whatever is otherwise so directly related to the proposed development and to the use of the land after its completion that the development ought not to be permitted without it; for example, the provision, whether by the developer or the authority at the developer's expense, of car parking in or near the development or reasonable amounts of open space related to the development (this is a more restrictive test than will be applied by the courts, as discussed above); or
4. whatever is designed in the case of mixed development to secure an acceptable balance of uses.

Even if the obligation passes one of these tests, it must be "fairly and reasonably related in scale and kind to the proposed development." Thus, contributions towards the cost of infrastructure should be directly related in scale and kind to the benefit which the proposed development will derive from the facilities to be provided.

Finally, the obligation must be a reasonable charge on the developer. In other words, the facility to be provided or financed should be directly related to the proposed development or the use of the land after development. The guidance states that it would not normally be reasonable to seek a contribution to road construction or improvement in the immediate vicinity of the proposed development unless the need for this arises wholly or substantially from the new development.

The recent study on planning agreements concludes that most agreements satisfy the requirements of the guidance that the obligations contained in an agreement should arise from or deal with a consequence of the development and be in proportion to the problems which they are intended to resolve. However, the test of need ("required to enable the development to proceed") is not always strictly applied.[11]

Effect of Section 50 Agreement

(a) Relevance of Agreement to Planning Application or Appeal

The extent to which the provisions of a section 50 agreement form a material consideration in the determination of a planning application or appeal has already been discussed. There must be some relationship between the provisions of the agreement and the development proposed in the application. The absence of such a relationship may give a third party, such as a rival developer, grounds for seeking judicial review of the decision to grant planning permission.

(b) Fettering of Discretion

In accordance with the general legal principle that decision-makers must not fetter their exercise of discretionary powers conferred by statute (Chapter 5), it is not competent for a planning authority to bind itself in a section 50 agreement to grant planning permission for a specified development.[12] Assuming that the terms of the agreement are a material consideration, the authority can take into account those terms when deciding the application. However, it must also take into account all other relevant considerations, which may dictate that permission should be refused.

In a similar way, the planning authority is obliged to take into account any material changes in circumstances arising between the time of the resolution to grant permission once a planning agreement is concluded and conclusion of that

[11] Rowan-Robinson and Durman, *op. cit.*, para. 27.0 *et seq.*

[12] TCPSA, s. 50(3); *Windsor and Maidenhead Royal Borough Council* v. *Brandrose* [1983] 1 W.L.R. 509.

agreement, and may refuse to grant permission on the basis of these changes.[13]

(c) Binding on the Land

The importance of section 50 agreements lies in the provisions allowing for recording of the completed agreement in the Register of Sasines or Land Register. Once the completed agreement has been recorded in the property register, its provisions bind in perpetuity the land to which it applies, applying to not only those persons who signed the agreement, but to all future parties who obtain an interest in the land notwithstanding their ignorance of the terms of the agreement, and it may be enforced against them by the planning authority.[14] In this way, it is similar to a grant of planning permission which attaches to the land rather than to the person who made the application. Other forms of planning agreements merely bind the signatories to the agreement.

The terms of the recorded agreement will not be enforceable against a third party who obtained an interest in the land in good faith prior to the agreement being recorded. This will apply whether or not the title of the third party was recorded before the recording of the agreement. This protection extends to any person who derives title from the bona fide third party. In such circumstances, the agreement will only be effective against the parties who signed it and, therefore, of little value to the authority.

Any future grant of planning permission cannot override the provisions of a section 50 agreement.[15]

(d) Enforcement of the Agreement

In the absence of any provision in the agreement regarding enforcement powers in the event of a failure to observe its terms, the agreement is treated as a contract and the normal

[13] *John G. Russell (Transport) Ltd.* v. *Strathkelvin D.C.* 1992 S.L.T. 1001.
[14] TCPSA, s. 50(2).
[15] *R.* v. *Tunbridge Wells B.C. ex p. Blue Boys Developments Ltd.* [1990] 1 P.L.R. 55.

contractual remedies are available to the planning authority without the necessity of following the enforcement procedures described in Chapter 7.[16] For example, the authority may seek a court order for specific implement of the obligations of the developer under the agreement or for interdict preventing the developer from acting contrary to the restrictions contained in the agreement, and damages. There are at least four instances of planning authorities obtaining interdict or specific implement in this manner in the sheriff court.[17]

(e) Variation and Discharge

Following recording in the property register, the provisions of the section 50 agreement bind the land in perpetuity. These provisions may be discharged or varied at any time and the appropriate legal document recorded in the property register, but only if all the parties to the agreement or their successors in title agree. If the parties cannot reach agreement on a discharge or variation, the agreement will remain undischarged or unamended. There is no possibility of a party applying to the Lands Tribunal for Scotland as its statutory jurisdiction does not extend to discharging obligations and restrictions contained in planning agreements unlike its equivalent body in England. It is, therefore, important that variation and discharge provisions be included in the agreement.

(f) Challenge of Agreement

There is no right of appeal to the Secretary of State against the terms of a planning agreement. However, the provisions of an agreement may be a relevant consideration in an appeal against the decision by the authority on an associated planning application.

It may be possible to apply to the Court of Session for judicial review of the decision of the planning authority to enter into the agreement, on the grounds that the authority

[16] *Avon C.C.* v. *Millard* [1986] J.P.L. 211.
[17] Rowan-Robinson and Durman, *op. cit.*, para. 17.2.

acted unreasonably or that the agreement does not serve a planning purpose or that the authority has exceeded the scope of its powers under section 50. However, any party who has signed the agreement may be personally barred from making such a challenge. Although in practice many agreements are imposed upon reluctant developers who feel that they have no choice but to enter into the agreement in order to obtain planning permission, signature of the agreement is a voluntary act and the courts are reluctant to allow parties to challenge agreements in such circumstances.

The Lands Tribunal for Scotland has no jurisdiction to discharge or vary the obligations contained in a section 50 agreement.

Drafting the Agreement

A recorded agreement applies to the land in perpetuity, thus an overly restrictive or badly drafted agreement may adversely affect the value of the land. It is important for all parties to ensure that the agreement records fully what has been agreed and that it will be effective in securing the performance of the obligations.

In most cases the agreement will be drafted by the planning authority once the principal obligations have been agreed. Inevitably the draft agreement will require some revision by the developer to avoid overly burdensome restrictions or obligations.

There is no prescribed form of planning agreement. The agreement must be expressed in clear and precise terms and any ambiguities avoided. In complex agreements, an interpretation clause defining the meaning of various key phrases is useful. To be accepted for recording in the property register, a section 50 agreement must identify the parties to the agreement, the land to which the agreement applies, and the obligations agreed between the parties.

(a) Parties

The agreement will normally be entered into by the planning authority dealing with the planning application associated with the agreement, although the regional council will be a party if the agreement provides for infrastructure works, such as roads improvements, which are the statutory responsibility of the regional council. If the application has been called-in for decision by the regional planning authority, that authority will enter into the agreement, possibly together with the district council depending upon the obligations contained in the agreement.

The other principal party to the agreement is the person or persons who have sufficient legal interest in the site to bind the land. Without the signature of all such persons, the agreement cannot be recorded in the property registers and can only be enforced against the parties who have signed the agreement.

An "interest" in land must be such as to enable that person to enter into an agreement which will bind future owners of the land. Clearly the owner of the land has sufficient interest for this purpose. The best practice must be to enter into section 50 agreements only with persons who have a title to the land which is recorded in the property register.[18]

It would seem inadvisable to enter into a section 50 agreement with a person whose ownership is based on an executed, but unrecorded disposition (legally described as an uninfeft proprietor). Such a person has sufficient interest to bind the land, but until the disposition is recorded in the property register there is a (slight) risk of a third party recording a title to the land before that disposition (and the section 50 agreement) is recorded, rendering any section 50 agreement recorded thereafter ineffective unless signed by that third party. Limited protection could be sought through a clause in the agreement prohibiting the party signing the agreement from selling the land prior to the recording of the agreement.

It is common for a sale of land to a developer to be agreed up to conclusion of missives, but the transfer of ownership not completed until planning permission is obtained. In such circumstances, the seller remains owner of the land until a signed disposition is delivered to the developer.[19] The only

[18] Circular 22/1984, para. 8. See Rowan-Robinson and Durman, *op. cit.*, para. 14.0 *et seq.*

[19] *Gibson* v. *Hunter Homes*, 1976 S.L.T. 94, *per* Lord President Emslie at p. 96.

right available to the developer under concluded missives is the right to demand performance of the contractual obligation to convey the land to him, and this is not an interest in land.[20] Thus a developer who has concluded missives, but has yet to complete the purchase cannot enter into a section 50 agreement, other than as a consenter (below). A person in this position may enter into an agreement with the planning authority undertaking to complete a section 50 agreement in specified terms as soon as a disposition in his favour has been delivered and recorded. Alternatively, in order to give sufficient confidence for the purchase transaction to be completed the planning authority may give an indication that planning permission will be forthcoming if a section 50 agreement is entered into (below).

The Scottish Office guidance suggests that a lessee under a recorded lease may also have a sufficient interest to enter into a section 50 agreement. In such circumstances, the landlord (and the owner if this is not the same person as the landlord) must consent to the agreement (below). Thus section 50 agreements are often entered into with tenants and landlords under minerals leases in connection with applications for permission for mineral extraction.

A section 50 agreement is not enforceable against any third party who in good faith onerously acquired right to the land prior to the recording of the agreement in the property registers, notwithstanding that the title of that third party has yet to be recorded. As a result, some persons who do not have sufficient interest to bind the land should be requested to sign the agreement as consentors. Their signature of the agreement will have the effect of binding them by its terms even before the agreement is recorded in the property register.

Possible consenting parties include heritable creditors, tenants, feudal superiors, parties with servitude rights over the site, purchasers under concluded missives and applicants for planning permission. Any restrictions contained in the agreement may significantly reduce the value of the land. Such a reduction in value may prejudice the interests of a

[20] *Margrie Holdings Ltd.* v. *Commissioners of Customs & Excise*, 1991 S.L.T. 38.

bank or other financial institution which has lent money and been granted a security over the land. This has already occurred in England where one financial institution withdrew from lending because the terms of an agreement providing for "low-cost" housing would have made it difficult to sell the property if it ever came to be repossessed by the institution. Any heritable creditors should be asked to indicate their consent to the agreement by signing it as consentors.

If the owner has leased part of the land and the agreement affects the tenant's enjoyment of the land, the landlord may require the consent of the tenant depending upon the terms of the lease. The consent of the feudal superior or those with servitude rights over the land may be required, depending on the provisions of the title to the land. If the owner of the land has concluded missives for its sale, the planning authority should consider seeking the purchaser's signature of the agreement as a consentor. The applicant for planning permission should sign the agreement.

In drafting (and revising) the agreement, it should be considered whether it is necessary for all signatories to be bound under all the obligations contained in the agreement. In particular, if some parties have an interest in only part of the site, they should ensure that they are bound only by the obligations in the agreement which apply to that part.

(b) The Land

To be accepted for recording in the property register, the planning agreement must contain a legal description of the land to which it is to apply. This description is prepared by reference to the previous title deeds, and may refer to a plan attached to the agreement. Unless the description is simple, it may be advisable for it to be contained in a separate schedule to the agreement.

(c) The Obligations

A wide range of obligations can competently form the basis of a section 50 agreement and new examples will continue to emerge. The only legal requirements are the need for a planning purpose and a rational decision (above).

For example, infrastructure improvements are a common subject of agreements. Developers often agree to pay the cost of the authority carrying out off-site infrastructure works in order to unlock the development potential of sites. Agreements can be used to phase-in parts of the development in conjunction with the provision of supporting infrastructure, or to prevent the construction of lucrative portions of the development ahead of parts of the development which the authority considers important to the community, for example, tying-in provision of a school to occupancy of a housing development.

Following the restrictions placed on the use of occupancy conditions, agreements can be used to regulate the occupancy of sheltered homes and retirement flats or provision of low-cost housing for local people. An agreement may contain restrictions on future sale of a property, for example, prohibiting the separate sale of farm cottages or granny flats.

The agreement may revoke existing, but unimplemented permission in return for a fresh grant of permission, or discontinue the existing use of premises once permission has been granted for the similar use of new premises. Where planning permission is granted for a replacement dwelling-house, an agreement may be used to secure demolition of existing buildings.

Some forms of development have almost standard provisions. Agreements in connection with retail developments may limit the range of goods which may be sold. Authorities frequently require agreements for provision of restoration bonds in connection with mineral workings.

Some authorities have even used agreements to require the developer to observe a local employment or local contractor preference. However, it may be difficult to prove that such requirements fulfil a planning purpose.

(d) Other Matters

In addition to identifying the parties, the land and narrating the obligations, the parties should consider the desirability of including other provisions.

The developer should consider including a clause in the agreement to the effect that it will only come into force if the grant of planning permission is implemented. This avoids the situation of the developer deciding not to proceed with the development, but the land remaining subject to the agreement.

If the agreement provides for a financial contribution to be paid, the purpose of the payment should be clearly specified and an obligation placed on the recipient to expend the money on that purpose. Provision should be made for a refund if this is not satisfied, either at all or within a specified period.

The normal contractual remedies are available to enforce the provisions of the agreement, but other remedies can be specified. For example, the agreement may empower the authority to carry out work and recover the cost from the developer if the work has not been commenced or completed within a specified time. Agreements in connection with mineral workings normally provide for sums to be paid to the authority if the developer fails to carry out restoration works or goes into liquidation. These payments are guaranteed under fidelity bonds issued by banks or insurance companies.

Alternatively, the agreement may allow the authority to treat any failure to observe the terms of the agreement as a breach of planning control entitling it to use the powers conferred by the planning enforcement regime (Chapter 7). The legality of such provisions is uncertain and developers should carefully consider their position before agreeing to such a provision.

More importantly, the agreement may provide that on any breach of its terms by the developer, the authority can revoke the grant of planning permission without compensation. This would terminate the development and any change of use would have to cease. It is doubtful whether it is competent for permission to be revoked in this way, but developers should seek the deletion of such a provision during the revisal of the draft agreement. An alternative to this draconian measure is for the agreement to provide for the effect of the planning permission to be suspended until the breach of the agreement is remedied.

In connection with powers to secure compliance with the terms of the agreement, ancillary powers should be provided. For example, planning officials should be given rights of entry to monitor compliance with the terms of the agreement and for the carrying out of any works upon which the developer has defaulted. Provision should be made for the authority to reclaim the cost of carrying out such works from the developer.

The agreement may provide that the planning authority is to be the sole judge of what constitutes a breach of the agreement, entitling it to exercise its enforcement powers under the agreement. Any provisions of this type, which give the planning authority complete discretion, should be resisted by the developer. An alternative is to provide for any disputes which arise in relation to the agreement to be settled through arbitration rather than legal action. An arbitration clause should be worded to include disputes relating to the interpretation as well as the level of compliance with the agreement. Careful consideration should be given to the profession from which the arbiter(s) is to be selected. The decision of the arbiter is normally declared to be final, although it may be challenged if the arbiter makes a legal error in the course of the decision. Provision should be made for payment of expenses.

If subsequent subdivision of the site is likely, the agreement should be drafted to avoid future difficulties regarding the enforcement and the distribution of obligations.

Following recording in the property register, the provisions of the section 50 agreement bind the land in perpetuity. Formal discharges of agreements or parts of agreements (which will then be recorded in the property register) should be obtained wherever possible to prevent legal difficulties arising in any future sale of the land. Positive obligations will usually be carried out shortly after the agreement is executed. Provision should be made in the agreement for a formal discharge of those obligations to be executed by the planning authority after the obligations have been carried out. In contrast, any restrictions on use will remain in force indefinitely, irrespective of any changes in circumstances. Although the provisions of the agreement may be varied or discharged with the agreement of all the parties, it is advisable for the agreement to specify procedures for its variation or discharge to protect the developer against future intransigence on the part of the authority.

In a similar way, the agreement may be drafted to include provision for reviews either at specified intervals or on the application of any party to the agreement, with a reference to an arbiter in the event of deadlock. Such provisions would avoid obsolete agreements continuing to affect land.

Timing of Agreement and Associated Planning Permission

Most section 50 agreements are entered into in the context of applications for planning permission. The planning authority will be unwilling to grant planning permission until the agreement has been executed, but the developer will be wary of entering into an agreement unless he can be certain that planning permission will be granted. Several solutions to this problem have been adopted in practice[21]:

(a) The planning authority may resolve to grant planning permission once the agreement has been concluded (sometimes referred to as a "minded to grant" letter), often delegating to the Director of Planning the power to grant permission once an agreement in appropriate terms has been executed. This is the most common method. There is no grant of planning permission until the decision notice is issued.[22] If there is a material change of circumstances in the period between the decision and completion of the agreement, the authority is obliged to take those circumstances into account and may refuse to grant the permission.[23] Any delay in concluding the agreement therefore risks losing the permission.

A variation on this procedure is for the application to be determined, but the decision notice left unissued until the agreement is executed. As planning permission is only granted once the notice is issued, this method must also carry the risk of losing the permission.

(b) The other common procedure is for planning permission to be granted subject to a condition requiring the applicant to enter into an agreement. Such a condition should specify all

[21] Rowan-Robinson and Young, *op. cit.*, p. 57.
[22] *R. v. West Oxfordshire District Council* [1986] J.P.L. 523.
[23] *John G. Russell (Transport) Ltd.* v. *Strathkelvin D.C.* (n. 13, *supra*).

the terms of the agreement or at least the heads of the agreement. It has been suggested that it would be illegal for a condition to require an applicant to enter into an agreement on matters outwith the legal scope of conditions.[24] There is also a danger for the authority that following a successful appeal, planning permission could be granted without the condition and, therefore, no requirement upon the developer to enter into the agreement.

Planning permission may also be granted subject to a suspensive condition providing that the grant of permission will not be effective until the agreement is executed or recorded. Alternatively, the condition could prevent commencement of development until specified works have been carried out, those works being the subject of the agreement.

(c) If the application for planning permission is not to be determined until the agreement is executed, the agreement will be expressed to be conditional on the grant (or implementation) of planning permission in the terms specified in a schedule to the agreement. This procedure will be appropriate only where the applicant has sufficient interest to enter into the agreement before planning permission is granted.

(d) The decision notice is issued on the strength of a formal undertaking by the developer to execute the agreement.

(e) The decision notice in respect of the application is incorporated into a schedule to the agreement.

Proposal for Agreement on Appeal

As most agreements are intended to remove planning disadvantages of proposed developments which might lead to a refusal of planning permission, the inability to reach agreement with the planning authority normally prevents any appeal. Although there is no duty on them to do so, reporters may encourage the parties to enter into negotiations with a view to concluding an agreement to remove an obstacle to a grant of planning permission, which cannot be removed by imposition of a condition. However, the reporter can play no

[24] Rowan-Robinson and Young, *op. cit.*, pp. 58–60.

part in the negotiations or specify the terms of the agreement, and the developer may be unable to reach agreement with the authority.

English law allows developers to side-step unco-operative planning authorities by entering into a unilateral planning obligation to provide planning advantages.[25] This obviates the need to reach agreement with the planning authority. The obligation will have an equivalent effect to a section 50 agreement. Most importantly, it will be a material consideration during the determination of the application for planning permission and in any appeal against refusal or deemed refusal of planning permission.

There is no equivalent provision in Scots law. However, promises are enforceable contracts in Scots law. It is conceivable, if unlikely, that a developer could draw up a legal document in the form of a promise which could, depending upon its content, form a material consideration which a reluctant authority would either be forced to consider when determining an application for planning permission, or face a successful appeal.

[25] Town and Country Planning Act 1990, s. 106A and 106B, as amended.

Chapter 7

DEVELOPMENT CONTROL IV — ENFORCEMENT

In order to control development effectively, planning authorities have sanctions to enforce planning control and prevent or stop unauthorised development. These enforcement powers were strengthened following the overhaul of the statutory enforcement system by the Planning and Compensation Act 1991 (amending the TCPSA), which adopted many of the recommendations of the Carnwath Report.[1] The procedures have been simplified, tougher penalties introduced, loopholes removed, and new powers conferred upon planning authorities.

Underlying Principles of Enforcement Powers

(a) Breach of Planning Control

The planning authority cannot exercise its enforcement powers unless there at least appears to have been a breach of planning control (a stricter requirement applies to the exercise of some powers). A breach of planning control occurs when development is carried out without first obtaining the required planning permission (Chapter 4), or contrary to any condition or limitation subject to which planning permission has been granted.[2] There is no statutory definition of "limitation." The Scottish Office guidance refers to the limitations which are imposed by the provisions for permitted development rights in the P.D.O. (Chapter 4).[3]

[1] Carnwath, *Enforcing Planning Control* (1989).
[2] TCPSA, s. 83A(1).
[3] Scottish Environment Department Circular 36/1992, "Planning and Compensation Act 1991—Lawful Development and Enforcement," para. 5.

(b) Enforcement Action

Although there is a wide range of enforcement powers available to planning authorities, only service of an enforcement or breach of condition notice constitutes taking enforcement action for the purposes of preventing a breach from becoming lawful development.[4]

(c) Lawful Development (Immunity from Enforcement Action)

A breach of planning control becomes lawful once the prescribed time limits (see below) for taking enforcement action have expired.[5] In consequence, there is no breach upon which to found enforcement action. In addition, permitted development rights under the P.D.O. may be utilised. A Certificate of Lawfulness of Existing Use or Development may be sought from the planning authority to establish conclusively the lawfulness of the use or development (Chapter 4).

Prior to the PCA reforms, a breach of planning control became immune from enforcement action after expiry of the time limit, but could never become lawful. As a result, permitted development rights could not be exercised and, in the event of compulsory purchase, there was no right to compensation for any value attributable to the activity.

The concept of lawful development does not extend to breaches of the statutory systems applicable to listed buildings, tree preservation, or advertisement control (Chapter 9). Breaches never become immune from enforcement action under these statutory systems, but may be immune from enforcement action under the planning system where there is an overlap in the statutory controls.

(d) Offences

A breach of planning control is not an offence in itself. In general, commission of an offence relates to a failure to

[4] TCPSA, s. 83A(2).
[5] s. 90(2), as substituted.

comply with the requirements of a notice served by the authority in exercise of its enforcement powers against the breach. Individual offences are created in relation to each enforcement power, and are examined in the appropriate part of this chapter.

All enforcement offences are subject to a six-month time limit for commencing summary court proceedings.[6] This period runs from the occurrence of the contravention. In the case of a continuing contravention, the six-month period runs from the last date of the contravention. There is uncertainty about the application of the six month period to planning offences. As enforcement offences do not relate to the breach of planning control, but to the non-compliance with the terms of the notice, the offence is a single one which can be charged by reference to a single day or longer period. It is therefore arguable that the six-month period runs from the date of the expiry of the period specified in the notice for compliance with its terms, notwithstanding that the breach of planning control continues. However, it is possible that this argument only applies to a notice requiring positive action (i.e. something to be done). If it requires negative action, such as cessation of an activity, the failure to comply with the requirement is a continuing offence and the six month time limit only runs from the date on which the activity ceases. This uncertainty can only be clarified by a court ruling or amendment of the law.

The PCA reforms also provide for prosecution for second or subsequent offences if the contravention of the notice continues after conviction.

Although the penalties for individual offences vary, the PCA reforms have increased the penalties to a maximum fine of £20,000 following summary conviction, or an unlimited fine after conviction on indictment. In addition, the court is directed to have regard to any financial benefit which has accrued or appears likely to accrue to the person in consequence of the offence. For example, where an enforcement notice requires use of a building for retail purposes to be stopped, the court may take into account the profits made from that retail business following expiry of the period for

[6] Criminal Procedure (Scotland) Act 1975, s. 331.

compliance with the requirements of the notice until conviction. There is no provision for imprisonment following conviction for an enforcement offence.

This system of enforcement offences is not without its problems. A planning authority intent on negotiating a solution to avoid the need for prosecution may fall foul of the six-month time limit. A substantial weight of corroborated evidence will be required to prove the case beyond reasonable doubt, including evidence on such prosaic matters as service of the notice upon the person charged with the offence. It is unclear whether the intent (*mens rea*) to commit the offence must be proved. A major hurdle is the apparent attitude of many procurator fiscals, who are responsible for prosecuting, and sheriffs, that planning offences are not true criminal matters. Indeed, the need to change this attitude was one of the underlying reasons for the increase in penalties for enforcement offences from £2,000 to £20,000. The hard-pressed fiscal with a heavy caseload of "real" criminal matters may decide that prosecution of an enforcement offence is not in the public interest and exercise his discretion not to prosecute. This decision is likely to be influenced by the generally low level of fines imposed by sheriffs in the few successful cases. It remains to be seen whether the PCA reforms will change these attitudes.

ENFORCEMENT ACTION: TIME LIMITS

Enforcement action must be taken within the following time limits, otherwise the breach of planning control will become lawful development[7]:

Four-Years Time Limit

(a) Building, engineering, mining or other operations (Chapter 4) undertaken without planning permission will become lawful development after four years from the date of substantial completion of the operations (such operations in breach of conditions or limitations are subject to the 10-year

[7] TCPSA, s. 83B.

time limit). Where an embankment was substantially completed within the four-year period, an enforcement notice requiring its demolition was upheld notwithstanding that parts of the embankment had been in place for over four years[8];

(b) A change of use of any building to use as a single dwelling-house will become lawful development after four years from the date of the change of use. It is irrelevant whether the building is converted into a single dwelling-house or an existing dwelling-house is subdivided into two or more separate dwelling-houses.[9] A house in multiple occupation with the occupants sharing facilities remains within the 10-year rule.

Ten-Year Time Limit

All other breaches of planning control become lawful development after 10 years from the date of the breach. This will include all material changes of use, and breaches of planning conditions, other than those relating to change of use of a building to a single dwelling-house.

This involves an extension of the four-year period which previously applied to building, engineering, mining or other operations in breach of conditions or limitations. As a transitional measure, any breach of condition or limitation relating to operational development immune from enforcement action in terms of the previous four-year limit will continue to be immune notwithstanding that it would now be subject to the 10-year limit.[10] The other main change is the substitution of the 10-year time limit for most changes of use. Previously only changes of use which had occurred prior to 1965 were immune.

Enforcement action against a change of use can require restoration of the land to its state prior to the change, thereby undoing any incidental operational development which may in itself not require planning permission or be lawful

[8] *Ewen Developments* v. *Secretary of State for the Environment* [1980] J.P.L. 404.
[9] *Van Dyck* v. *Secretary of State for the Environment; Doncaster B.C.* v. *Secretary of State for the Environment* [1993] J.P.L. 565.
[10] PCA, s. 36(2).

development. The laying of hardcore was an integral part of an unauthorised change of use for the parking of lorries and enforcement action against that change of use could validly require removal of the hardcore notwithstanding that it had been laid more than four years previously and was therefore immune from enforcement action in itself.[11]

If an enforcement notice has been served within the time limit and is still in effect, it is competent for the planning authority to serve a breach of condition notice in respect of the same breach of planning control, notwithstanding that the time limit for enforcement action has expired. Further enforcement action is also possible where the planning authority have taken or purported to take enforcement action against the breach within the previous four years. This extends the time limit for a further four years to allow a planning authority to issue a fresh enforcement or breach of condition notice where the previous notice was withdrawn or found to be null.

[It should be noted that different time limits apply to mining operations.]

Enforcement Powers

All enforcement powers are discretionary and the planning authority can choose not to take enforcement action. Equally, the authority may choose to under-enforce by taking enforcement action against only part of the breach. Such decisions can only be challenged by applying to the Court of Session for judicial review on the grounds that the decision is unreasonable (in the special legal sense, Chapter 8).

The Scottish Office guidance states that in considering any enforcement action the decisive issue for the planning authority should be whether the breach of control would unacceptably affect public amenity or the use of land and buildings meriting protection in the public interest. Enforcement action should always be commensurate with the breach of planning control to which it relates.[12]

[11] *Murfitt* v. *Secretary of State for the Environment* [1980] J.P.L. 598.

[12] Scottish Office Environment Department Circular 8/1992, "Enforcing Planning Control," para. 7.

The first phase of enforcement action is likely to be service of a planning contravention notice requiring provision of further information. Planning officers may exercise rights of entry to ascertain whether there has been a breach. If a breach of planning control appears to have occurred, the person responsible for the apparent breach may be encouraged to apply for retrospective planning permission (Chapter 5) or a Certificate of Lawfulness of Existing Use or Development (Chapter 4) with a view to regularising the position. If the person refuses, or the case is serious, the authority may take further enforcement action to require the breach to be remedied.

Only service of an enforcement or breach of condition notice within the prescribed time limits prevents a breach of planning control becoming lawful development (above).

The methods of serving notices are dealt with at the end of this chapter.

If there is failure to comply with the requirements of the notice, the planning authority may report the matter to the procurator fiscal for a decision on prosecution, or take direct action to carry out the requirements and recover the cost from the recipient of the notice (this power to take direct action only arises following failure to comply with an enforcement or wasteland notice).

Planning Contravention Notices

The power to serve a planning contravention notice was introduced by the PCA. It is intended to enable planning authorities to seek information where there is a suspected breach of planning control. The notice should also encourage discussion with the planning authority by acting as a warning of enforcement action, and provide an opportunity to regularise the situation. The power to serve a planning contravention notice may in practice replace the more general power to seek information as to interests in land.[13]

A planning contravention notice may be served by the planning authority where it appears that there may have been

[13] TCPSA, s. 270, as amended.

a breach of planning control (above) in respect of any land.[14] A mere suspicion of a breach, following upon a complaint by a member of the public, may be enough. Service of this notice does not affect any other power exercisable in respect of any breach of planning control. It is not an essential prerequisite to enforcement action that a planning contravention notice has been served.

The notice is served on the owner or occupier or any person with another interest in the land, or any person carrying out operations on the land or using it for any purpose.

The notice may require the person on whom it is served to give information so far as he is able about any specified operations, uses or activities being carried out on the land (the requirement to specify these matters should act as an obstacle to a planning authority using the notice as a fishing expedition for information). It may also require provision of information regarding any matter relating to conditions or limitations imposed upon a grant of planning permission. These requirements are complied with by giving information in writing to the planning authority.

For example, the notice may require the person to state whether or not the land is being used for any specified purpose or any operations or activities are being or have been carried out on the land. It may also require him to state when any use, operations or activities began, and to give the name and address of any person known to him to use or have used the land for any purpose or to be carrying out, or have carried out, any operations or activities on the land. In addition, it may require any information he holds as to any planning permission for any use or operations or any reason for planning permission not being required for any use or operation. He may also be required to state the nature of his interest (if any) in the land and the name and address of any other person known to him to have an interest in the land.

The notice must inform the person on whom it is served of the likely consequences of his failing to respond to the notice, and in particular, that enforcement action may be taken. It must also inform the person that failure to respond to the

[14] s. 83C.

notice may result in the loss of the right to compensation following service of a stop notice (below). The notice may also give notice of a time and place at which the authority will consider any representations which may be made in connection with the notice. This will give an opportunity for negotiation with the planning authority to avoid enforcement action.

Failure to comply with a planning contravention notice within 21 days of its service is an offence carrying liablity on summary conviction to a fine not exceeding level 3 on the standard scale.[15] This offence may be committed in the space of a day or over a longer period of time and a person may be convicted again if he fails to comply with the notice following conviction. It will be a defence to prove that there was a reasonable excuse for failing to comply with the requirement.

It is also an offence knowingly or recklessly to make a statement purporting to comply with a requirement of the notice, which is false or misleading in a material particular. A person convicted of this offence will be liable on summary conviction to a fine not exceeding level 5 on the standard scale.

There is no statutory right of appeal to the Secretary of State against a planning contravention notice. However, a petition for judicial review may be brought before the Court of Session alleging that the notice is invalid (Chapter 8). Alternatively, the notice may be ignored and any prosecution defended on the basis that the notice is invalid.

Rights of Entry for Enforcement Purposes

A person duly authorised in writing by the planning authority has the right to enter any land at any reasonable hour if there are reasonable grounds for entering for the purpose in question. This right of entry may be exercised to ascertain whether there is or has been a breach of planning control, determine whether and how any enforcement powers should be exercised, or ascertain whether there has been compliance with any requirement imposed as a result of the exercise of

[15] s. 83D. Appendix I contains details of the standard scale for fines.

enforcement powers.[16] The right of entry extends to neighbouring land, whether or not it is in the same ownership or occupation. Where admission is sought to a dwelling-house, 24-hours notice of the intended entry must be given to the occupier. Where admission has been refused, or a refusal is reasonably apprehended, or the case is one of urgency, a warrant authorising entry may be issued by a sheriff.

The land should be left as effectively secured against trespassers as when entry was taken. Compensation is payable for any damage caused. It is an offence to disclose details of manufacturing processes or trade secrets obtained while exercising the right of entry, other than in the course of duty. It is an offence wilfully to obstruct exercise of the right of entry, punishable on summary conviction by a fine not exceeding level 3 (Appendix 1).

Enforcement Notices

Service of an enforcement notice prevents a breach of planning control becoming lawful development (above) and therefore is one of the main enforcement powers (the other being the power to serve a breach of condition notice). Service of an enforcement notice may be combined with a stop notice (below).

(a) Power to Serve Enforcement Notice

An enforcement notice may be issued by the planning authority where it appears that there has been a breach of planning control and that it is expedient to issue the notice, having regard to the provisions of the development plan and to any other material considerations (Chapter 5).[17] The authority therefore has the discretion to ignore a breach of planning control, or under-enforce (below).

Regional planning authorities have power to serve an enforcement notice where a breach of planning control

[16] ss. 91A, B and C.

[17] s. 84; with the introduction of the plan-led system (Chapter 3), the authority will require to act in accordance with the provisions of the development plan, unless the material considerations dictate otherwise — s. 18A.

materially prejudices an approved structure plan.[18] The Secretary of State also has a default power to serve an enforcement notice.[19]

One enforcement notice may be served in respect of several breaches of planning control.[20] Following service of an invalid enforcement notice, the authority may serve a fresh notice, subject to the prescribed time limits (above).[21]

Planning authorities now have the power to withdraw an enforcement notice, or waive or relax any requirement of such a notice.[22] In particular, the time limit for taking steps to comply with the notice may be extended. This power to vary or withdraw may be exercised whether or not the notice has taken effect. The planning authority is required to give notice of the variation or withdrawal to every person served with a copy of the enforcement notice, and to any person who would be served with a copy if the notice was re-issued. Withdrawal of an enforcement notice will not prejudice the power of the planning authority to issue a further notice within the prescribed time limits (above).

(b) Effect of Enforcement Notice

The enforcement notice must specify the date upon which it will take effect. Any appeal against the enforcement notice must be lodged prior to that date. Lodging an appeal prevents the notice taking effect until the appeal has been determined or withdrawn.

Once the enforcement notice comes into effect, it will apply permanently to the land (unless withdrawn), even if there has been full compliance with its requirements, other than to the extent that its terms are inconsistent with the terms of any planning permission granted subsequent to service of the notice.[23] Thus any requirement to discontinue a use will

[18] s. 84A.
[19] s. 260(5), as amended.
[20] *Valentina of London Ltd.* v. *Secretary of State for the Environment* [1992] J.P.L. 1151.
[21] *R.* v. *Wychavon D.C. and Secretary of State for the Environment* [1992] J.P.L. 753.
[22] TCPSA, s. 84AB.
[23] ss. 89 and 89A.

operate as a permanent restriction, and any resumption of the discontinued use will be in contravention of the notice and, therefore, an offence. In particular, any reinstatement or restoration of buildings demolished or altered in compliance with an enforcement notice, will be in contravention of that notice notwithstanding that its terms are not apt for this purpose. A person who carries out such reinstatement or restoration shall be guilty of an offence and liable on a summary conviction to a fine not exceeding level 5 on the standard scale (Appendix 1).

In certain limited circumstances, compliance with the terms of an enforcement notice results in a deemed grant of planning permission. Where the planning authority chooses to under-enforce by requiring only partial remedying of the breach of planning control and all the requirements of the enforcement notice have been complied with, planning permission is deemed to have been granted in respect of any construction of buildings or carrying out of activities in respect of which the authority could have taken enforcement action. In addition, where an enforcement notice requires construction of a replacement building and all the requirements of that notice have been complied with, planning permission is deemed to have been granted in respect of that construction.[24]

There are various offences which may be committed once an enforcement notice has taken effect. The owner of the land, or lessee under a lease with at least three years still to run, commits an offence if the period specified in the enforcement notice for complying with its requirements has expired without those requirements being satisfied in full.[25] In contrast to the previous law, this offence also includes any failure to cease a specified activity. It is a defence for the owner to show that he did everything he could be expected to do to secure compliance with the notice. If the occupier is preventing the owner from carrying out work required by an enforcement notice, a Sheriff may issue a warrant authorising the owner to go onto the land and carry out the work.[26]

[24] ss. 84AA(11) and (12).
[25] s. 86.
[26] s. 88(3), as substituted.

It is also an offence for any other person who has control of or an interest in the land to carry on, or cause or permit to be carried on, after the end of the period for compliance any activity which an enforcement notice requires to be ceased. Occupiers, lessees and other persons (conceivably even heritable creditors) may therefore be guilty of an offence. However, only the owner/lessee can be prosecuted for failing to take the active steps required by the notice, such as demolition of a building. The liability of other parties is confined to failing to cease an activity which the notice required to be discontinued.

The offences may be committed in the course of a single day or any longer period. A person may be convicted of a second or subsequent offence if he continues the failure to comply with the requirements of the notice following conviction. It is a defence that the person was unaware of the existence of the notice, but only if that person was not served with a copy and the notice was not contained in the register of enforcement notices which must be kept by the planning authority (below).[27] Summary prosecution for these offences must commence within six months (above).

The decision to prosecute and the choice of summary or solemn procedure lies with the procurator fiscal. On summary conviction, a fine not exceeding £20,000 may be imposed (previously £2,000), but an unlimited fine may be imposed following conviction on indictment. In determining the level of fine, the court must have regard to any financial benefit which has accrued or appears likely to accrue to the person in consequence of the offence. For example, where an enforcement notice requires use of a building for retail purposes to be stopped, the court may take into account the profits made from that retail business following expiry of the period for compliance with the requirements of the notice.

If the steps detailed in the enforcement notice have not been taken within the specified period, the planning authority may take those steps, including action to discontinue a use, and recover any expenses reasonably incurred from the

[27] s. 87A, as inserted.

person who is then the owner or lessee of the land.[28] It is an offence to obstruct the authority from taking such steps. If that person failed to exercise his right to appeal to the Secretary of State against the notice (below), he is prevented from disputing the validity of any such action taken in accordance with the notice by the authority. The planning authority is also given the power to sell any materials removed by it from the land, unless claimed by the owner within three days. Given the budgetary restraints upon local government, and the difficulties of recovering money from reluctant persons through the courts, it is unlikely that these powers will be exercised (although it is understood that at least one Scottish planning authority has a practice of taking this form of direct action, with a high success rate in recovering its expenses).

Where the owner, lessee or occupier incurs expenses for the purpose of complying with an enforcement notice or reimburses the expenses of the planning authority, these sums may be recovered from the person by whom the breach of planning control was committed.[29]

(c) Service of Enforcement Notice

Copies of the notice must be served in the required manner on the following persons within 28 days after its date of issue and at least 28 days before the date on which it is to take effect:

(i) the owner of the land, which includes a lessee under a lease with at least three years left to run[30];
(ii) the occupier of the land — whether a person is an occupier is a question of facts and circumstances, and squatters have been considered occupiers by virtue of the length of their occupation[31]; and
(iii) any other person having an interest in the land which the planning authority believes is materially

[28] s. 88.
[29] s. 88(2) as amended.
[30] s. 275(1).
[31] *Scarborough B.C.* v. *Adams* [1983] J.P.L. 673.

affected by the notice, for example, heritable creditors and landlords.

Thus the enforcement notice is directed against the persons who may have the power to secure the result required by the notice and all other parties who have an interest in the land which requires that they be made aware of the notice. The latter parties may have the ability to force the former to comply with the terms of the notice, for example, through the terms of a lease. A planning contravention notice may be used to establish the identity of these parties (above).

In an appeal to the Secretary of State against an enforcement notice, any failure to serve the notice on the appellant or another person may be disregarded if no substantial prejudice has been caused by the failure to serve. An enforcement notice was not null where the failure was the result of a mistaken belief that another party served with the notice was the owner.[32] In contrast, failure to serve an enforcement notice on a person known by the authority to be the owner of the land rendered the notice null.[33] If a failure to serve renders the notice null, the planning authority can serve a fresh enforcement notice on all parties, subject to the prescribed time limits.

Details of the notice should also be recorded in the register available for public inspection. Failure to do so may create a defence to any prosecution (above).

(d) Content of Enforcement Notice

Prior to the PCA, the requirements governing the content of enforcement notices were a happy hunting ground for lawyers seeking to challenge notices. The overhauled system is designed to reduce the legal complexity surrounding the content of enforcement notices, coupled with increased powers for planning authorities and reporters on appeal to vary or correct notices. As a result of these changes, much of

[32] *R.* v. *Greenwich L.B.C., ex p. Patel* [1985] J.P.L. 851.

[33] *McDaid* v. *Clydebank D.C.*, 1984 S.L.T. 162; J.P.L. 579, but see the compulsory purchase case of *Martin* v. *Bearsden & Milngavie D.C.*, 1987 S.L.T. 300.

the previous case law on the content of enforcement notices must now be treated with caution.

There is no prescribed form of enforcement notice, but each notice must state the following[34]:

(i) the matters which appear to the planning authority to constitute the breach (or breaches) of planning control, but only in sufficient detail or with sufficient precision to enable the recipient to know what these matters are;
(ii) whether the breach consists of carrying out development without the required planning permission, and/or failing to comply with any condition or limitation attached to a grant of planning permission. Thus the notice need only identify the general nature of the alleged breach;
(iii) the steps required to be taken or the activities which must cease in order to wholly or partly remedy the breach or remedy any injury to amenity which has been caused by the breach. This is considered in detail below;
(iv) the date on which the notice is to take effect, which must be at least 28 days after the last date of service of the enforcement notice[35];
(v) the period at the end of which any steps are required to have been taken or any activities ceased. Different periods may be specified for different steps or activities; and
(vi) the reasons why the planning authority considers it expedient to issue the notice, and a description of the precise boundaries of the land to which the notice relates, by reference to a plan or otherwise. The enforcement notice must be accompanied by an explanatory note giving prescribed information as to the right of appeal.[36]

[34] TCPSA, s. 84AA. Model enforcement notices are attached to Circular 8/1992, Appendices 2–4.
[35] s. 84(3)(b).
[36] Town and Country Planning (Enforcement of Control) (No. 2) (Scotland) Regulations 1992 (1992 S.I. 2086), regs. 3 and 4.

In most cases, the land to which the notice is directed will be the planning unit (Chapter 4) within which the alleged breach has or is taking place. However, the notice may be validly directed against a greater or lesser area than the planning unit.[37] The only requirement is that the area involved be sufficiently identified to tell the recipient what he has done wrong and what he must do to remedy that wrong.

Remedying the breach will involve making the developer comply with the terms and conditions of any planning permission by discontinuing any use of the land or by restoring the land to its condition before the breach took place, or remedying any injury to amenity which has been caused by the breach. The steps should not strike at an activity which is not part of the breach. An enforcement notice requiring discontinuation of a retail use went too far as it prevented continuation of the ancillary retail use attached to the previous main agricultural use.[38] However, the steps may include reversal of any development integral to the breach, notwithstanding that the development would not require planning permission in its own right or is lawful.[39]

The required steps may include the alteration or removal of any buildings, the carrying out of building or other operations, or the modification of contours of a deposit of refuse or waste materials by altering the gradient of its sides. The notice may specify restrictions on the carrying on of activities on the land. If the breach of planning control consisted of demolition of a building, the notice may require construction of a replacement building as similar as possible to the demolished building. Once the replacement building has been constructed in compliance with the enforcement notice, planning permission is deemed to have been granted for its construction.

Care will still require to be taken to describe precisely the steps to be taken to remedy the breach, and avoid exceeding what is necessary for this purpose, particularly in light of the potential criminal liability attached to the notice. Requiring the installation of "satisfactory sound-proofing of a compressor

[37] *Rawlins* v. *Secretary of State for the Environment* [1990] 1 P.L.R. 110.
[38] *Mansi* v. *Elstree Rural District Council* (1964) 16 P. & C.R. 153.
[39] *Murfitt* (n. 11, *supra*).

and for all possible action to be taken to minimise the effects created by acrylic paint" was hopelessly imprecise.[40] An enforcement notice requiring removal of stone from the foreshore was invalid because it was impossible to tell from the notice which of the stone was to be removed.[41]

In addition to the discretion to ignore a breach of planning control and not serve an enforcement notice, the authority may decide to under-enforce by serving an enforcement notice requiring only partial remedying of the breach. This allows the authority to take a practical view of what can be achieved through issuing an enforcement notice. Under-enforcement is not without consequences. If an enforcement notice could have required the removal of any buildings or cessation of activity, but the authority chose to under-enforce, as soon as the requirements of the enforcement notice have been complied with planning permission is deemed to have been granted for the development consisting of the construction of the buildings or carrying out of the activities.[42] Thus an ill-considered enforcement notice will prevent any future enforcement action. Planning authorities must therefore be sure to identify the full extent of breaches of planning control prior to issuing an enforcement notice.

(e) Appeal Against Enforcement Notice

At any time before the date specified in the notice on which it will take effect, any person served with a copy of the notice or any other person having an interest in the land may appeal to the Secretary of State against the enforcement notice.[43]

Lodging an appeal prevents the enforcement notice coming into force on the date specified in the notice. As a result, until the enforcement notice is upheld on appeal there is no requirement to take the steps specified in the notice to remedy the breach of planning control. Exercise of the right of appeal may therefore provide a further period for negotiation to resolve any dispute between the planning authority and

[40] *Metallic Protectives* v. *Secretary of State for the Environment* [1976] J.P.L. 166.
[41] *McNaughton* v. *Peter McIntyre (Clyde) Ltd.*, 1981 S.P.L.P. 15.
[42] TCPSA, s. 84AA(11).
[43] TCPSA, s. 85, as amended.

the landowner, during which the alleged breach may continue. Most authorities would prefer to agree a solution, thereby avoiding the necessity of continuing with an appeal. Submission of an appeal would also provide sufficient time to lodge an application for retrospective planning permission or apply for a Certificate of Lawfulness of Existing Use or Development.

The right of appeal is open to abuse by persons seeking to continue a profitable activity, which is in breach of planning control, for as long as possible. Appeals may take up to a year to be determined. Such abuses can be prevented by the planning authority serving a stop notice with the enforcement notice, with the effect that the use or operation is prohibited from continuing pending determination of the appeal. Most authorities are reluctant to serve stop notices because of the potential liability to pay compensation. Alternatively, an interdict could be sought to prevent the activity from continuing, but the authority could be liable to pay damages if the interdict was wrongfully obtained (below).

The grounds of appeal are:

(i) planning permission ought to be granted in respect of the breach of planning control constituted by the matters specified in the notice, or the condition or limitation concerned ought to be discharged;
(ii) the matters stated in the notice have not occurred;
(iii) these matters do not amount to a breach of planning control, including development which has become lawful because no enforcement action has been taken within the prescribed time limits (above);
(iv) at the date when the notice was issued no enforcement action could be taken against the breach of planning control. This either refers to lawful development or to the time limit for further enforcement action (above);
(v) copies of the enforcement notice were not served as required by the TCPSA;
(vi) the requirements of the notice exceed what is necessary to remedy any breach of planning control or to remedy any injury to amenity which has been caused by any such breach;

(vii) any period specified in the notice for compliance with its requirements falls short of what should reasonably be allowed.

An appeal is lodged by giving written notice of appeal to the Scottish Office Inquiry Reporters (referred to as SOIR),[44] before the date specified in the enforcement notice as that on which it is to take effect. The appeal will have been lodged timeously if the notice was sent in a properly addressed and pre-paid envelope posted in sufficient time for it to be delivered before that date in the ordinary course of the post (overturning a court ruling that the effective date is the date of receipt and not the date of posting).

There is no prescribed form of notice of appeal and a short letter stating the appellant's wish to appeal to the Secretary of State against the enforcement notice will be sufficient. A written statement of the grounds of appeal and a brief statement of supporting facts may be submitted at the same time as the notice of appeal or not later than 14 days after being requested by SOIR.[45] The appeal may be dismissed if the appellant fails to comply with this time limit. The appellant will also be requested to indicate whether he wishes the appeal to follow the written submissions procedure or be heard at a public inquiry (Chapter 8). Both the appellant and the planning authority have an absolute right to request a public inquiry.

By lodging an appeal, the appellant is deemed to have made an application for planning permission and a fee must be paid to SOIR accordingly. This requirement applies whether or not one of the grounds of appeal is that planning permission ought to be granted, but if that is one of the grounds the appeal and application will lapse if the fee is not paid within the period specified in a written notice from the SOIR to the appellant. No fee is payable if, prior to service of the notice, an application for planning permission for the development remains undetermined or an appeal has been

[44] 2 Greenside Lane, Edinburgh EH1 3AG, Tel: 031 556 8400, Fax: 031 244 5680.

[45] See n. 36, *supra* and reg. 5, *ibid*.

lodged against the decision of the planning authority on such an application.[46]

The planning authority must submit a statement within 28 days of receiving notification of the appeal from SOIR, and send a copy to the appellant. This statement includes a summary of the response of the authority to each ground of appeal and will indicate whether the authority would be prepared to grant planning permission for the matters alleged to constitute a breach of planning control. If the authority fails to submit the statement within the time limit, the Secretary of State may proceed with the appeal and quash the enforcement notice.

In determining an appeal against an enforcement notice, the Secretary of State has power to:

(i) correct any defect, error or misdescription in the notice, or vary its terms, if he is satisfied that the correction or variation will not cause injustice to the appellant or the planning authority (previously this power was limited to correcting any non-material informality, defect or error);
(ii) disregard the failure to serve a copy of the notice on any person, if neither the appellant or that person has been substantially prejudiced by this failure;
(iii) give directions to give effect to his decision on the appeal, including directions for quashing the notice;
(iv) grant planning permission in respect of any of the matters stated in the enforcement notice as constituting a breach of planning control;
(v) discharge any condition or limitation subject to which planning permission was granted, and may substitute any other condition or limitation;
(vi) grant permission for such other development on the land to which the enforcement notice relates as appears appropriate; and
(vii) determine whether on the date on which the appeal was made, any existing use of the land,

[46] TCPSA, s. 85(7) and (7A) as amended, and Town and Country Planning (Fees for Applications and Deemed Applications) (Scotland) Regulations 1990, as amended, reg. 10.

operations, or any matter constituting a failure to comply with a condition or limitation attached to a grant of planning permission, were lawful, and grant a Certificate of Lawfulness of Existing Use or Development accordingly.

In considering whether to grant planning permission, the Secretary of State must have regard to the provisions of the development plan, so far as material to the subject-matter of the enforcement notice, and to any other material considerations.

Aside from the grounds of appeal, the Secretary of State may find that the enforcement notice is a nullity. For example, the notice may fail to specify the date upon which it is to take effect and, therefore, cannot take effect. If the notice is a nullity, it does not exist and there is no notice upon which to determine the appeal.[47]

Any person aggrieved by the decision of the Secretary of State on appeal may challenge the validity of that decision in the Court of Session.[48] This right of challenge is subject to a six-week time limit from the date of the decision letter. The court is only concerned with the validity (or legality) of the decision and will not interfere with its merits (Chapter 8). The decision must therefore be challenged on the grounds that it is null or invalid as outwith the powers (*ultra vires*) of the Secretary of State. For example, the Secretary of State may have misused his statutory powers by failing to take into account a relevant factor.

(f) Challenge of Enforcement Notice in the Courts

Any challenge to the validity of an enforcement notice under grounds (ii) to (v) is only competent as part of an appeal to the Secretary of State (challenge on the other grounds would relate to the merits of the notice rather than to its validity and would, therefore, be outwith the jurisdicition of the courts).[49]

[47] *Encyclopaedia of Planning Law,* Vol. 2, para. 173.09.
[48] TCPSA, s. 233.
[49] s. 85(10).

This provision prevents any challenge to the validity of an anticipated enforcement notice by interdict[50] or challenge as part of a defence to a prosecution.[51]

Notwithstanding this statutory provision, an enforcement notice may be challenged through an application for judicial review in the Court of Session on the grounds that the notice is null or invalid because it was *ultra vires* or outwith the powers of the planning authority to serve the notice.[52] However, as a general rule, judicial review procedure will not be available in circumstances where there is a statutory remedy available. As a result, most challenges of enforcement notices will be by way of appeal to the Secretary of State.

Stop Notices

The PCA reforms also amended the provisions relating to stop notices. For example, in special circumstances, a stop notice can now take effect immediately upon service; and a stop notice can prohibit use of residential caravans. After four years, an unauthorised use cannot be prohibited by service of a stop notice. The circumstances in which compensation will be payable following service of a stop notice are more restricted. Finally, the penalties for ignoring a stop notice have been increased.

(a) Power to Serve Stop Notice

The power to serve a stop notice may be exercised only in association with service of an enforcement notice, where the planning authority considers it expedient that any activity (or ancillary or associated activity), which the enforcement notice requires to be ceased should cease before the expiry of the period for compliance with the enforcement notice.[53] A stop notice may be served at the same time as the enforcement notice or at any time thereafter until the enforcement notice takes effect. Lodging an appeal against an enforcement notice

[50] *Barrie* v. *Lanark D.C.*, 1979 S.L.T. 14.
[51] *R.* v. *Keeys* [1989] J.P.L. 28.
[52] For example, *McDaid* v. *Clydebank D.C.* (n. 33, *supra*).
[53] TCPSA, s. 87.

will prevent that notice from taking effect, leaving the planning authority with the option of serving a stop notice. Scottish Office guidance states that planning authorities should ensure that the requirements of a stop notice prohibit only what is essential to safeguard amenity or public safety in the neighbourhood, or to prevent serious or irreversible harm to the environment in the surrounding area.[54]

The effect of a stop notice is to prohibit the carrying out of the activity on the land to which the enforcement notice relates or on any part of the land specified in the stop notice. The stop notice can also require cessation of activities which are ancillary to or associated with the activity struck at by the enforcement notice, in other words, activities associated with (but not part of) the breach of planning control.

The stop notice may prohibit some, but not all of the activities which the enforcement notice requires to cease, or particular aspects of a single activity. It may also require cessation of activity on part, but not all of the land specified in the enforcement notice. This ability to under-enforce by selecting which of the activities specified in the enforcement notice should be prohibited by the stop notice enables the planning authority to prevent a clear breach of planning control from continuing, pending an appeal against the enforcement notice, but avoid liability to pay compensation for preventing an activity which is less obviously a breach.

A stop notice cannot prohibit use of any building as a dwelling-house. However, the restriction on prohibiting use of a residential caravan has been removed. A stop notice also cannot prohibit any use carried out (whether continuously or not) for more than four years prior to the date of service of the notice. In calculating the four years, no account is taken of any period during which the use was authorised by planning permission, such as a temporary permission. This four-year rule applies to uses and does not extend to building, engineering, mining or other operations or the deposit of refuse or waste materials.

The effect of serving a stop notice underlines the limitations of enforcement notices. An enforcement notice takes at least

[54] Circular 8/1992, Pt. II, para. 71

28 days to come into effect and provides a further period for compliance with its terms, during which time the breach of planning control may continue. Lodging an appeal to the Secretary of State against the enforcement notice suspends its effect until the determination or withdrawal of the appeal. Service of a stop notice prevents the breach of planning control from continuing until the enforcement notice comes into effect.

Stop notices have their own limitations. A stop notice has a negative character and can only be used to prohibit activity rather than to achieve positive action or remedy the breach of planning control. As the effect of a stop notice is limited to requiring complete cessation of an activity, stop notices cannot be used to keep an activity within reasonable bounds. In addition, unlike an interdict, a stop notice cannot be used to prohibit a threatened breach: it can only by served with or after an enforcement notice once there appears to have been a breach of planning control. The usefulness of the power to serve a stop notice is reduced further by the potential liability for compensation (below).

A stop notice ceases to have effect once the period for compliance with the enforcement notice has expired and an offence is being committed for non-compliance with the terms of the enforcement notice. It also ceases to have effect if the enforcement notice to which it relates is withdrawn or quashed on appeal. Where the enforcement notice is varied so that it no longer relates to an activity prohibited by the stop notice, the stop notice will cease to have effect in relation to that activity. A stop notice is not invalidated by any failure to serve the enforcement notice on all parties, provided the planning authority shows that it took all reasonably practicable steps to effect proper service.

The stop notice may be withdrawn at any time by the planning authority without prejudicing its power to serve a fresh notice. Withdrawal is effected by giving notice to all persons served with a copy of the stop notice and displaying this notice in place of any site notices. There is no statutory power to vary a stop notice.

It is an offence for a person to contravene, or cause or permit contravention of, the provisions of a stop notice after a site notice has been displayed or the notice has been served on him. This offence may be committed in the course of a day or a longer period of time. Continued contravention of the stop notice following conviction is also an offence. It will be a defence for the accused person to prove that the stop notice was not served on him and that he had no reasonable cause to believe that the activity was prohibited by the stop notice. Display of a site notice may be an important factor in determining reasonable cause. The decision to prosecute and the choice of procedure rests with the procurator fiscal, with liability to a fine not exceeding £20,000 on summary conviction and an unlimited fine following conviction on indictment. In determining the level of fine the court will have regard to any financial benefit which has accrued or appears likely to accrue to the person in consequence of the failure to comply with the stop notice.

(b) Service of Stop Notice

A stop notice may be served on any person who appears to the planning authority to have an interest in the land or be engaged in activities which constitute or involve the breach of planning control alleged in the enforcement notice. In comparison, the enforcement notice is served on the owner and occupier of the land. The stop notice may be served at the same time as the enforcement notice or at a later date before the enforcement notice takes effect.

The planning authority may also display a site notice on the land, stating the requirements of the stop notice, the persons on whom it has been served, and the consequences of contravening the stop notice. Display of a site notice may widen the categories of persons against whom prosecution for contravening the notice may be successful (above).

(c) Content of Stop Notice

There is no prescribed form of stop notice,[55] but it must specify the date upon which it is to take effect. In normal circumstances, this date must be between three and 28 days

[55] Circular 8/1992, Appendix 5 contains a model stop notice.

after the date of service. However, a stop notice may take earlier effect if the planning authority considers that there are special reasons why an earlier date should be specified. The Scottish Office guidance gives as an example the need to protect areas of great landscape value or conservation areas from harmful operational development.[56] For the notice to take earlier effect in this way, the authority must serve a statement of these special reasons along with the notice. There is no longer a requirement that the stop notice refer to and enclose a copy of the enforcement notice.

(d) *Challenge of Stop Notice*

There is no statutory right of appeal to the Secretary of State or the Court of Session against a stop notice. However, a petition for judicial review may be brought before the Court of Session alleging that the notice is invalid on legal grounds (Chapter 8). It may be difficult to obtain an interdict to prevent service of a stop notice or to suspend its effect pending the decision of the court, as there is a right to compensation if the stop notice is eventually quashed.[57] An alternative but risky option to applying for judicial review is to ignore the notice and defend any prosecution on the basis that the notice is invalid.

(e) *Compensation and Stop Notices*

The potential liability to pay compensation has acted as a deterrent to use of stop notices. Compensation is payable where a stop notice has ceased to have effect (above) in the following circumstances[58]:

> (i) the enforcement notice is quashed on appeal as invalid, other than on the ground that planning permission ought to be granted for the activity or the condition or limitation discharged; or

[56] *Ibid.*, Pt. II, para. 76.

[57] *Central R.C.* v. *Clackmannan D.C.*, 1983 S.L.T. 666; contrast *Shanks & McEwan* v. *Gordon D.C.*, 1991 S.P.L.P. 32:15.

[58] TCPSA, s. 166, as amended.

(ii) the enforcement notice is varied to omit the requirement to cease the activity prohibited by the stop notice; or

(iii) the enforcement notice is withdrawn, other than in consequence of a grant of planning permission by the planning authority for the development to which the notice relates; or

(iv) the stop notice is withdrawn.

For these purposes, a prohibition in a stop notice shall be treated as dependent on an allegation in an enforcement notice if, and to the extent that, the activities to which the prohibition in the stop notice relates are the same as those alleged in the enforcement notice to constitute a breach of planning control, or are so closely associated therewith as to constitute substantially the same activities.

Following the PCA reforms, no compensation will be payable where the stop notice prohibits any activity which at any time when the stop notice is in force constitutes or contributes to a breach of planning control. Thus, even if the enforcement notice fails, the ludicrous situation will not arise of the planning authority being liable to pay compensation for prohibiting an activity which is a breach of planning control. The right to compensation is also excluded where any loss or damage suffered could have been avoided if the claimant had provided information sought under statutory powers, such as a planning contravention notice (above), or had otherwise co-operated with the planning authority when responding to the notice. Finally, no compensation is payable if either the planning authority decides to grant planning permission and, therefore, withdraws the enforcement notice or the Secretary of State, in determining the appeal, decides to grant planning permission and so quashes the enforcement notice.

Compensation may be claimed by a person who had an interest in the land to which the stop notice related when it was served. There is no requirement that the person must have been served with a copy of the notice. Interests in land will include those of an owner or occupier and possibly other parties such as lessees and heritable creditors who had a legal interest in the land.

Compensation is payable in respect of any loss or damage directly attributable to the prohibition contained in the notice, including any sum payable in respect of a breach of contract caused by taking action necessary to comply with the prohibition. The initial claim for compensation in respect of a stop notice must be submitted within six months, but will be valid for 20 years.[59]

Breach of Condition Notice

The Carnwath Report recommended that there should be a remedy to enforce a condition without enabling the merits to be reopened in an enforcement notice appeal (implementation of the permission is taken to imply acceptance of all conditions attached to it). This recommendation has led to the introduction of the breach of condition notice, which joins the enforcement notice as the other main form of enforcement action which prevents a breach of planning control from becoming lawful development.

As a result of the lack of a right of appeal against a breach of condition notice, a grant of planning permission should not be implemented until consideration has been given to the appropriateness of any conditions attached to the permission. Any purchase of land should involve careful scrutiny of planning conditions and warranties should be obtained from the seller that no conditions have been breached.

(a) Power to Serve Breach of Condition Notice

A breach of condition notice may be served by the planning authority where there is non-compliance with any of the conditions or limitations regulating the use of land imposed upon a grant of planning permission.[60] Thus, a notice may be served only if there is actual non-compliance (an objective test), whereas an enforcement notice may be served where it "appears" to the authority that there has been a breach of planning control (a subjective test). This suggests that more

[59] *Holt* v. *Dundee D.C.*, 1990 S.L.T. (Lands Tr.) 30.
[60] TCPSA, s. 87AA.

proof will be required before the breach of condition notice may be served.

The Scottish Office guidance states that the decisive issue should be whether public amenity or the use of land or buildings meriting protection in the public interest is unacceptably affected. A breach of condition notice should only be served where the condition is legally valid, satisfies the criteria for imposition of conditions (Chapter 6), and has clearly been breached on the available evidence.[61]

The planning authority has power to withdraw the notice without prejudicing its power to serve a fresh notice within the prescribed time limits. There is no specific power to vary the notice. However, the time limit for compliance may be extended.

In contrast to an enforcement notice, a breach of condition notice comes into effect on the date of service. If, after the period allowed for compliance has expired, any of the conditions specified in the notice is not complied with and the steps specified in the notice have not been taken or the activities have not ceased, the person served with a copy of the notice is in breach of its terms and guilty of an offence. It is not clear whether compliance with the terms of the notice has the effect of discharging the notice, or whether a breach of condition notice has a similar effect to an enforcement notice and will remain in force to catch any future breaches following compliance.

Any person found guilty of such an offence shall be liable on summary conviction to a fine not exceeding level 3 on the standard scale (Appendix 1). This offence may be committed in the course of a day or over a longer period. Further offences will be committed if there is non-compliance with the notice following conviction. It will be a defence to prove that all reasonable measures were taken to secure compliance with the conditions specified in the notice, or that the accused no longer had control of the land where the notice was purportedly served upon him as the person having control thereof.

[61] Circular 36/1992, "Planning and Compensation Act 1991, Lawful Development and Enforcement," paras. 9 and 24.

A breach of condition notice will cease to have effect where the condition is discharged, or so far as the notice is inconsistent with a subsequent grant of retrospective planning permission.[62] However, this will not affect liability for a previous failure either to comply or to secure compliance with the notice.

There is no provision enabling the planning authority to take the steps specified in a breach of condition notice and recover its expenses from the person served with the notice.

(b) *Service of Breach of Condition Notice*

The breach of condition notice may be served upon any person who is carrying out or has carried out the development, or who has caused or permitted another to do so. In the case of conditions regulating the use of the land, the notice may be served upon the person who has control of the land. Thus, unlike an enforcement notice which is served on the owner and occupier, the objective seems to be that a breach of condition notice is served upon the person responsible for the breach of condition or the person who can secure compliance with the condition. It also seems that the planning authority has an element of discretion in deciding the person(s) to be served with a breach of condition notice.

The example given by the Scottish Office guidance is a condition requiring completion of a landscaping scheme in association with a housing development. This type of condition does not regulate the use of land. Thus a breach of condition notice cannot be served upon the individual homeowners (it would be possible to serve enforcement notices), but must be served upon the original developer.

(c) *Content of Breach of Condition Notice*

The notice must specify the planning permission to which it relates, the conditions which have not been complied with (which need not be all the conditions), and the steps which the authority consider ought to be taken, or the activities

[62] TCPSA, s. 89A.

which the authority considers ought to cease, to secure compliance with these conditions. The period for compliance must be at least 28 days from the date of service of the notice, as specified in the notice.

It may be within the discretion of the planning authority to ignore non-compliance with some or all of the conditions imposed upon a grant of planning permission. However, unlike the power to serve an enforcement notice, the statutory wording does not explicitly permit service of a breach of condition notice requiring partial and not full compliance with a condition.

(d) Challenge of Breach of Condition Notice

There is no statutory right of appeal to the Secretary of State or the Court of Session against a breach of condition notice. It will therefore be impossible to challenge the merits of the notice, but may be possible to challenge its validity. An invalid notice could be ignored and its invalidity raised as a defence to any prosecution for non-compliance with its terms. Alternatively, a petition for common-law judicial review may be submitted to the Court of Session on the ground that the notice is beyond the powers (*ultra vires*) of the planning authority to serve (Chapter 8). The Court of Session may refuse a petition for judicial review on the ground that the statutory procedures for challenging conditions should have been utilised (Chapter 6). Invalidity of the notice will not prevent the planning authority serving a fresh notice within the prescribed time limits.

The option of negotiating with the planning authority must always be borne in mind. Negotiations may lead to submission of an application for planning permission without compliance with the condition (Chapter 5).

Interdict

Following the PCA reforms, planning authorities have a statutory power to seek interdict from the sheriff court or the

Court of Session to restrain or prevent any actual or apprehended breach of planning control.[63] Interdict is a court order requiring an activity to be stopped or preventing an activity from starting (known as an injunction in England and Wales). It has a negative character and is not appropriate for requiring an activity or works to be carried out. Breach of interdict amounts to contempt of court and may result in a fine and/or imprisonment.

It is irrelevant to the exercise of this power that the authority has exercised or proposes to exercise other enforcement or planning powers. Interdict can, therefore, be used in conjuction with other enforcement action, for example, to prevent the lodging of an appeal from delaying the requirement of an enforcement notice to cease an unauthorised activity. This power may be used to avoid the potential liability for compensation which follows service of a stop notice in such a situation (below). However, planning authorities should note that interim interdict is granted *periculo petentis*, with the result that there will be liability to pay compensation in the form of damages if the interim interdict is later proved to be excessive. An interdict may be sought in circumstances where a stop notice cannot be served, such as before there has been an actual breach of planning control, or after an enforcement notice has come into effect.

Application for interdict may be made to either the Sheriff Court or the Court of Session. The choice of court will depend on factors such as the seriousness of the case, convenience and cost. The court may grant such interdict as it thinks appropriate for the purpose of restraining or preventing the breach.[64] Refusal of the application for interdict will continue to be within the discretion of the court. For example, it is possible that the court may refuse to grant an interdict in circumstances where a stop notice could be served, on the grounds that the more specific power provided by Parliament should be exercised, especially since it carries provisions for payment of compensation.

[63] s. 260A.

[64] *City of London Corporation* v. *Bovis Construction* [1989] J.P.L. 263 shows the circumstances in which the courts in England and Wales will grant an injunction.

Wasteland Notices

The planning authority has power to serve a wasteland notice where it appears that the amenity of any part of its district is adversely affected by the condition of any land or buildings within the district. Unlike the other enforcement powers, this power may be exercised in the absence of a breach of planning control. The notice is served on the owner, lessee and occupier of the land or building, and requires specified steps to be taken to abate the adverse effect. The effect of the notice is similar to an enforcement notice. An appeal against the notice may be submitted to the Secretary of State at any time until the notice takes effect. Failure to comply with the requirements of the notice is not declared to be an offence. If the required steps are not taken, the only sanction available to the authority is to enter the site and take those steps itself, recovering the costs of doing so from the owner or lessee of the site.[65]

Discontinuance Order

The planning authority has power to require discontinuance of any use of land, alteration or removal of any buildings or works, or to impose conditions on the continuance of a use of land.[66] This power is exercised in the interests of the proper planning of its area (including the interests of amenity). Regard must be had to the development plan and to any other material considerations. The order will not take effect until confirmed by the Secretary of State. There is provision for a hearing to be held at the request of the owner, lessee or occupier of the land, or any other person affected by the order. If the order is confirmed, there is a right to compensation for depreciation of the value of an interest in land, or disturbance in the enjoyment of the land.[67] The cost of carrying out works in compliance with the order can also

[65] TCPSA, s. 63, as amended.
[66] s. 49, as amended.
[67] s. 159, as amended.

be recovered from the planning authority. It is an offence not to comply with the order.[68]

Other Enforcement Matters

Service of Notices

Service of a notice is achieved by delivering it to the person, by leaving it at their usual or last known place of abode, or by sending it by recorded delivery or registered mail to that address. Where the valuation roll shows a person to have an interest in the land, the notice should be served at the address on the roll for that person. Service on companies is effected by delivery to the secretary or clerk of the company at its registered or principal office, or by registered letter/recorded delivery addressed to the secretary or clerk at that office. If the planning authority is unable to identify after reasonable enquiry the persons entitled to service, the notice may be addressed to "the owner," "the lessee," or "the occupier" of the land and served as above. If any part of the land is unoccupied, the notice may be addressed to "the owners and any lessees and occupiers" and affixed in a conspicuous manner to some object on the land, but must be served upon any person who has given to the authority an address for service.[69]

Register of Notices

Prescribed details of every wasteland notice, enforcement notice, breach of condition notice, and stop notice, served in relation to land in its district must be entered by the planning authority into a register as soon as practicable and, in any event, within nine days. The register must be available for public inspection at all reasonable hours. Provision is made for removal of entries following withdrawal of a notice, a

[68] s. 100, as amended.
[69] s. 269.

decision on appeal to quash the notice, or its reduction by the Court of Session.[70]

Personal Bar

There are certain limited circumstances in which the planning authority will be personally barred from exercising its enforcement powers (the equivalent principle in English law is estoppel).

Where an appeal has been upheld on the substantive issues, the legal principle of *res judicata* (finality of determination) applies and it is not open to the planning authority to serve fresh notices alleging similar breaches of planning control based on the same facts and circumstances.[71] However, this principle does not prevent service of a fresh notice within the time limits where a previous notice was quashed on procedural grounds or as a nullity.[72]

The other instance in which personal bar may be an issue is where a planning officer indicates that planning permission is not required for a proposed development. The problem is whether such a statement can personally bar the planning authority and prevent it from taking enforcement action against the development, which has commenced without permission in reliance upon this indication. Previously it could be argued that where the authority had delegated powers to the officer to make decisions on its behalf a written statement in this form amounted to a section 51 determination which bound the authority. With the replacement of the formal procedure for obtaining Certificates of Lawfulness of Proposed Use or Development (CLOPUD) for the informal section 51 determinations, there is no longer a mechanism for obtaining informal, but binding decisions. In the absence of delegated powers, statements by its planning officers do not bind the authority.[73] However, in a recent decision the ostensible or apparent authority of the officer to make the

[70] s. 87A, as amended and Enforcement No. 2 Regulations 1992, reg. 7, (see n. 36, *supra*).
[71] *Thrasyvoulou* v. *Secretary of State for the Environment* [1990] 2 A.C. 273.
[72] *R.* v. *Wychavon D.C.*, (n. 21, *supra*).
[73] *Western Fish Products* v. *Penwith District Council* [1981] 2 All E.R. 204.

decision prevented the authority from taking enforcement action.[74] In light of this uncertainty, it is clearly unsafe to rely upon any assurances from planning officers regarding the need for planning permission and consideration should be given to applying for a CLOPUD.

[74] *Camden L.B.C.* v. *Secretary of State for the Environment* [1993] J.P.L. 1049.

Chapter 8

CHALLENGE OF PLANNING DECISIONS

Prior to embarking on a challenge of a planning decision, it is essential to identify the result that is sought and determine which, if any, procedure could achieve this result. For example, despite a successful judicial review petition, the Secretary of State or planning authority in re-deciding the matter may be free to reach the same decision, provided the decision is taken in the correct manner. Judicial review is, therefore, not always the most appropriate procedure for challenging decisions.

Other relevant factors in deciding which procedure to use include the existence of time limits and the availability of the remedy in the circumstances. The degree to which professional assistance will be necessary, with the resultant cost implications, will be an important consideration. None of the procedures discussed in this chapter necessarily require such assistance, and indeed some are deliberately informal to avoid intimidating non-professionals, but many persons will be unwilling to act without professional advice. The likelihood of a successful challenge using the procedure must also be assessed.

This chapter concentrates upon the options available to a person who wishes to challenge a decision upon a planning application, either at first instance or on appeal. However, procedures for challenging the exercise of other planning powers share the same general characteristics.

Negotiation

Chapter 5 commenced with a reminder of the importance of consulting the planning authority for its views in advance of submitting a planning application. It is equally advisable to explore the possibility of negotiating a solution with the planning authority before formally challenging a decision. Formal procedures are expensive and time-consuming for both challenger and planning authority, and each should recognise the importance of compromise and avoidance of appeals.

If valid grounds of challenge can be shown, the planning authority may be willing to negotiate a compromise. Alternatively, the authority may be willing to give an informal indication that a revised proposal may be successful. Such an indication would enable submission of a fresh application for planning permission rather than a challenge to the original decision. Additional information not before the planning authority at the time of the decision may also provide scope for negotiation.

The procedures to commence a challenge may be begun during negotiations to place more pressure on the planning authority to agree a compromise. However, such action carries the risk that the authority will withdraw from further negotiations. Whatever tactics are employed, care must be taken to ensure that any time limit for commencing the challenge does not expire. If necessary, a challenge can be commenced to prevent expiry of the time limits while the negotiations continue. If negotiations will be lengthy, the parties can agree that the challenge be sisted (suspended) in the meantime. Applicants who anticipate difficulties in obtaining planning permission often submit duplicate applications, permitting them to lodge an appeal in connection with one application while continuing negotiations with the authority on the other application (Chapter 5).

As a result of the inability of the planning authority to revoke a grant of planning permission without paying compensation or re-determine the matter in the absence of a fresh planning application, for all practical purposes negotiation with the authority is not a worthwhile option for third parties wishing to challenge a decision on a planning application. Such parties may, however, wish to seek reassurance on future decisions or that compliance with conditions attached to a grant of permission will be monitored and enforcement action taken against any breaches.

Appeal to the Secretary of State

Applicants for planning permission have a statutory right of appeal to the Secretary of State in respect of the decision on their application by the planning authority. There are rights of appeal to the Secretary of State in connection with other forms of planning decisions. Unless otherwise stated, these follow a similar procedure. In most cases, the power of the Secretary of State to determine appeals has been delegated to full-time qualified officials known as reporters (equivalent to the inspectors in England and Wales).[1] The Secretary of State retains the power to recall for decision exceptional or important cases within the classes of delegated appeals. These cases, together with non-delegated appeals, are decided by the Secretary of State after consideration of the report made by the reporter who heard the appeal. The administration of planning appeals is handled by the Scottish Office Inquiry Reporters (SOIR).

Availability

The applicant for planning permission (and no other person) has a right of appeal to the Secretary of State against:

(i) a refusal of permission or other approval by the planning authority, or against any conditions imposed on the grant of permission or approval.[2] (Procedures for challenging planning conditions are examined in Chapter 6.); and

(ii) a deemed refusal of permission, where the planning authority has failed either to notify the applicant of its decision on the application, or give notice that it has exercised its power to decline to determine the

[1] TCPSA, Sched. 7, as amended; Town and Country Planning (Determination of Appeals by Appointed Persons) (Prescribed Classes) (Scotland) Regulations 1987 (S.I. 1987 No. 1531), as amended.

[2] s. 33, as amended.

application, or that the application has been called-in by the Secretary of State for decision (Chapter 5).[3]

Time Limit

The notice of appeal must be lodged within six months of[4]:

(i) the notice of the decision of the planning authority on the planning application; or

(ii) in the case of a deemed refusal, the expiry of two months from the date of receipt of the application (four months if the application includes an environmental statement, and three months from the call-in date when the application is called-in for decision by the regional planning authority), or the expiry of any extended period agreed upon in writing by the applicant and the planning authority. The date of receipt of the application is the date by which the following have been lodged: any fee for the application together with the cost of any advertisement payable by the applicant, and the certificates required in connection with the application.[5] This will often be earlier than the date of registration.

This time limit is absolute and any appeal lodged late will be rejected as invalid.

Grounds of Challenge

In most appeals to the Secretary of State there is essentially only one ground of challenge: that planning permission ought to be granted for the proposed development. It would be competent but inadvisable for the appellant to do no more

[3] s. 34, as amended.
[4] Town and Country Planning (General Development Procedure) (Scotland) Order 1992 (D.P.O.), art. 23.
[5] D.P.O., art. 14.

than state this ground. The Secretary of State (or his reporter) has power to deal with the application afresh, as if it had been made to him in the first instance.[6] The planning merits of the application may, therefore, be assessed without any further input from the appellant other than the information which appears in the planning application. This is the inevitable result of the presumption in favour of development (Chapter 5), which is the usual starting point for grounds of appeal.

It is advisable for the appellant to expand on the reasons why planning permission ought to be granted to ensure that all the relevant points are put before the reporter. Rather than rely on the presumption in favour of development, the appellant may wish to stress the reasons why permission should be granted for the proposed development, by reference to the material considerations outlined in Chapter 5. Alternatively, or in addition, the appellant can argue that the reasons given by the planning authority for its decision are wrong, based on erroneous information, or insufficient to overcome the presumption. There is no single correct approach, but all the grounds of appeal must be stated on the form before the appeal is submitted.

Unlike a challenge in the courts, the grounds of appeal may involve discussion of the planning merits of the application and other factual matters. The planning merits of a proposed development stem from the provisions of the development plan and other material considerations (Chapter 5). Appropriate reference can therefore be made to relevant law, policies in the structure and local plans, any other relevant policies of the planning authority, and the advice given to planning authorities by the Secretary of State through circulars and other documents (Chapter 2). The report to the planning committee on the application, prepared by the planning officer and obtainable by members of the public through the access to information rules, is a useful starting point for gathering this information. The complexity or importance of the proposed development will dictate how much reference to such documents is required.

[6] TCPSA, s. 33(3).

Initial Procedure

The appeal is lodged by submitting the following documents to SOIR within the six month time limit:

(i) The notice of appeal normally in the form of a completed Form P/PPA, copies of which are provided by SOIR on request. If time is short, however, it is possible to submit a statement of the grounds of appeal and complete the form thereafter. The appellant is required to send a copy of the notice to the planning authority at the same time and, thereafter, the appellant and the authority are required to copy all correspondence with SOIR to each other[7];

(ii) a copy of the application which is the subject of the appeal and documents submitted along with it, including the section 24 certificate relating to notification of owners and agricultural tenants, and any neighbour notification certificate (Chapter 5);

(iii) a copy of the decision notice informing the applicant of the decision of the authority on the application, unless the appeal is against a deemed refusal;

(iv) copies of all other relevant correspondence with any planning authority;

(v) a section 24 certificate in respect of the appeal, in the form of a completed Certificate A, B, C or D (supplied with Form P/PPA). By completing Certificate A, the appellant certifies that at the time of submitting the appeal and within the previous 21 days nobody except the appellant was the owner of the site of the proposed development. Certificate B states that notice has been served on the owners named therein. Certificate C or D states that all reasonable steps (specifying these steps) have been taken to find out the names and addresses of the owners but without success, other than those named on whom notice has been served, and that notice of the appeal has been published in a local newspaper in the form of Notice No. 2 (supplied along with Form

[7] D.P.O., art. 23(3).

P/PPA). All these certificates state that the site does not form part of an agricultural tenancy or that the named agricultural tenant(s) has been notified of the appeal.

Notice is given to owners and agricultural tenants by serving a completed copy of Notice No. 1 (also supplied along with Form P/PPA) in the ways described in Chapter 7. This notice alerts these persons to their opportunity to make representations to the Secretary of State about the appeal within 21 days of the date of service. As any representations which they made in connection with the application which is the subject of the appeal will be forwarded to the SOIR by the planning authority and considered by the Secretary of State/reporter, it may not be necessary for them to lodge further representations.

Unlike submission of planning applications, there is no requirement to notify neighbours, but any representations lodged by neighbours in connection with the application will be forwarded by the planning authority and considered as part of the appeal.

(vi) an indication that the applicant wishes the appeal to be determined on the basis of written submissions or by a hearing, which in the vast majority of cases will be in the form of a public local inquiry (below). If the appellant opts for the written submissions procedure, a full statement of his case should be submitted along with the notice of appeal.

Many of these items may need to be obtained from the planning authority. If the time limit is looming, the appeal should be lodged along with an explanation that the papers are being sought from the planning authority.

Either the appellant or the planning authority is entitled to require that the appeal be the subject of a public inquiry.[8] In other words, the appellant's choice of written submissions procedure can be overriden by the planning authority exercising its right to ask for a public inquiry to be held. Even if both parties opt for the written submissions procedure, the Secretary of State may require that a public inquiry be held, perhaps because of the complexity of the matter or the degree

[8] TCPSA, s.33(4).

of public interest (the provisions empowering the Secretary of State to set up a special inquiry in the form of a Planning Inquiry Commission have never been exercised). Once the written submissions procedure has begun, it is still open to either party or the reporter to request that a public inquiry be held. During the course of a public inquiry, it is competent for the parties to agree that, thereafter, the appeal be disposed of on the basis of written submissions.

The determining issues in selecting which appeal procedure to request are the complexity and importance of the issues involved, any dispute as to the facts, and the suitability of written submissions for deciding these issues. It may also be relevant that the written submissions procedure is quicker. A decision by written submissions procedure took a median time of 21 weeks in 1991 compared to 37 weeks for inquiry procedure.[9] If the applicant is paying for professional advice or assistance, written submissions procedure will also be considerably cheaper.

Written Submissions Procedure

The written submissions procedure is available for most forms of planning appeals[10] and is used in the vast majority of appeals (87 per cent in 1990). It is quicker, simpler and cheaper than the public inquiry procedure. Instead of the appeal being heard in a court-room style setting of a public inquiry, the arguments are presented in written form and the decision reached on the basis of these submissions and a site visit. Planning authorities have been urged to make use of this procedure as much as possible.[11]

The written submissions procedure is based around a timetable for lodging documents. Interestingly, the requirement is for documents to be sent rather than received within the specified time limits. Although there is provision made for late submissions to be excluded from consideration when

[9] Draft NPPG, "The Planning System," para. 31.

[10] Town and Country Planning (Appeals) (Written Submission Procedure) (Scotland) Regulations 1990 (S.I. 1990 No. 507) and Circular 7/1990, "Written Submissions Procedure."

[11] S.D.D. Circular 26/1984, "Planning Appeals," para. 8.

deciding the appeal, there is normally some leeway allowed. Indeed lack of resources often results in planning authorities lodging submissions late. The Secretary of State has the power to extend the time limits at the request of either party, and can set later time limits in particular cases. Any failure to comply with the procedural rules which causes substantial prejudice may result in the decision being quashed by the Court of Session. In addition, the rules of natural justice apply.

(a) Notification

Within 14 days of receiving either the notice of appeal or an indication of the applicant's choice of the written submissions procedure, if this is not included in the notice, the planning authority must give notice of the appeal to those persons or bodies notified or consulted by the authority (other than by newspaper advertisement), and who made representations in connection with the application. The authority must also serve notice on any other persons who lodged representations or, if a large number of representations were received, the authority may advertise the appeal in a local newspaper.

The notice/advertisement must state the name of the appellant and the address of the appeal site, describe the application, and explains that the representations submitted in connection with the application will be considered by the Secretary of State, unless the person requests otherwise in writing within 14 days of the date of receipt of the notice. It must also state that any written representations in relation to the appeal must be sent to the Secretary of State within 14 days of receipt of the notice or date of publication of the advertisement.

(b) Appeals Questionaire

Within the same 14-day period, the planning authority is also required to send a completed appeals questionnaire to SOIR, and a copy to the appellant. The questionnaire seeks confirmation from the authority of its agreement to the use of written submissions procedure and information on consultation responses and representations received in connection with the application. It is returned by the planning authority together with copies of all documents relating to the case and which are referred to in the completed questionnaire, other than any confidential written representations. These documents will normally include the planning officer's report to the committee on the application, and copies of all consultation responses and representations received.

(c) Written Submissions

Unless the planning authority elects to treat the questionnaire and supporting documents as its written submissions, the authority is required to send its written submissions to SOIR, and a copy to the appellant, within 28 days of receipt of the notice of appeal, or the applicant's choice of written submissions procedure.

Any interested party may make written submissions within 28 days of the date of the receipt of the appeal by the Secretary of State. Copies of these submissions will be sent by SOIR to the appellant and planning authority, both of whom will be given 14 days to lodge any response.

(d) Further Procedure

The appellant has 14 days from receipt of the authority's written submissions to lodge a response with SOIR, sending a copy of the response to the authority. The authority will normally be given an opportunity to respond, although this is not provided for in the procedure rules.

(e) Site Visit

Although there is no provision in the rules, the reporter determining the appeal will usually visit the site of the proposed development accompanied by the appellant and a representative of the authority. The date of this visit will be arranged with them by SOIR. If other parties have made representations in relation to the appeal, they will be notified of the site visit. The purpose of the site visit is for the reporter to view the physical characteristics of the site and surrounding area and seek clarification from the parties in relation to any of these characteristics mentioned in their submissions. The site visit is not a forum for discussing the grounds of appeal or making statements in support of or against the appeal, and the reporter will intervene to stop any such discussion or statement.

(f) Decision

Following the site visit, the decision of the reporter on the appeal will be issued. Copies of the decision letter are sent to the appellant, planning authority and any parties who lodged representations in relation to the appeal.

Where there have been significant delays on the part of one or both parties in lodging their submissions, the reporter has the power to ignore any written submissions sent outwith the relevant time limits. If the authority fails to send its written submission/questionnaire within the time limit, the appeal may be determined on the basis of the applicant's grounds of appeal alone, provided written notice of the intention of the reporter to so determine the appeal has been given to the appellant and the authority.

Public Local Inquiry

Where complex or contentious issues are involved, or there is a dispute on the facts, it is more appropriate for the appeal to be heard at a public local inquiry. Such an inquiry must be held if either party requests it. Even if both parties request that the appeal be decided by written submissions, the Secretary of State may insist that a public local inquiry be held because of the complexity of the matter or the degree of public interest. At a public local inquiry the issues are presented through the giving of evidence by and cross-examination of witnesses.

All public inquiries are based on the principles of natural justice, broadly defined as openness, fairness and impartiality.[12] The Court of Session may quash the decision if there

[12] Memorandum of Guidance attached to S.D.D. Circular 14/1975, "Public Inquiry Procedures," para. 53.

has been a failure to comply with the procedural rules which has caused substantial prejudice or a breach of natural justice (below). Compliance with the rules does not necessarily prevent a breach of natural justice.

There are several general principles underlying the public local inquiry procedure. Appellants should give full public explanation of their proposals and planning authorities should discuss the proposals thoroughly with appellants and with objectors, to improve public understanding, open the way to compromise and avoid the need for an inquiry. As much written evidence as possible should be circulated in advance of the inquiry, and the use of surprise evidence for tactical advantage is discouraged. Repetitious cross-examination during the inquiry should be avoided. The reporter conducting the inquiry is not confined to the role of the silent listener and may seek any clarification he deems necessary or direct questions to issues not adequately covered in the evidence. Above all, the procedure adopted at the inquiry should be as informal as possible.[13]

There are different rules applicable to public local inquiries for planning appeals which are delegated by the Secretary of State to reporters for decision[14] and for appeals which are decided by the Secretary of State after considering the report prepared by the reporter.[15] Most forms of appeals are now delegated to reporters for decision, although the Secretary of State retains the power to recall any delegated case for his own decision.

The detailed procedures laid down in both sets of rules are broadly similar until the close of the inquiry, as examined below. The procedure commences once the planning authority receives notification that the appellant has chosen for the appeal to be heard at a public local inquiry, or the authority indicates that it wishes such an inquiry to be held. Most

[13] Circular 14/1975.

[14] Town and Country Planning Appeals (Determination by Appointed Persons) (Inquiry Procedure) (Scotland) Rules 1980 (S.I. 1980 No. 1677), as amended by Amendment Rules 1987 (S.I. 1987 No. 1522), referred to as Delegated Appeals Rules (D.A.R.).

[15] Town and Country Planning (Inquiries Procedure) (Scotland) Rules 1980 (S.I. No. 1676), referred to as Inquiries Procedure Rules (I.P.R.).

authorities submit a completed appeals questionnaire at this stage, although this is not required by the rules. At least 28 days before the inquiry the planning authority lodges its written statement of observations. Productions are exchanged between the parties 10 days in advance of the inquiry. Where witnesses are to speak from prepared statements (referred to as precognitions), these are exchanged when the inquiry starts, normally just before the witness is to give evidence. Inevitably, documents are lodged on the last possible date, notwithstanding exortations to avoid surprise tactics. Correspondence from SOIR will normally inform parties of what is expected of them.

(a) Procedure: Preliminary Information

The planning authority is notified by SOIR that the appeal is to proceed to a public local inquiry. SOIR gives the authority the names and addresses of all section 26 parties. These are the persons who have made representations, either to the authority in relation to the application or to the Secretary of State in connection with the appeal, within the 21 day period allowed for such representations, in their capacity as owners or agricultural tenants of any part of the land to which the appeal relates. The planning authority must inform SOIR of any such persons who have made representations to the authority, and provide the appellant with the names and addresses of all section 26 parties.

In addition, if the Secretary of State, a government department, local authority or new town development corporation made representations or issued a direction as to how the application should be determined, the planning authority must notify that person or body that the direction or expression of view is relevant to the inquiry, and that person or body must provide the authority with a written statement of the reasons for the view or direction, if this has not already been done.

(b) Notification of Identity of Reporter

SOIR give written notice to the appellant, the planning authority and the section 26 parties, informing them of the name of the reporter appointed to hear the appeal. If a replacement reporter is appointed close to the date of the inquiry, it will be sufficient for this reporter to announce his own name and the fact of his appointment at the inquiry.

(c) *Notification of Inquiry*

SOIR put forward suitable dates for the holding of the inquiry and liaise with the appellant and the planning authority to reach agreement on the dates and anticipated length of the inquiry. For major inquiries, these details are decided at the pre-inquiry procedure meeting (below). The accomodation in which the inquiry is held is normally arranged by SOIR and located within the district in which the appeal site is situated. At least 28 days written notice of the date, time and place must be given to the appellant, the planning authority, the section 26 parties, and any person who had lodged objections to the appeal which have not been withdrawn[16] (shorter notice may be given with the written agreement of the appellant and the planning authority). The reporter may vary the date, time and place where it becomes necessary or advisable to do so. Reasonable notice of the variation must be given.

SOIR usually arranges for publication of notice of the inquiry in an advertisement in a local newspaper circulating in the district within which the appeal site is situated. The reporter also has the power to require the planning authority to publish notices of the inquiry in local newspapers, to serve notice of the inquiry on specified persons or classes of persons, or post notices of the inquiry in conspicuous places near to the appeal site.

For major inquiries, a pre-inquiry procedural meeting is held to identify the issues, define areas of agreement and disagreement between parties, determine the likely programme of the inquiry, and agree a timetable for advance circulation. The procedure meeting is open to the public and notice will be given of the meeting by newspaper advertisement.

[16] TCPSA, s. 267(3).

(d) *Preparation for a Public Local Inquiry*

The preparatory work for a public local inquiry is greater than that for a written submissions appeal, mainly because more complex appeals will always be heard at an inquiry. The exact details of this preparatory work varies between the parties. The appellant will have submitted his grounds of appeal and any supporting statement, and is left to consider selecting witnesses and gathering any evidence to be lodged as productions. The planning authority must consider the grounds of appeal and prepare its statement of observations. Third parties can focus on the inquiry itself, unless they intend to lodge productions. In major inquiries there will be more onerous advance circulation requirements, and, therefore, greater preparatory work all round.

Selecting witnesses is an important consideration. It is common for expert evidence to be given by a planning witness, who may be a planning consultant or perhaps a landscape architect. Roads engineers are often called as expert witnesses to give evidence on traffic issues. There are a myriad of other possible expert witnesses, depending upon the nature of the development and its proposed location. It will be clear from the grounds of refusal which aspects of the proposed development may require expert evidence. The appellant is not required to call expert witnesses and is free to limit his case to the evidence which he will give himself, as he benefits from the presumption in favour of development and is under no obligation to prove his case (although this should not be relied upon in practice).

Expert witnesses are entitled to express their professional opinion on the issues involved in the appeal which are within the area of their expertise. However, this can be a double-edged sword. During cross-examination an expert witness can be asked for his professional opinion on a point, and will be forced to voice this opinion even if it is contrary to the case being pursued by the party who called the witness to give evidence. Questioning during the cross-examination of an expert witness may therefore provide support for the opposing case.

The planning authority will normally call the planning officer who dealt with the application (or his superior) as the main witness. However, if the decision reached on the application was contrary to that recommended by the planning officer in the report on the application (Chapter 5), the Royal Town Planning Institute (RTPI) advises the officer to refuse to appear as a witness as this would involve supporting a decision contrary to his recommendation. In the absence of a planning officer, one option is to call a member of the planning committee as a non-expert witness.

(e) Statements to be Served Pre-Inquiry

It is a general principle of the inquiry procedure that there should be advance circulation among the parties of the written statements of their cases or objections, the precognitions of witnesses, the documents to be founded on, and the written statement of any national or local policy which may be relevant.[17] In particular, if an objector intends to refer to an alternative site, he should notify the reporter as soon as possible.[18]

In all but major inquiries (and inquiries in connection with called-in applications, see Chapter 5), the requirement for advance circulation is as follows. At least 28 days before the date of the inquiry, the planning authority must send to the reporter a written statement of the observations which the authority proposes to put forward at the inquiry, together with copies of all representations received by it in relation to the appeal. Copies of the statement and representations must also be served on the appellant and all section 26 parties, although the reporter can authorise the authority to serve a notice on the section 26 parties stating the times and places at which the statement and representations may be inspected.

Where the Secretary of State has given a direction which applies to the proposed development which is the subject of the appeal, the planning authority must refer to the direction in the statement sent to the reporter and include a copy of the direction and the reasons given for it. Similarly, where any government department, local authority or development

[17] Memorandum of Guidance attached to S.D.D. Circular 14/1975, "Public Inquiry Procedures," para. 8.
[18] *Ibid.*, para. 14.

corporation has expressed in writing to the planning authority a view on the application, and the planning authority proposes to rely on the expression of view in its submissions at the inquiry, the authority must include it in its statement. The authority is obliged to include in its statement any view expressed which favoured granting the application for planning permission. The planning authority must send a copy of the statement to the government department, local authority or development corporation concerned within the notice period.

If the authority intends to refer to documents, photographs, maps or plans, or put them in evidence at the inquiry, a list of these documents should be included with the statement, together with a notice stating the time and place at which these documents may be inspected. The authority must afford a reasonable opportunity to the appellant, section 26 parties and any other interested persons, to inspect these documents and, where practicable, take copies.

The appellant's case is contained in the grounds of appeal and any other written statement lodged with the appeal, and it is unusual for the appellant to lodge any further statement. However, the reporter has power to require the appellant to serve a written statement of the observations which he proposes to put forward at the inquiry.

It is customary for the planning authority and the appellant to exchange productions 10 days before the inquiry, with copies sent to SOIR for the reporter's use. The productions consist of any documents which are to be referred to or put in evidence at the inquiry. It is competent to list productions which are bulky, expensive to copy, or subject to copyright, and offer a reasonable opportunity to inspect and, where practicable, copy the documents. Copies of the productions, or a list of them and notification of where a set may be inspected, must be sent to the section 26 parties.

For major inquiries, a timetable for advance circulation is agreed at the pre-inquiry procedural meeting. Each party submits in advance a statement of the case which it will present at the inquiry, thereby giving notice of the general issues which it intends to raise. Unlike most inquiries, the advance circulation extends to written statements of what each witness will say at the inquiry.

(f) Participants in the Inquiry

Public local inquiries are open to the public. However, only certain persons are permitted to participate in the inquiry. Those entitled to participate are: the appellant, the planning authority, a representative of the Secretary of State (where he gave a direction affecting the application) or government department (where the department's view is referred to in the planning authority's statement), any local authority, the development corporation (where the land is in an area designated as the site of a new town), all section 26 parties, and any person to whom the reporter required notice of the inquiry to be served. In non-delegated appeals, any person who has lodged an objection in respect of the appeal which has not been withdrawn is entitled to participate in the inquiry. In both delegated and non-delegated appeals, any other person may appear at the inquiry at the discretion of the reporter.

Persons may appear on their own behalf or be represented by a solicitor, advocate or any other person (a local authority or development corporation may be represented by one of its officers). The reporter will usually allow, and indeed encourage, one or more persons to appear on behalf of a group of persons who have a similar interest in the matter.

(g) Procedure at Inquiry

Apart from the requirements imposed by the rules, the procedure adopted at the inquiry is at the discretion of the reporter. The emphasis should be on informality. At the commencement of the inquiry the reporter must state the procedure which he proposes to adopt. The reporter will also normally ask the persons attending the inquiry to identify themselves and state whether they intend to participate. If any person entitled to appear at the inquiry fails to do so, it is within the discretion of the reporter to proceed with the inquiry.

The usual format for an inquiry is a morning session between 10am and 1pm, followed by an afternoon session from 2pm until 5pm. This timing may vary to avoid breaks in the evidence of a witness. More frequent breaks may be taken during long inquiries. Participants are normally free to enter and leave the room when the inquiry is sitting.

The evidence on behalf of the appellant is normally heard first. This is followed by the evidence of the other parties in such order as the reporter may determine. If the planning authority is the only other principal party, it is customary for the authority's evidence to follow that of the appellant, with the evidence of third parties heard last. Hearing the evidence in this order has the benefit that all the detailed evidence has been presented before members of the public give evidence. The procedure rules provide for closing statements to be made in the same order, with the appellant having the right to reply to the closing statements made by the other parties, although closing statements are often made in reverse order, enabling the appellant to respond during his closing statement to the closing statements made by the other parties.

Evidence is given through testimony of witnesses, who may be experts or lay people involved in the matter which is the subject of the appeal. A person participating in the inquiry may give evidence as a witness. It is normal practice for each witness to give evidence by reading a prepared written statement, known as a precognition, copies of which are circulated just before the witness begins to speak. The function of the precognition is simple: it saves the reporter from having to write notes throughout the testimony given by the witness. At major inquiries the precognitions are circulated in advance.

Each witness begins by identifying himself and narrating any qualifications which he holds. Where appropriate, their evidence should refer to the productions lodged prior to the inquiry. It is not generally acceptable for any written evidence which has not been lodged as a production to be referred to during evidence, although it may be admitted with the consent of the other participating parties. Maps and photographs can be used to good effect during evidence. The evidence must be relevant to the subject-matter of the inquiry, not repetitous, and should not stray beyond the issues stated in the grounds of appeal and any supporting statement, or in the planning authority's statement of observations.

Once the evidence of the witness has been heard (what lawyers refer to as the examination-in-chief), the other parties participating in the inquiry are given the opportunity to cross-examine the witness. Cross-examination is not limited to matters covered in examination-in-chief and may include matters favourable to the case of the party cross-examining the witness. Cross-examination is normally restricted to opposing parties, although a witness on behalf of a supporting party may be cross-examined either to clarify matters raised or where parts of the witness's evidence are hostile to the cross-examining party. Cross-examination is used to clarify issues, highlight areas of agreement, and undermine the credibility of the evidence by exposing weakness or flaws. Expert evidence may be undermined by exposing incomplete research or faulty conclusions. The reporter may prohibit further cross-examination of a witness which would lead to undue repetition.

Following cross-examination by the other parties, the witness may be re-examined by the party on whose behalf the witness is giving evidence. Re-examination cannot be used to introduce matters which were not raised in the course of the witness' evidence or cross-examination. The purpose of re-examination is to clear up difficulties or ambiguities which arose during the cross-examination, and repair any flaws in the evidence. Finally, the reporter may ask the witness questions on matters which he considers to be relevant to the inquiry. The next witness is then called and the procedure repeated.

The rigid evidential rules applicable to court procedures do not apply to inquiries. Witnesses are not normally put on oath. Corroboration of evidence is not required. Hearsay evidence, such as a report of a conversation which the witness did not hear but which was reported to him, or written evidence from a person who is not called as a witness, will be admissible even though it cannot be tested by cross-examination.[19] Comments can be made which are not supported either by documentary evidence or any expertise or experience claimed by the witness. However, less weight may be attributed to such evidence as a result.

The reporter has the discretionary power to require appearance of witnesses or production of evidence, either on

[19] *T.A. Miller* v. *Minister for Housing and Local Government* [1968] 1 W.L.R. 992.

the request of any party or of his own accord. However, any person may refuse to answer a question or produce evidence on the ground of the legal rules relating to privilege or confidentiality. The reporter may administer oaths and examine witnesses on oath and may accept, in lieu of evidence on oath by any person, a statement in writing by that person.[20]

The reporter must not require or permit the giving or production of any written or oral evidence which would be contrary to the public interest. This may include information relating to the estimated profitability of the proposed development.[21] A representative of the Secretary of State or government department cannot be required to answer a question which is, in the reporter's opinion, directed to the merits, as opposed to the facts, of government policy. Such a question should be disallowed by the reporter as Parliament is the proper forum for raising such questions.[22] However, this principle should not preclude discussion at the inquiry of whether a policy should be departed from in the particular circumstances of the appeal.

Any evidence is admitted at the discretion of the reporter, who may direct that documents tendered in evidence be made available for inspection by any person entitled or permitted to participate in the inquiry and that facilities be provided for taking or obtaining copies. The reporter may take account of any written representations or statements received by him before the inquiry from any person, subject to disclosure at the inquiry and circulation in advance, where practicable. The reporter may allow the planning authority or appellant to alter or add to the statement of observations or any list of documents accompanying the statement, so far as may be necessary to determine the questions in controversy between the parties. However, the reporter must give the appellant or planning authority, and section 26 parties, an adequate opportunity to consider such fresh observations or document. If such an adequate opportunity requires adjournment of the

[20] TCPSA, s. 267.
[21] *Wordie Property Co. Ltd.* v. *Secretary of State for Scotland*, 1984 S.L.T. 345.
[22] D.A.R., r. 9(4) and I.P.R., r. 8(4).

inquiry, the reporter may make a recommendation to the Secretary of State regarding payment of any additional expenses occasioned by the adjournment.

By applying in writing to the Secretary of State not later than 14 days prior to the inquiry, any of the persons entitled to appear may require the appearance of a representative on behalf of the Secretary of State, where he has given a direction affecting the application, or a government department, where the statement of observations by the planning authority includes the written views of the department. An application may be made to the reporter to require the appearance of a representative of a local authority where the statement of observations by the planning authority includes the written views of that local authority. The representative will state the reasons for the direction or view expressed, and give evidence and be subject to cross-examination in the same way as other witnesses.

The reporter may adjourn the inquiry and provided the date, time and place of the adjourned inquiry are announced before adjournment, no further notice shall be required.

(h) Site Inspection

The reporter may make an unaccompanied inspection of the site of the proposed development at any time, without giving notice to persons entitled or permitted to participate in the inquiry. It is usual for an accompanied site inspection to be carried out at a suitable time during or after the inquiry (such an inspection can be required by either the appellant or planning authority). The date and time of this inspection is announced by the reporter during the inquiry. The appellant, planning authority, section 26 parties and any other party to the inquiry are entitled to accompany the reporter on the inspection, and the suitability of the date and time are usually confirmed with all these parties. It is within the discretion of the reporter to proceed with the inspection if any of these parties is not present at the time appointed.

The purpose of the accompanied site inspection is to enable the reporter to clarify, in the presence of the parties, the physical characteristics of the site. It is not an opportunity to place evidence before the reporter or for a discussion of the issues, and the reporter will intervene to prevent either of these situations from continuing.

(i) Procedure after Close of Inquiry

The determination of most planning appeals is delegated by the Secretary of State to the reporters. In these delegated appeals, the reporter prepares his decision letter after the close of the inquiry. In making a decision on the appeal, the reporter may take into consideration any new evidence not raised at the inquiry which he considers to be material. The new evidence may include expert opinion on a matter of fact or any new issue of fact, other than a matter of government policy. Notification of the substance of the new evidence or of the new issue of fact must be given to the appellant, the planning authority and any section 26 party who participated in the inquiry, giving them an opportunity within 21 days to make written representations and/or require the reopening of the inquiry. Even if there is no request from the parties, it is within the discretion of the reporter to reopen the inquiry, if he thinks fit. The procedure for giving notice of the date, time and place of the reopened inquiry is the same as for the original inquiry, except the minimum period of notice is reduced to 21 days.

A different procedure applies where the appeal is determined by the Secretary of State. After the close of the inquiry, the reporter prepares the first part of his report, which includes a list of the parties which participated, together with a list of the witnesses; brief summaries of the evidence and of the main contentions of each party; and the findings of fact. The summary of evidence is not intended to be an exhaustive narrative, and points may be grouped under either subject or issue headings. The reporter is not required to make a finding-in-fact on every disputed issue.[23] Any party has the opportunity to request a copy of the first part of the report, in which case a copy is provided to every party to the inquiry, with an opportunity to lodge comments within 14 days. The report may be amended to take into account any such

[23] *London & Clydeside Properties* v. *City of Aberdeen District Council*, 1984 S.L.T. 50.

comments, provided that the reporter has consulted all the other parties regarding these comments. A matter not raised at the inquiry may not be included in the report except with the consent of all parties. The second part of the report contains the reporter's reasoning and recommendations. This two-part division has led to much litigation on the questions of whether a matter is a finding-in-fact or a conclusion/recommendation, and whether the findings-in-fact provide sufficient foundation for the recommendations.[24] The full report is submitted to the Secretary of State who will use it to decide the appeal. The Secretary of State is not bound to follow the recommendation made by the reporter.

After submission of the report, if the Secretary of State differs from the reporter either on a finding of fact or proposes to take into consideration any new evidence or any new issue of fact, other than a matter of government policy, which was not raised at the inquiry and as a result will disagree with the reporter's recommendation, he must notify the appellant, the planning authority and participating section 26 parties of his disagreement and the reasons for it. An opportunity must be given for them to make written representations within 21 days. In the case of new evidence or issue of fact, the parties have the right to require the reopening of the inquiry. Even in the absence of such a request, the Secretary of State may reopen the inquiry if he thinks fit. The procedure for giving notice of the date, time and place of the reopened inquiry is the same as for the original inquiry, except the minimum period of notice is reduced to 21 days. Even if the new evidence does not persuade the Secretary of State to disagree with the recommendation, the rules of natural justice may still require him to provide the parties with an opportunity to lodge representations in respect of that evidence.

(j) Notification of Decision

The decision on the appeal, made by either the reporter or the Secretary of State, and written reasons for that decision are

[24] Young and Rowan-Robinson, *Scottish Planning Law and Procedure* (1985) p. 503 *et seq*.

notified to the appellant, the planning authority, all section 26 parties, and any person who participated in, or was represented at the inquiry, and asked to be notified. Any of the persons notified of the decision may apply in writing to the Secretary of State within six weeks of notification for an opportunity to inspect any documents listed in the notification and the Secretary of State is required to give the opportunity accordingly.

The reasons should be proper, intelligible and adequate. They should deal with the substantial points raised in the appeal and enable the reader to know what conclusion the decision-maker has reached on the principal controversial issues, and understand on what grounds the appeal has been decided. The degree of particularity required will depend entirely upon the nature of these issues. Decision letters will not be construed as if Acts of Parliament and should be read as a whole. The central question is whether the deficiency of the reasons given has caused substantial prejudice.[25]

Reporter's Role

The reporter is the master of the procedure at the inquiry, and is frequently called upon to make rulings during the inquiry. He is entitled to adopt an interventionist role and ask witnesses questions, rather than merely note the evidence brought out during examination. Following the conclusion of the inquiry or the exchange of written submissions, the reporter either determines the appeal or makes recommendations to the Secretary of State on how the appeal should be decided. In reaching these conclusions, the reporter is entitled to make use of his planning experience and expertise. In common with the planning authority, the reporter is obliged to take account of all material considerations and not merely those raised by the parties at the inquiry or in their written submissions.[26] However, where the reporter identifies a planning issue which he considers may be material to the

[25] *Save Britains Heritage* v. *Secretary of State for the Environment* [1991] 2 All E.R. 10; *Wordie Property Co. Ltd.* v. *Secretary of State for Scotland*, (n. 21, *supra*).
[26] But see *Anwar* v. *Secretary of State for Scotland*, 1992 S.C.L.R. 875.

decision on the appeal, but which had not been addressed by either party, the reporter is not entitled to reach a conclusion on that issue and found upon it as a factor material to his determination of the appeal, without giving the parties an opportunity of commenting on it.[27] The weight to be attached to the material put before him is a matter for the reporter and he is not bound to accept evidence presented by a party even though it is not contested.[28]

Undue Delay

If the appellant appears to be responsible for undue delay in the progress of the appeal, whether by the written submission procedure or public local inquiry, the Secretary of State/reporter may give the appellant notice at any time before or during the determination of the appeal that it will be dismissed, unless the appellant takes specified steps for the expedition of the appeal within a specified time limit.[29] For example, the notice may require the appellant to agree an inquiry date. The Secretary of State/reporter has a discretionary power to dismiss the appeal if these steps are not taken within the time limit. As planning authorities would then have the power to decline to determine any similar application within the next two years (Chapter 5), appellants should comply with these notices.

Appeal Decision

The appeal may be allowed or dismissed, and any part of the decision of the planning authority may be reversed or varied, irrespective of what aspect of the decision is challenged.[30] However, an opportunity to make representations must be given to the planning authority and appellant if the Secretary of State/reporter proposes to reverse or vary any part of the decision to which the appeal does not relate.

[27] *Anduff Holdings* v. *Secretary of State for Scotland*, 1992 S.L.T. 696; *cf. Ladbroke Racing Ltd.* v. *Secretary of State for Scotland* 1990, S.C.L.R. 705.
[28] *Narden Services* v. *Secretary of State for Scotland*, 1993 S.L.T. 871.
[29] TCPSA, s. 33(7A).
[30] s. 33(3).

Before embarking on an appeal against a condition or part of the decision of the planning authority, the disappointed applicant will have to consider the risk of either losing the entire permission, or being burdened with a more onerous condition. This situation has given rise to a practice of making duplicate planning applications (Chapter 5). This enables the decision on one application to be appealed in the knowledge that it is possible to fall back on the decision on the second application if the appeal is unsuccessful.

If planning permission could not have been granted by the planning authority or could not have been granted without the conditions imposed by it, the Secretary of State may decline to determine the appeal or to proceed with the determination.[31]

The Secretary of State/reporter may intimate to the parties, before issuing the decision letter, that he is minded to grant planning permission if a section 50 agreement is concluded (Chapter 6). This gives the parties an opportunity to enter into such an agreement, but this will require the co-operation of the planning authority which may be unforthcoming, given the expectation that the appeal will be dismissed if no agreement can be put in place.

Withdrawal of Appeal

An appeal may be withdrawn in writing at any time prior to issue of the decision letter. However, if the appeal is withdrawn at a late stage the appellant may become liable to pay the expenses of the planning authority.

Expenses

Unlike court cases, expenses do not follow success and the parties involved in a planning appeal are normally expected to meet their own expenses. An award of expenses will only be made if there has been unreasonable behaviour which has caused the party applying for the award to incur unnecessary expense, either because it should not have been necessary for

[31] s. 33(7), as amended.

the case to come before the Secretary of State for determination or because of the manner in which the party against whom the claim is made has conducted his part of the proceedings.[32]

What amounts to unreasonable behaviour will depend on the circumstances of each case. Some of the examples given in the Scottish Office guidance of unreasonable behaviour on the part of the planning authority include failing to give complete, precise and relevant reasons for refusal of an application; reaching its decision without reasonable planning grounds for doing so; refusing an application because of local opposition, where that opposition is not founded upon valid planning reasons; refusing an application where it is clear from the decision on an earlier appeal against the refusal of a similar application that no objection would be seen to a revised application in the form submitted; and failing to take account of relevant statements of government policy in departmental circulars or of relevant precedents of which the planning authority was aware.

Unreasonable behaviour on the part of the appellant may include pursuing an appeal in circumstances where there is no reasonable likelihood of success, for example, as a result of a previous appeal decision in respect of a similar development on the same site; withdrawing the appeal without giving sufficient time for reasonable notice of the cancellation of the inquiry to be given to the parties; and deliberately unco-operative behaviour, including refusing to explain the grounds of appeal or refusing to discuss the appeal.

Unreasonable behaviour on the part of either party may include introducing a new matter at a late stage in the proceedings; refusing either to supply adequate grounds of appeal, or to co-operate in settling agreed facts or supplying relevant information all of which unnecessarily prolongs the proceedings; failing to comply with the requirements of any statutory procedural rules (account will be taken of the extent to which an appellant has taken professional advice); and failure to comply with procedural requirements to the serious prejudice of the other party and leading to the adjournment

[32] ss. 267(7) and 267A; S.D.D. Circular 6/1990, "Awards of Expenses in Appeals."

of the inquiry (an award may be made relating to the extra expense arising from the adjournment).

In exceptional circumstances, such as unreasonable conduct at a public inquiry which causes unnecessary expense, awards of expenses may be made in favour of or against parties other than the appellant and planning authority. In general, third parties will not be eligible to receive expenses where unreasonable behaviour by one of the main parties relates to the substance of that party's case.

Application for expenses should be made to the reporter prior to conclusion of the inquiry, to enable the reporter to hear the parties' arguments on the application. In the case of an appeal by written submissions, application may be made at any time until submission of the party's final written submission. The decision on the application for expenses will be taken on the basis of a further exchange of written submissions. In either procedure, later applications will only be entertained if good reason can be shown for not submitting the application earlier.

Once a full or partial award of expenses has been made, the parties must agree the amount of expenses incurred in relation to the appeal. If they fail to agree, the matter is referred to the Auditor of the Court of Session for decision. A decision to award expenses can only be challenged by judicial review.[33]

Challenge in the Court of Session — Review Proceedings

The Court of Session in Edinburgh has jurisdiction to hear challenges of planning decisions or actions, either by way of the statutory review procedure or under its common-law (non-statutory) judicial review procedure.

Although an application for review is often referred to as an appeal, there are important legal differences between review by the Court of Session and an appeal decided by the Secretary of State. In deciding an appeal, the Secretary of State has the power to declare the original decision wrong,

[33] *City of Aberdeen* v. *Secretary of State for Scotland*, 1993 S.L.T. 1149.

whether as a matter of policy or on the merits of the case, and substitute his own decision in place of that originally reached. In essence, the appeal involves a rehearing and re-decision of the application. In contrast, the Court of Session, as a review body, has no power to rule on the merits or correctness of the original decision. The judges can only decide whether or not the decision was made in a legal manner, and have no power to intervene where a "wrong" decision has been made in a legal manner. Even where a decision is held to be illegal and quashed, the Court of Session has no power to substitute its own decision and must refer the case back to the decision-maker for a fresh decision to be reached. At this stage it is open to the decision-maker to reach the same decision, but in a legal manner. A successful challenge in the Court of Session may, therefore, be a pyrrhic victory.

Unlike a public local inquiry (above), a challenge by statutory review procedure will be subject to the legal rules of evidence and procedure common to all court actions.

Statutory Review

The term statutory review is used here to denote the review powers of the Court of Session conferred by the TCPSA.

Types of Challengeable Decision

There is a statutory right of challenge in the Court of Session against orders[34]:

(a) revoking or modifying planning permission (Chapter 5);
(b) requiring discontinuance of use or alteration or removal of buildings or works (Chapter 7);
(c) prohibiting resumption of or suspending the winning and working of minerals (Chapter 9);
(d) tree preservation orders (Chapter 9);
(e) defining areas of special control of advertisements (Chapter 9); and
(f) revocation of listed building consent (Chapter 9).

[34] s. 233.

The right of statutory challenge in the Court of Session also extends to decisions by the Secretary of State/reporter in connection with:

(a) a called-in application for planning permission (Chapter 5);
(b) a planning appeal, including appeals against waste-land notices (Chapter 9), enforcement notices (Chapter 7), and listed building enforcement notices (Chapter 9), and against the refusal or partial refusal of a certificate of lawful use or development (Chapter 4);
(c) confirmation of a completion notice (Chapter 5);
(d) an application for hazardous substances consent (Chapter 9);
(e) an application for consent under a tree preservation order or advertisement control regulations, or relating to any certificate or direction under any such order or regulations, whether his decision is made on appeal or on an application referred to him for determination in the first instance (Chapter 9);
(f) confirmation or refusal to confirm a purchase notice or listed building purchase notice (Chapters 5 and 9); and
(g) an application for listed building consent referred to him for decision or on an appeal (Chapter 9).

The statutory review procedure also extends to challenges relating to both structure and local plans.[35] These challenges share many of the characteristics discussed below, but the particular issues involved are examined in Chapter 3.

Standing — Persons who may Challenge

Standing (*locus standi*) is the legal term used to describe the classes of person who have a legal right to challenge a decision. If a person has no standing in connection with the court action, the court will refuse to consider his challenge.

[35] s. 232, as amended.

The statutory review procedure can be used by the planning authority directly concerned with one of the decisions/orders specified above, and by any person "aggrieved" by the decision/order.[36] In the absence of any statutory definition, it is impossible to identify all the instances when persons are aggrieved. It is clear, however, that mere dissatisfaction is not enough and some connection to the decision or order will be required, most commonly through participation in the process leading up to that decision or order. Persons "aggrieved" by an appeal decision include persons who have been given notice of a public local inquiry in connection with the appeal, have submitted observations to a public local inquiry and who would have been entitled to participate in the inquiry.[37] Where adjacent proprietors, the planning authority which decided the application, and the regional council, as water and drainage authority, had participated in a public local inquiry, they were held to be persons aggrieved.[38]

Most recently, the Court of Session has taken a broad approach to the question of when a person is aggrieved. A third party who had not objected to an application was held to be a person aggrieved by the appeal decision in relation to the application in the exceptional circumstances where the application and newspaper advertisement failed to give full notice of the proposed development and deprived the third party of his opportunity to make representations.[39]

To identify persons aggrieved, some assistance may be sought from the decisions on title and interest for the purposes of common-law judicial review (below).

Time Limits

Application to the Court of Session for statutory review of an order or action must be made within six weeks from the date

[36] s. 233(1) and (2); Young, "Aggrieved Persons in Planning Law" (1993) S.L.T. (News) 43.
[37] *Strathclyde Regional Council* v. *Secretary of State for Scotland (No. 2)*, 1990 S.L.T. 149 at p. 154E.
[38] *North-East Fife D.C.* v. *Secretary of State for Scotland*, 1992 S.L.T. 373.
[39] *Cumming* v. *Secretary of State for Scotland*, 1993 S.L.T. 228.

on which the order is confirmed or the action is taken.[40] In relation to a decision of the Secretary of State/reporter, the period commences from the date on which the letter recording the decision is typed, signed and date-stamped, and not when notification of the decision is received by the parties.[41] Christmas day and bank holidays are included within the six week period.[42]

Grounds of Challenge

The validity of the order or action can be challenged on either of two grounds[43]:

> (a) that the order or action was not within the statutory powers; or
> (b) that the interests of the challenger have been substantially prejudiced by a failure to comply with any of the relevant requirements in relation to that order or action.[44] This is a reference to the requirements of the TCPSA and the Tribunals and Inquiries Act 1992, and any rules made under those Acts, including the statutory procedures applicable to planning appeals.

Interpretation of these grounds has proved a problem for the courts. However, it is now accepted that under the first ground of challenge,[45]

> "the court can interfere with the Minister's decision if he has acted on no evidence; or if he has come to a conclusion to which, on the evidence, he could not reasonably come; or if he has given a wrong interpretation to the words of a statute; or if he has taken into consideration matters which he ought not to have taken

[40] TCPSA, s. 233(1).
[41] *Griffiths* v. *Secretary of State for the Environment* [1983] 1 All E.R. 439; J.P.L. 237.
[42] *Stainer* v. *Secretary of State for the Home Department* [1994] J.P.L. 44.
[43] TCPSA, s. 233(1)(a) and (b).
[44] s. 233(4)(b).
[45] *Ashbridge Investments* v. *Minister of Housing* [1965] 1 W.L.R. 1320, *per* Lord Denning at p. 1326.

> into account, or vice versa; or has otherwise gone wrong in law."

This wide approach has been summarised into a checklist of four principles known as the Ashbridge formula[46]:

> (a) the decision-maker must not act perversely. In other words, the decision may be overturned if the court considers that no reasonable person in the position of the Secretary of State, properly directing himself on the relevant material, could have reached the conclusion which he did reach;
> (b) he must not take into account irrelevant material or fail to take into account that which is relevant. Provided the Secretary of State/reporter takes account of a matter, the court will not interfere with the weight he gives to that matter in the decision, partly because the court has no opportunity to hear the witnesses or re-examine the evidence;
> (c) he must abide by statutory procedures; and
> (d) he must not depart from the principles of natural justice.

In addition, in non-delegated appeals (above) to differ from the reporter in a finding of fact, the Secretary of State must have sufficient material.[47]

The Secretary of State/reporter must give proper and adequate reasons for the decision, which are clear and intelligible and deal with the substantial points which have been raised. The decision letter should not be subjected to the rigorous interpretation appropriate to the determination of the meaning of a contract or statute.[48]

The Ashbridge formula closely corresponds to the common-law grounds for judicial review. The first ground of statutory challenge will, therefore, be used to review all errors of law

[46] *Per* Forbes J. in *Seddon Properties* v. *Secretary of State for the Environment* [1978] J.P.L. 835.
[47] *Coleen Properties* v. *M.H.L.G.* [1971] 1 W.L.R. 433.
[48] For example, *City of Glasgow District Council* v. *Secretary of State for Scotland and William Hill (Scotland) Ltd.*, 1992 S.C.L.R. 453; S.P.L.P. 36:56.

which are reviewable under the common-law judicial review procedure (below).

As a result of the width of the first ground of challenge, the second ground is only likely to be used where there is a procedural defect which does not amount to an error of law and is, therefore, not reviewable under the first ground (or the common-law judicial review procedure), such as breach of a non-mandatory procedural requirement[49] or failure to give reasons as required by statute or regulations.[50] For a successful challenge under the second ground, the interests of the challenger must have been substantially prejudiced as a result of the failure to comply with the relevant requirements. It seems that any defect in procedure which is more than a technical or insignificant defect will be assumed to have caused substantial prejudice.[51] It is not necessary for the challenger to show that the decision would have been different if the statutory requirements had been complied with — "the loss of a chance of being better off" will be enough to constitute substantial prejudice.[52]

Powers of the Court

The Court of Session has the power to suspend, by interim order, the operation of the order (except a tree preservation order) or action which is the subject of challenge until the final determination of the proceedings.[53]

If the Court determines that the order or action in question is not within the powers of the Act or that the interests of the applicant have been substantially prejudiced by a failure to comply with any of the relevant requirements, it has the discretion to quash that order or action.[54] The court may

[49] For discussion of mandatory and directory requirements, see *London & Clydeside Estates* v. *Aberdeen District Council* [1980] 1 W.L.R. 182, *e.g. per* Lord Hailsham L.C. at p. 189H; *James* v. *Secretary of State for Wales* [1966] 1 W.L.R. 135, *per* Lord Denning M.R. at p. 142.

[50] *Wordie Property Co. Ltd.* v. *Secretary of State for Scotland*, 1984 S.L.T. 345.

[51] *Ibid., per* Lord President Emslie at p. 356.

[52] *Hibernian Property* v. *Secretary of State for the Environment* (1973) 27 P. & C.R. 197, *per* Browne J. at p. 218.

[53] TCPSA, s. 233(4)(a).

[54] s. 233(4)(b).

decide not to quash the order or action on the grounds that the same decision would have been reached in any case, or that the decision was correct, but for the wrong reasons.[55] With the exception of tree preservation orders and orders designating areas of special control under the advertisement control regulations, the court has no power to quash only part of the whole order or action.[56]

Following the quashing of a decision, the matter is referred back to the decision-maker for a fresh decision to be reached. Where a fundamental error of law has been made, it may be necessary to start the decision-making process afresh.[57] Any new evidence or circumstances which had arisen in the meantime, such as the adoption of different policies, must be considered and new arguments can be raised by the parties. However, a fresh start may not always be required. For example, if the challenger has not been given an opportunity to make representations on a point, it may be sufficient to give the challenger that opportunity and to allow the other parties an opportunity to comment on those representations.

The powers of the court expose the limitations of statutory review proceedings for challenging planning orders or actions. Even if the decision is challenged successfully, the court may refuse to exercise its discretionary power to quash the decision. If the court quashes the decision, it is open to the decision-maker to reach the same decision as before, but in a legal manner. It is, therefore, possible that the challenger may be able to achieve nothing more than obtain further time for negotiation.

Expenses

Unlike planning appeals (above), the successful party in the Court of Session will normally be awarded his expenses against the other party (expenses follow success). Before commencing court action, the challenger must consider whether, if his challenge is unsuccessful, he can afford to pay

[55] *Glasgow D.C.* v. *Secretary of State for Scotland*, 1982 S.L.T. 28.

[56] B.A.A. v. *Secretary of State for Scotland*, 1979 S.C. 200.

[57] *Kingswood District Council* v. *Secretary of State for Environment* [1988] J.P.L. 248.

the costs incurred by the other party (or parties) in relation to the court action. However, the costs of preparing for court action and the danger of liability to pay the costs of a successful challenger may persuade the decision-maker to negotiate a compromise.

Judicial Review

In addition to the statutory review jurisdiction discussed above, the Court of Session has a common-law supervisory jurisdiction to review decisions of inferior courts, tribunals and other administrative and public bodies to ensure that they do not exceed or abuse their statutory jurisdiction, powers or authority. This jurisdiction also allows the court to insist upon standards of rationality and fairness of procedure (for example, the rules of natural justice), in addition to what is expressly required by statute. In the exercise of this jurisdiction, as with statutory review, the court acts as a review body and cannot substitute its own decision for the decision which is challenged (the distinction between review and appeal procedure is discussed above).[58]

The supervisory jurisdiction of the court is exercised through decisions on petitions for judicial review. This judicial review procedure offers a quick decision on the challenge, and a wider range of remedies than is available to the court under the statutory review procedure. However, there are limitations on the availability of judicial review procedure. If there is a statutory remedy available to the challenger, judicial review may be excluded as a result of a statutory ouster clause or the duty to exhaust a statutory remedy. Any person seeking to use judicial review procedure must also establish that they have sufficient standing to challenge the decision and that they have not delayed in making their challenge.

Types of Decision

Planning is a statutory function, with powers conferred upon planning authorities and the Secretary of State by statute and

[58] *West* v. *Scottish Prison Service*, 1992 S.L.T. 636.

exercised for the public benefit. Planning decisions are, therefore, a prime example of decisions which are susceptible to judicial review under the common-law supervisory jurisdiction. In general, all forms of planning decisions, orders and actions are susceptible to judicial review, although a petition for judicial review must always satisfy the restrictions examined below.

Ouster Clauses: Exclusion of Judicial Review

Where provisions in Acts of Parliament have sought to oust completely the jurisdiction of the court by precluding the courts from entertaining a challenge at any time (such provisions are known as ouster clauses), the courts have been willing to resist the exclusion of their judicial review powers and find jurisdiction to hear the challenge. In contrast, where a statutory review procedure offers the courts a limited opportunity to review the decision, the courts have accepted restrictions on their common-law jurisdiction. This latter approach has been consistently taken by both the Scottish and English courts towards challenges of planning decisions.

As well as providing a statutory review procedure, the TCPSA states that the orders and actions which may be challenged under that procedure cannot be questioned in any other legal proceedings.[59] As a result, any common-law judicial review proceedings to question the validity of such an order or action will not be competent, whether or not the six-week time limit for commencement of statutory review proceedings has expired.[60] For these purposes, it is irrelevant that the challenger had no knowledge of the matter complained of during that six-week period.[61]

Duty to Exhaust Alternative Remedies

Even in the absence of an ouster clause, the existence of a statutory procedure to challenge a decision may exclude any

[59] TCPSA, s. 231(1).
[60] *Pollock* v. *Secretary of State for Scotland*, 1993 S.L.T. 1173; 1993 S.P.L.P. 38:19.
[61] *Martin* v. *Bearsden & Milngavie District Council*, 1987 S.L.T. 300.

petition for judicial review of that decision.[62] The well-established principle, that failure to exercise a statutory remedy bars resort to the common-law supervisory jurisdiction of the Court of Session, is incorporated into its rules governing judicial review procedure.[63] As a result, judicial review procedure is generally unavailable where there is a statutory right of appeal.[64] The rules specifically state that the availability of the statutory review procedure for planning decisions (albeit for six weeks only) excludes judicial review, emphasising that the common law and statutory procedures are mutually exclusive.

This strict position means that any petition for judicial review will be incompetent where a statutory remedy exists. For example, the applicant for planning permission has a statutory right of appeal against the decision of the planning authority on the application. Thus, any challenge attempted under judicial review procedure would be incompetent as the applicant must first exhaust the statutory remedy. Third parties have no statutory right to challenge the decision of the authority and are, therefore, free to apply for judicial review. An extreme example of the strictness of this position lies in the decisions that judicial review of the decision to serve a stop notice is incompetent, notwithstanding the lack of a statutory means of appealing, on the grounds that there is a right to compensation for loss due to the stop notice.[65]

An exception is made to this duty to exhaust an alternative remedy in "exceptional circumstances." The extent of this exception is uncertain and the decisions of the court on this point very much depend upon the facts and circumstances of each case. The seriousness of the alleged illegality and the effectiveness of the statutory procedure to remedy the illegality may be important factors. However it is clear that the "exceptional circumstances" test creates a strong presumption in favour of exhaustion of the statutory remedy.

[62] See generally, Collar, "Judicial Review: The Significance of an Alternative Remedy" (1991) J.L.S.S. 299.

[63] Rule of Court 260B(3).

[64] *Bellway Homes* v. *Strathclyde Regional Council*, 1979 S.C. 92, 1980 S.L.T. 66.

[65] *Central Regional Council* v. *Clackmannan District Council*, 1983 S.L.T. 666; *Earl Car Sales* v. *Edinburgh District Council*, 1984 S.L.T. 8. See also Chap. 7.

Standing

The petitioner must have standing, or title and interest to sue, before the court has jurisdiction to hear the challenge. As a general rule, title and interest is a preliminary matter which should not be determined by favourable or adverse decision on the merits of the case (there is no Scottish equivalent of the English procedure for seeking leave to apply for judicial review, which requires the court to reach a preliminary conclusion on the merits of the case). The obvious illegality of the decision sought to be challenged will not relieve the petitioner of the requirement to show title and interest to challenge the decision.

Title has been described as "some legal relation which gives him (the challenger) some right which the person against whom he raises the action either infringes or denies."[66] Where a decision by the Secretary of State on another appeal prejudged an appeal by the petitioners, their title to seek judicial review of that decision was derived from their pending appeal.[67] The existence of a statutory right of objection against a decision seems to confer title to sue in respect of that decision.[68] Thus, the lack of any statutory right of objection against a decision by the regional council to call-in an application meant that the petitioners had no title to challenge that decision.[69] While previously a neighbour had no title to challenge a grant of planning permission,[70] the introduction of the neighbour notification process, which gives notifiable neighbours a statutory right of objection to planning applications, gives notifiable neighbours title to sue.[71] Third parties now have a greater statutory role in the planning process and this will give such persons more extensive title to challenge decisions. It seems that any person who lodges an objection to an application for planning permission may have title to challenge a decision relating to

[66] *D. & J. Nichol* v. *Dundee Harbour Trustees*, 1915 S.C. (H.L.) 7, *per* Lord Dunedin at p. 12.
[67] *Lakin* v. *Secretary of State for Scotland*, 1988 S.L.T. 780.
[68] *Black* v. *Tennent* (1899) 1 F. 423.
[69] *Bellway Homes* v. *Strathclyde Regional Council* (n. 64, *supra*).
[70] *Simpson* v. *Edinburgh Corporation*, 1960 S.C. 313. See also Chap. 5.
[71] *Pollock* v. *Secretary of State for Scotland* (n. 60, *supra*).

that application.[72] The court has stated that there seems no reason, in principle, why an individual should not sue to prevent breach by a public body of a duty owed by it to the public,[73] and that the concept of title should not be limited to a statutory right of appeal.[74]

In addition to title to sue, the petitioner must also establish "interest." This requirement was formerly described as relating to the petitioner's "pecuniary right and his status,"[75] but could now be described as sufficient interest.[76] It seems certain that, depending upon the circumstances of the case, the following parties will have sufficient interest: the applicant for permission, the planning authority and notifiable neighbours. Other third parties may have sufficient interest, but pressure groups cannot expect to prove a legal interest merely by alluding to the objects and work of the group.[77] This must surely raise a question mark over the rights of third-party groups, such as amenity and conservation societies, to challenge planning decisions by petition for judicial review, unless they have a statutory right of objection. (However, a statutory right of objection could arise merely through the newspaper advertisement of the application, Chapter 5.)

When considering standing for these purposes, the decisions relating to persons aggrieved in relation to standing for statutory review should be of general assistance. These were discussed earlier in this chapter.

Time Limits

There is no Scottish equivalent to the (broadly) three-month time limit for making an application for judicial review to the English courts. As a result, the right to challenge a decision

[72] *Pickering* v. *Kyle & Carrick District Council*, 1991 G.W.D. 7–361; *Trusthouse Forte (U.K.) Ltd.* v. *Perth & Kinross District Council*, 1990 S.L.T. 737; *James Aitken & Sons (Meat Producers)* v. *City of Edinburgh District Council*, 1990 S.L.T. 241.

[73] *Wilson* v. *I.B.A.*, 1979 S.L.T. 279.

[74] *Per* Lord Clyde in *Scottish Old Peoples Welfare Council Petitioners*, 1987 S.L.T. 179.

[75] *Swanson* v. *Manson* (1907) 14 S.L.T. 737 at p. 738.

[76] *Per* Lord Clyde in *Scottish Old Peoples Welfare Council Petitioners*, *op. cit.*

[77] For example, *Scottish Old Peoples Welfare Council Petitioners*, *ibid.*

by judicial review is only extinguished by prescription after 20 years, but may be barred within the 20-year period by mora, taciturnity and acquiescence.[78]

The essence of the plea of mora, taciturnity and acquiescence is that, by reason of delay, the petitioner has abandoned his right of challenge and is personally barred from seeking to challenge the decision by way of judicial review. Whereas the time limit for statutory review may expire before the challenger is aware of reasons for challenging the decision, the plea of mora, taciturnity and acquiescence requires knowledge on the part of the challenger. However, it must be emphasised that, even if the delay does not bar judicial review, the court may exercise its discretion to refuse to overturn a decision if substantial hardship or prejudice, or detriment to good administration might be caused by the delay involved.

There is little case law on this plea, but it seems that it has three elements: the petitioner must have knowledge of the decision and why it is unsatisfactory to him, but not necessarily knowledge of legal grounds of challenge; he must delay challenging the decision after gaining this knowledge; and, finally (although this element may not be essential), he is silent in the face of actions by other parties on the faith of the validity of the decision.

While a delay of 10 months barred a petition for judicial review in one case,[79] in another a delay of seven months was not immediately fatal even although the applicants had been aware of the grounds of challenge during the whole of that period and there had been substantial actions on the part of the planning authority and the developer on the strength of the validity of the decision.[80] This may indicate a general reluctance to disqualify a challenge at the first hurdle before the merits of the case have been discussed. However, the only safe course for potential challengers is to seek legal advice as soon as they are aware that a decision is

[78] See generally; Collar, "Mora and Judicial Review," 1989 S.L.T. (News) 309 and "Mora and Judicial Review — Some Further Thoughts," 1992 S.L.T. (News) 335.

[79] *Hanlon* v. *Traffic Commissioner*, 1988 S.L.T. 802.

[80] *Pickering* v. *Kyle & Carrick District Council*, 1991 G.W.D. 7–361.

unsatisfactory. Legal advisors must ensure that a petition for judicial review is lodged as soon as possible thereafter.

Grounds for Judicial Review

The grounds for judicial review are based upon *ultra vires* (literally "beyond powers") conduct, where the decision-maker has acted illegally by acting outwith its powers. The grounds for judicial review frequently overlap and new grounds are always developing. Indeed, it is often difficult to identify the particular grounds at issue in a court case. Traditionally, the grounds for judicial review were classified under three heads: jurisdiction, discretion and natural justice, but have recently been reclassified under the heads of illegality, irrationality, and procedural impropriety.[81]

(a) Illegality

The decision-maker must understand the law that regulates its decision-making power and give effect to it. This includes the need to keep within its jurisdiction and not act outwith its statutory powers, to avoid acting in bad faith, and the requirement that any statutory discretionary power be exercised properly.

Many planning powers are discretionary and seem to confer unfettered power upon decision-makers. However, limits to the exercise of these powers have been developed by the courts, allowing them to intervene to prevent abuse of discretionary powers. For example, when determining applications for planning permission, planning authorities have the statutory power to impose "such conditions as they think fit." Although the wording of this statutory power would seem to give authorities absolute discretion, the courts have evolved a series of legal restrictions on the exercise of this power (Chapter 6).

[81] *Per* Lord Diplock in the G.C.H.Q. case — *C.C.S.U.* v. *Minister for the Civil Service* [1985] A.C. 374 at p. 410–11.

Each individual exercise of discretion must be free and not pre-judged. It is well-established that each planning application must be decided upon its individual merits. The concept of precedent, whereby the planning authority is bound to act in accordance with previous similar decisions, has no place in planning law (although consistency in decision-making is encouraged by the Scottish Office). Similarly, the decision-maker may formulate a policy for dealing with future decision-making, but the possibility of making an exception to that policy must be considered in each case, otherwise the policy has fettered the exercise of discretion. Thus although a presumption is to be introduced that planning applications will be determined according to the policies expressed in development plans, provision is made for material planning considerations in individual cases to overcome this presumption (Chapter 5). In addition, unless authorised by statute, the decision-maker must not delegate its discretion and must always make the final decision itself (Chapter 5). A planning authority cannot bind itself in a section 50 agreement to grant planning permission (Chapter 6).

Discretionary powers must also be exercised reasonably, in the special legal sense of Wednesbury reasonableness. This requires the decision-maker to take into account all material considerations and ignore all irrelevant matters or ulterior motives. Powers conferred by the planning legislation must, therefore, be exercised for a planning purpose, otherwise an ulterior motive has been taken into account. For example, the discretionary power to impose conditions upon a grant of planning permission was illegally exercised when a condition was imposed upon a housing development requiring that the houses should first be occupied by persons on the council's housing waiting list, because the power was exercised to require the developer to assume the duty of the council at his own expense.[82]

The court will quash the decision only if the consideration which was ignored or the irrelevant factor which was taken into account influenced the decision, and the same decision

[82] *R.* v. *Hillingdon London Borough Council, ex p. Royco Homes* [1974] 2 All E.R. 643.

would not have been reached on other valid reasons.[83] However, the consideration need not have been the dominant reason for the decision; provided it was not an insignificant or insubstantial factor in the decision reached, there will be no requirement to prove that a different conclusion would have been reached had it not been taken into account.[84]

(b) *Irrationality*

"Irrationality" is defined as:

> "a decision which is so outrageous in its defiance of logic or of accepted moral standards that no sensible person who applied his mind to the question to be decided could have arrived at it."

Previously this formed part of the concept of Wednesbury reasonableness: "a conclusion so unreasonable that no reasonable authority could ever have come to it." The requirement for such an extreme degree of unreasonableness should act as a safeguard to prevent the court from interfering with the merits of a decision.

(c) *Procedural Impropriety*

The supervisory jurisdiction allows the court to insist on standards of procedural fairness beyond what is expressly required by statute. Judicial review on this ground does not relate to the content of the decision, rather to the manner in which it was reached. The decision is tainted by a flaw in the decision-making process. Judicial development of this area of the law has given rise to suggestions that there is a duty to act fairly.[85] The degree of procedural fairness required varies depending upon the circumstances of each decision. For

[83] *R.* v. *Broadcasting Complaints Commission ex p. Owen* [1985] Q.B. 1153.
[84] *Simplex* v. *Secretary of State for the Environment* [1988] 3 P.L.R. 25.
[85] *Per* Lord Roskill in G.C.H.Q. case (n. 81, *supra*) at p. 414; *Lakin* v. *Secretary of State for Scotland*, 1988 S.L.T. 780.

example, an oral hearing cannot be demanded in every circumstance.

Included under the head of "procedural impropriety" are failures to observe statutory procedural rules, and breaches of the rules of natural justice, which form a procedural code implied by the common law and supplementing any statutory provisions. There are two limbs to the rules of natural justice: the right to be heard and the rule against bias.

The right to be heard (*audi alteram partem*) includes the right to have the opportunity to present your case and know the basis of the case presented by the other side, as well as the right to a fair hearing — each party should have a "fair crack of the whip."[86] Some planning authorities give applicants the opportunity either to respond formally to objections made to a proposed development or to amend the application to counter the objections. It may be arguable that such an opportunity must be offered to ensure that the applicant is given a fair hearing. Similarly, if the application is amended, but not to such an extent that the planning authority require a fresh application to be submitted, there may be a duty to inform all those who lodged objections to the original application of the amendments and allow them to make further representations.[87] The law has not evolved to the extent that definite limits may be expressed. The only safe course is for the planning authority to assess at each stage in the progress of the application whether it has acted fairly in respect of all parties. In one case, by representing to the councillors determining the application that the outstanding problem had been resolved, without drawing attention to the representations maintained by an objector, the planning officers had not allowed a fair opportunity for the objections to be considered.[88]

In the context of planning appeals, the right to be heard extends to the right to request a public local inquiry (above). The written submissions procedure (above) provides a good example of the procedures necessary to ensure that each party

[86] *Fairmount Investments* v. *Secretary of State for the Environment* [1976] 2 All E.R. 865.
[87] *Lochore* v. *Moray District Council*, 1992 S.L.T. 16.
[88] *Castelow* v. *Stirling D.C.* 1992 G.W.D. 19–1139.

is given a fair hearing. Where an appeal was determined on issues not raised by either party and no opportunity was offered for submissions to be made by the parties on these issues, there was a breach of natural justice.[89]

The other limb to natural justice is the rule against bias (*nemo judex in re sua*). Mere suspicion of bias influencing the decision may be sufficient for the decision to be declared illegal[90]: justice must not only be done, but be seen to be done. An example of this principle can be seen in the non-statutory code of conduct whereby any councillor who has an interest, financial or otherwise, in a planning application, should declare the existence of the interest and take no part in the discussion and determination of that application. This system is voluntary and individual councillors must decide whether their interest in the application is sufficiently close to warrant self-disqualification. Inevitably, in smaller communities it is more difficult to avoid conflicts of interest arising and this may have to be recognised when assessing suspicion of bias. There may be a suspicion of bias where a councillor is a business competitor of the applicant and, therefore, has an interest in the failure of a business-related planning application, although the courts have ruled that is would be going too far to say that this necessarily disqualified him.[91]

The rule against bias does not prevent the grant of planning permission for development of land owned by the planning authority, even in circumstances where the authority has agreed to lease the land to the applicant if the planning application is successful.[92] Special procedural rules apply to proposals for development by the planning authority (Chapter 9).

The reporter hearing a planning appeal must also avoid creating any suspicion of bias. A conversation between a reporter and officials of the planning authority following the close of an inquiry created such a suspicion and, therefore,

[89] *Anduff Holdings* v. *Secretary of State for Scotland* 1992 S.L.T. 696.

[90] *Steeples* v. *Derbyshire C.C.* [1984] 3 All E.R. 468; *Simmons* v. *Secretary of State for the Environment*, [1985] J.P.L. 253.

[91] *R.* v. *Holderness B.C., ex p. James Roberts Developments Ltd., The Times*, December 22, 1992.

[92] *R.* v. *St. Edmundsbury B.C., ex p. Investors in Industry* [1985] 3 All E.R. 234; *cf. Steeples* v. *Derbyshire C.C.* (n. 90, *supra*).

amounted to a breach of natural justice.[93] Where the reporter and both parties indulged in a drink after the inquiry, it was considered inadvisable for a reporter to remain for a fresh drink after the departure of one party, although there was no breach of natural justice.[94] Similarly, there was doubtful wisdom in the reporter lunching with and travelling to the site visit with a planning authority witness, even with the consent of the appellant.[95]

As part of the requirement for procedural fairness, the law protects legitimate expectations. A legitimate expectation is normally equated with a right to be heard or a duty to consult, although the concept is wider.[96] Legitimate expectations can be created by promise or by an established practice which it is reasonable to expect will continue. If a planning authority undertakes to consult a person on a planning application or has always consulted that person on similar applications, that person may have a legitimate expectation of being consulted prior to determination of the application. Failure to fulfil that expectation may result in a challengable decision. It is unfortunate that diligent planning authorities, which consult widely to gauge public reaction to planning proposals, may create enforceable legitimate expectations of consultation, whilst authorities which rarely consult any persons other than statutory consultees will avoid creating such expectations.

If the decision-maker creates an express legitimate expectation that a policy will be followed, then the policy cannot be changed without giving an opportunity to discuss this change to those with the expectation. However, the courts have rejected the argument that this could extend to a legitimate expectation that the Secretary of State would follow previous indications of policy and grant planning permission.[97] The expectation does not prevent a change in policy, but merely

[93] *Simmons* v. *Secretary of State for the Environment* (n. 90, *supra*).
[94] *Cotterell* v. *Secretary of State for the Environment* [1991] J.P.L. 1155.
[95] *Fox* v. *Secretary of State for the Environment* [1993] J.P.L. 448.
[96] R. v. *Secretary of State for the Home Department, ex p. Ruddock* [1987] 2 All E.R. 518.
[97] *R.* v. *Secretary of State for the Environment, ex p. Barratt (Guildford)* [1990] J.P.L. 25. See also *R.* v. *Great Yarmouth Borough Council, ex p. Botton Bros. Arcades* [1988] J.P.L. 18.

requires the decision-maker to consult with the person holding the legitimate expectation before making the change and to allow representations to be made regarding the change.[98] An appeal decision was quashed on the ground of unfairness where, by reason of the decision-maker's inconsistency in the interpretation and application of his policy, a person dealing with him had been taken by surprise and had had no adequate opportunity to meet the new approach before the relevant decision was made.[99]

Legitimate expectation is a developing area of the law and the courts have yet to issue a judgment explaining its limits in planning. Clearly much will depend on the circumstances of individual cases. From recent decisions, it seems that legitimate expectations overlap with the duty of fairness. Where the applicants for planning permission failed to carry out their legal duty to notify a neighbour of the application, the neighbour drew this to the attention of the planning authority and indicated that he wished to object to the application, but reserved the statement of his reasons until he had been properly notified. The applicants then submitted an amended application in respect of which the neighbour was not notifiable and for which the planning authority granted permission two days later. This grant of planning permission was declared illegal because the planning authority had prejudiced the legitimate expectation of the neighbour of being able to lodge an objection against the application.[1]

Another decision of the Court of Session indicates that in circumstances where only one type of development can proceed in an area, such as a superstore, applicants whose applications have been called-in or are the subject of appeal, may have a legitimate expectation of a hearing being held to consider the merits of all sites.[2] An applicant whose appeal against refusal of planning permission was pending sought to challenge the Secretary of State's decision not to call-in

[98] *R.* v. *Secretary of State for Health, ex p. United States Tobacco International Inc.* [1992] 1 Q.B. 353.

[99] *Barnet Meeting Room Trust* v. *Secretary of State for the Environment* [1993] J.P.L. 739.

[1] *Lochore* v. *Moray District Council* (n. 87, *supra*).

[2] *Lakin Ltd.* v. *Secretary of State for Scotland* (n. 85, *supra*).

another superstore application. The court held that the applicant had been deprived of its legitimate expectation of having its appeal determined at a public local inquiry and the Secretary of State had prejudged the issue and pre-empted the appeal. In considering the merits of the alternative site, which was the subject of the applicants' appeal, the Secretary of State failed to give them a fair hearing and, therefore, acted illegally. The decision would probably have been valid if the Secretary of State had ignored the existence of alternative sites completely, even although this would still have effectively prejudged the outcome of the applicant's appeal.

As the concept of legitimate expectation demonstrates, the boundaries of the grounds for judicial review are continually developing.

Procedure

An application for judicial review is made by petition to the Court of Session. There is a special accelerated procedure intended to promote flexibility and rapid decisions where required.[3] The requirement that the petition be signed by an advocate or solicitor acts as a practical (rather than a legal) obstacle to lay persons representing themselves (referred to as party litigants) in a judicial review case.

Powers of the Court

The discretionary powers of the Court of Session under judicial review procedure are wider than its statutory review powers (above). In addition to quashing an illegal decision, either in whole or in part, judicial review procedure allows the court to prevent an illegal decision being made or restrain illegal conduct (by interdict), to force a body to carry out a stated duty (by specific implement), to declare the true legal position (make a declaration), and to award damages.[4] It also has power to make any interim order which it thinks fit, pending determination of the action.

[3] R.C. 260B, introduced in 1985. See, St. Clair and Davidson, "Judicial Review in Scotland" (1986), Chap. 2.

[4] R.C. 260B(4)(b).

Expenses

The normal rule of expenses following success applies: the successful challenger will normally obtain an order of expenses against the decision-maker, while the unsuccessful challenger will be liable to pay the costs of the other parties involved in the court action, in addition to his own.

Other Methods of Challenge

Ombudsman

Complaints relating to decisions and actions of planning authorities on planning applications can now be made direct to the Commissioner for Local Administration in Scotland (known as the ombudsman).[5] The jurisdiction of the Commissioner is limited. There is a twelve-month time limit from the day on which the complainer first had notice of the matters alleged in the complaint. If there is a legal remedy available, the Commissioner will investigate the matter only if, in the circumstances, it is not reasonable to expect the complainer to resort to that remedy. There must be "maladminstration" leading to "injustice." Although the Commissioner has substantial powers of investigation, there is no power to enforce his/her decisions or recommendations. However, recommendations for compensation or redress are frequently implemented by planning authorities.

Sue for Negligence or Breach of Contract

Planning authorities are subject to the ordinary law of delict and contract. Thus, where an individual has suffered harm as a consequence of either the unlawful actions or the omissions of a public official or public body, an action for damages may be available. However, the current trend is to deny any liability in negligence of public authorities for the exercise of their statutory powers.[6] Where a person fails to fulfil the

[5] Local Government (Scotland) Act 1975, Pt. III, as amended. The Commissioner can be contacted at 23 Walker Street, Edinburgh EH3 7HX.
[6] *Ryeford Homes* v. *Sevenoaks D.C.* [1990] J.P.L. 36; 1989 S.P.L.P. 27:53.

conditions of a section 50 agreement, the normal remedies for a breach of contract will be available to the other parties to the agreement (Chapter 6).

European Law

European Community law has already introduced the environmental assessment procedure (Chapter 5) and several statutory designations protecting areas of land (Chapter 9). The Maastrict Treaty recognises the competence of the Community (now the European Union) in relation to planning and land-use policies. As the role of the European Community in planning law increases, there is the prospect of an individual bringing a case before the European Court of Justice alleging a failure to fulfil Community obligations in relation to planning.

It is already possible for an individual to bring a case involving planning law before the European Court on Human Rights, for example, alleging a breach of article 8 of the European Convention on Human Rights: "Everyone has the right to respect for his private and family life, his home and his correspondence."[7] However, if planning powers are exercised in the public interest and in accordance with the law, any petition is unlikely to be successful.

[7] Evans and Watchman, "European Convention on Human Rights and Fundamental Freedoms — A New Dimension to Planning Law?" (1981) 4 S.P.L.P. 65 and 1983 S.P.L.P. 44.

Chapter 9

PARTICULAR CONTROLS

The provisions examined in the previous chapters generally have universal application. The TCPSA also contains particular controls which apply to items of special significance, such as listed buildings, or to designated areas, such as conservation areas, or to specific forms of development, such as mineral extraction, or to classes of developers, such as the Crown and planning authorities. The following examination of these often complex controls necessarily takes the form of an overview rather than a complete and detailed exposition.

Listed Buildings

The Secretary of State has the power to compile lists of buildings of special architectural or historic interest, referred to as listed buildings.[1] There are currently some 39,500 listed buildings in Scotland. Historic Scotland is the Scottish Office Department with responsibility for listed buildings.[2]

The term "building" includes any structure or erection, and items such as telephone boxes and bridges have been designated as listed buildings. Any object or structure fixed to the listed building, or which falls within its curtilage and has formed part of the land since before July 1, 1948 is treated as part of the building.[3] The primary test of what is listed is the circumstances of the site at the date of statutory listing. There is no statutory definition of "curtilage," but this term broadly includes any land or building used for the comfortable enjoyment of the listed building or serving its purpose in

[1] TCPSA, s. 52(1), as amended.
[2] Contact at 20 Brandon Street, Edinburgh EH3 5RA; tel: 031 556 8400.
[3] s. 52(7), as amended.

some necessary or reasonably useful way, although not marked off or enclosed in any way (Chapter 4). A listed building may, therefore, include stables, mews blocks or garden walls within its grounds, notwithstanding that these have passed into separate ownership since the date of listing, but not buildings erected within its curtilage since July 1, 1948. Importantly, listing covers the interior as well as the exterior of the building irrespective of whether the list contains a detailed interior description.

It is open to planning authorities or any person or body to suggest to the Secretary of State/Historic Scotland that a building be listed. When considering whether to list a building, the Secretary of State may take into account not only the building itself, but also the contribution of its exterior to the architectural or historic interest of any group of buildings of which it forms part.[4] He may also consider the desirability of preserving any feature of the building on the ground of its architectural or historic interest. Before compiling or approving the list, persons or bodies with special knowledge or interest in buildings of architectural or historic interest must be consulted. There is no right of appeal against listing, but representations can be made to the Secretary of State. Listed buildings may be removed from the list, either following representations by an interested party or the demolition or alteration of the building.

Listed buildings are divided into three non-statutory categories according to merit:

A — buildings of national or international importance; either architectural or historic, or fine little-altered examples of some particular period, style or building type.

B — buildings of regional or more than local importance; or major examples of some period, style or building type which may have been somewhat altered.

[4] Further principles of listing are specified in para. 1.7 of the Memorandum of Guidance on Listed Buildings and Conservation Areas (new edition, 1993) published by Historic Scotland.

C(S) — buildings of local importance; lesser examples of any period, style or building type, whether as originally constructed or as the result of subsequent alteration; simple, well-proportioned traditional buildings, often forming part of a planned group, e.g. an estate or an industrial complex or grouping well in association with buildings in a higher category.
(The previous C category has been phased out.)

These categories have no legal effect, but are used as a guide to the importance of the listed building and might, therefore, suggest the degree of difficulty which may be anticipated in obtaining listed building consent in relation to the building.

After the list has been compiled and approved, a copy of the relevant part is deposited with the planning authority, which is responsible for serving notice on the owner, lessee and occupier of the building intimating its listing. Copies of the list of such buildings must also be made available for public inspection.

Listed Building Control

(a) *Listed Building Consent*

Listed building consent is required in advance for demolition of a listed building or its alteration or extension in any manner which would affect its character as a building of special architectural or historic interest.[5] The need for listed building consent is not satisfied by a grant of planning permission, nor an express or deemed consent under the control of advertisement regulations. It is an offence to carry out demolition or such works without listed building consent, or to fail to comply with conditions attached to such a consent (below). An application may be made for retrospective consent to authorise works already done.[6] Unlike planning permission, a failure to obtain listed building consent can

[5] TCPSA, s. 53(1) and (2), as amended.
[6] s. 53(2A).

never become immune from enforcement action through the passage of time.

The requirement for consent extends to objects or structures which are fixed to a listed building, or come within its curtilage and have done so since before July 1, 1948. In consequence, buildings which were originally ancillary to the listed building, but are now under separate ownership can continue to be regarded as listed buildings on the basis of location within the curtilage of the principal building.

It is important to note that, unlike planning permission, consent may be required for internal alterations to a listed building irrespective of whether the internal features are described in the listing.

There are guidelines for identifying whether works affect the character of a listed building and, therefore, require consent.[7] For example, stone cleaning and proposals to replace traditional windows with modern forms of glazing will usually require listed building consent. Staircases, chimney pieces, panelling, doors and door furniture, dadoes, plasterwork and other interior features can all form part of the character of the listed building, and any changes to these items may require consent. The opinion of the planning authority on the need for consent should be sought in advance of any works.

Listed building consent is not required (although it may be necessary to obtain planning permission) if the building is[8]:

1. an ecclesiastical building used for ecclesiastical purposes (other than wholly or mainly as a residence for a minister);
2. included in the Schedule of monuments (scheduled monument consent is required instead);
3. for the erection of a modern free-standing building in the curtilage of a listed building, or works to objects or structures which have been within its curtilage only since July 1, 1948 and are not physically attached to the building; or
4. for works by the Crown to listed Crown buildings.

[7] Memorandum of Guidance (n. 4, *supra*), Appendix 1.
[8] TCPSA, ss. 53, 54(1) and 253.

Application for listed building consent is made to the planning authority, on the form obtainable from the authority. It is not competent to apply for consent in principle (referred to as outline consent), and full details of the proposed works must be given in the application. If planning permission is also required for the work (Chapter 4), application for both consents is normally made on the same form. The applications can be processed simultaneously, but separate decisions must be issued.

When applying for listed building consent, the applicant is required to complete a certificate stating either that he is the owner of the building or any part of the building to which the application relates, or has served notice of the application on the owner(s) named in the certificate or, despite taking specified steps, has been unable to trace any or all of the owners (Chapter 5). Copies of the form of notice to be served upon the owners are included with the application form obtained from the planning authority. In the event that any or all of the owners cannot be traced, the applicant must publish notice of the application in a local newspaper.[9] In contrast to planning applications, there is no form of neighbour notification for listed building consent applications.

The planning authority must advertise the application in both a local newspaper and the Edinburgh Gazette, and display a site notice for at least seven days. The advertisement and site notice must include a description of the works and name a place where plans of the works can be inspected. The application cannot be determined until 21 days after the date of the advertisement or the posting of the notice. In contrast to planning applications, the authority is not obliged to consult appropriate bodies for their views, although this may be done as a matter of good practice.

In determining the application, the authority must take into account any representations relating to the application received during the 21-day period and, in particular, any representations made by a person who satisfies them that he is owner of part of the building. Special regard must be paid

[9] Town and Country Planning (Listed Buildings and Buildings in Conservation Areas) (Scotland) Regulations 1987 (S.I. 1987 No. 1529), reg. 6.

to the desirability of preserving the building or its setting or any features of special architectural or historic interest which it possesses.[10] Scottish Office policy specifies a presumption in favour of preservation of listed buildings, and continuation of their original use wherever possible, and requires evidence that every possible attempt has been made to find a suitable alternative use.[11] However, exceptions to this rule may be justified by the special circumstances of the site.[12] Planning authorities are directed to be flexible in dealing with applications for changes of use of listed buildings. Where application is made for the alteration or extension of any listed building, planning authorities should always seek to preserve the architectural integrity of the building and encourage its restoration where some of that integrity has been lost.

In most cases the authority may not grant consent without notifying the Secretary of State/Historic Scotland, who has 28 days to consider calling-in the application for his own decision (but can extend this period indefinitely by giving notice to the authority). The date of the grant of listed building consent by the authority is the date on which the decision notice bears to have been signed.

Listed building consent may be granted subject to conditions. In the absence of any express conditions, a grant of listed building consent is deemed to be subject to a condition requiring commencement of the works authorised by the consent within five years (three years in the case of pre–1980 consents). If the works have not commenced within that period, the consent expires.[13] Other conditions may reserve specified minor details of the work for subsequent approval of the planning authority; preserve particular features of the building; require the making good, after the works are completed, of any damage caused to the building by the works; or provide for the reconstruction of the building or any

[10] TCPSA, s. 54(3), as amended.

[11] Memorandum of Guidance (n. 4, *supra*), para. 2.10 *et seq.*

[12] *Save Britains Heritage* v. *Secretary of State for the Environment* [1991] 1 W.L.R. 153.

[13] TCPSA, ss. 54A and 54B.

part of it following the execution of any works, with the use of original materials so far as practicable and with specified alterations to its interior. It is also competent for the authority to impose a condition preventing demolition of the listed building until it is satisfied that the site will be redeveloped in accordance with a current planning permission, either through a section 50 agreement (Chapter 6) and/or the placing of contracts for redevelopment work.[14] Any person with a legal interest in a listed building may apply to the planning authority for variation or discharge of conditions attached to a grant of listed building consent.[15]

Where consent has been granted for demolition of a listed building, work cannot commence until at least three months after the Royal Commission on the Ancient and Historical Monuments of Scotland has been notified by the applicant (the appropriate form should be sent to the applicant by the planning authority along with the grant of consent). The Commission must either have been given access to record the building, or have stated in writing that its recording is complete or that it does not wish to record it.[16]

The applicant has a right of appeal to the Secretary of State against[17]:

1. a refusal of listed building consent or of approval of subsequent details required in terms of a condition attached to the original grant of consent, or the grant of consent or approval subject to conditions;
2. a refusal of an application to vary or discharge conditions, or any fresh conditions imposed following such an application; and
3. a failure of the planning authority to determine the application, or give notice that the application has been called-in by the Secretary of State, within two months of the date of receipt of the application or any extended period agreed in writing with the applicant (known as a deemed refusal appeal).

[14] ss. 54(4), (4A) and (5), as amended.
[15] s. 54D.
[16] s. 53(2), as amended.
[17] Sched. 10, paras. 7 and 8, as amended, and as applied by s. 54D(2).

The appeal must be submitted within six months of notice of the decision or expiry of the two-month period.[18] The wording of the regulations leaves it uncertain whether the six month period runs from the date of the notice or the date on which it is received. The procedure is similar to that for planning appeals described in Chapter 8. In addition to the normal grounds of appeal, the appellant may allege that the building is not of special architectural or historic interest and, therefore, ought not to be listed. In determining the appeal, the Secretary of State may reverse or vary any part of the decision by the authority, whether the appeal relates to that part or not, and may deal with the application as if it had been made to him in the first instance. As part of the appeal decision, the Secretary of State can also "de-list" the building by removing it from the list.[19]

The Secretary of State's decision on the merits of the appeal or called-in application is final. However, the legality of the decision may be challenged in the Court of Session under the statutory review procedure, but only within six weeks of the decision (Chapter 8).

(b) Enforcement

A listed building enforcement notice may be served where it appears to the planning authority, or the Secretary of State, that any works have been or are being executed to a listed building in contravention of the requirement to obtain listed building consent, or of the conditions attached to a consent. In making its decision, the authority has regard to the effect of the works on the character of the building as one of special architectural or historic interest.[20] A failure to obtain listed building consent can never become immune from enforcement action through passage of time, unlike work carried out without planning permission.

The notice specifies the alleged contravention and the steps required, within a given period, either to restore the building to its former state, or to bring it to the state in which it would

[18] Listed Buildings Regulations (no. 9, above), reg. 8.
[19] TCPSA Sched. 10, paras. 7(2) and (3).
[20] ss.92 and 96(1), as amended.

have been if the terms and conditions of any listed building consent for the works had been complied with. Alternatively, where it appears to the authority that complete restoration of the building to its former state is undesirable or not reasonably practical, the notice can specify steps to alleviate the effects of works executed without listed building consent, in a manner acceptable to it. The notice must specify the date upon which it is to take effect, and the period within which the steps are required to be taken. Different periods may be specified for different steps.

A copy of the listed building enforcement notice is served on the current owner, lessee and occupier of the building and on any other person who has an interest in the building which, in the opinion of the planning authority, is materially affected by the notice. (Methods of service are discussed in Chapter 7.) Details of the building in respect of which the notice has been served must be entered in a list available for public inspection.

Withdrawal of the notice by the planning authority is competent at any time, whether or not it has taken effect, and without prejudice to its power to serve another. The authority may also waive or relax any requirement of the notice and, in particular, extend any period for taking the steps specified in the notice. Notification of its withdrawal, or any waiver or relaxation of its terms, must be given to every person served with the notice.

The owner of the land is guilty of an offence if at the end of the period for compliance with the notice, any step required to be taken in terms of the notice has not been taken.[21] Such an offence may be charged by reference to any day or longer period of time. It is a defence to show that everything was done that he could be expected to do to secure that all the required steps were taken, or that he was not served with a copy of the notice and was not aware of it. On summary conviction, there is liability to a maximum fine of £20,000, and to an unlimited fine following conviction on indictment. In determining the level of fine the court shall in particular have regard to any financial benefit which has accrued or appears

[21] s. 94(1), as substituted.

likely to accrue to the person in consequence of the offence. Following conviction, further offences are committed if there is a continuing failure to take any step.

If the steps required by the listed building enforcement notice have not been taken within the specified period, the planning authority may enter the land and take those steps, recovering any expenses reasonably incurred in this process from the person who is then the owner or lessee of the land. Such expenses are deemed to have been incurred on behalf of the person who carried out the unauthorised works, but there is no specific provision for recovery from that person. It is an offence to wilfully obstruct the exercise of this right of entry.[22]

Any person on whom the notice was served or any other person having an interest in the building to which it relates may lodge an appeal to the Secretary of State against the notice.[23] Such an appeal follows a similar procedure to an appeal against a planning enforcement notice (Chapter 7) and prevents the requirements of the notice from coming into force pending determination or withdrawal of the appeal. Written notice of the appeal must be lodged with SOIR before the notice takes effect (on the expiry of the period specified in the notice), or sent in a properly addressed and pre-paid envelope posted at such a time that, in the ordinary course of post, it would be delivered before that date.

The grounds of appeal are:

1. the building is not of special architectural or historic interest;
2. the matters alleged to constitute a contravention of the requirements to obtain listed building consent, or of the conditions of a consent, do not involve such a contravention;
3. that those matters (if they occurred) do not constitute such a contravention;
4. the works were urgently necessary in the interests of safety or health or for the preservation of the building, and it was not practicable for this purpose to carry out repairs or works for affording temporary

[22] s. 95, as amended.
[23] s. 93, as amended.

support or shelter, and that the works were limited to the minimum measures immediately necessary;

5. listed building consent ought to be granted for the works, or any relevant condition of such consent which has been granted ought to be discharged or different conditions substituted;
6. the notice was not served in accordance with the statutory provisions;
7. the requirements of the notice exceed what is necessary for restoring the building to its condition before the works were carried out;
8. the period specified in the notice as the period within which any steps required thereby are to be taken falls short of what should reasonably be allowed;
9. the steps required by the notice to be taken would not serve the purpose of restoring the character of the building to its former state;
10. the steps specified exceed what is necessary to bring the building to the state it would have been in if the listed building consent had been complied with;
11. the steps specified exceed what may reasonably be required to alleviate the effects of works executed without listed building consent.

In the course of the appeal, the Secretary of State may correct any defect, error or misdescription in the notice or vary its terms, provided he is satisfied that the correction or variation will not cause injustice to the appellant or planning authority. He may also disregard a failure to serve the notice on any person where that person has not suffered material prejudice as a result. In deciding the appeal, the Secretary of State may either quash the notice and grant listed building consent for the works to which the notice relates, or discharge any condition subject to which such consent was granted and substitute any other condition, whether more or less onerous, or uphold the notice. In addition, he may de-list the building by removing it from the list of buildings of special architectural or historic interest. The legality of the decision of the Secretary of State on the appeal may be challenged in the Court of Session using the statutory review procedure (Chapter 8).

(c) Offences

It is an offence to carry out demolition or works which require listed building consent without obtaining such consent, or to fail to comply with conditions attached to a consent. It is a defence to show that the works were urgently necessary in the interests of safety or health or for the preservation of the building, and that it was not practicable to secure these interests by repair works or works providing temporary support or shelter, that the works were limited to the minimum measures immediately necessary and written notice justifying the need for the works was given to the planning authority as soon as reasonably practicable. A person guilty of such an offence is liable on summary conviction to imprisonment for up to six months and/or a maximum fine of £20,000, and for conviction on indictment up to two years imprisonment and/or an unlimited fine. In determining the level of fine to be imposed, the court is directed to have regard to any financial benefit which has accrued or appears likely to accrue to that person in consequence of the offence.[24]

Failure to comply with a listed building enforcement notice is also an offence (above), together with doing or permitting to be done any act, other than that authorised by a grant of planning permission and/or listed building consent, which causes or is likely to result in damage to a listed building with the intention of causing such damage (below).

Other Consequences of Listing

(a) Permitted Development

The permitted development rights conferred by the Permitted Development Order (Chapter 4) apply more restrictively to listed buildings, with the result that planning permission is required for a wider scope of activities. For example, permitted development rights for painting the exterior of a building do not apply to listed buildings, with the result that planning permission will be required for the painting work if

[24] s. 53(1), (5) and (6), as amended.

the external appearance of the listed building will be materially affected as a result of that work.[25]

(b) Protection of Setting

If the planning authority considers that the setting of a listed building would be affected by a development for which an application for planning permission has been made, the application should be advertised in a local newspaper and a site notice displayed for at least seven days, and 21 days allowed for representations to be lodged. When deciding whether to grant planning permission for such a development, the planning authority must take into account any representations received following the advertisement and site notice.[26]

The Scottish Office guidance suggests that development within the curtilage (Chapter 4) should always be regarded as affecting the setting unless the curtilage is very large and the new building is not intervisible with the listed building. New buildings outwith the curtilage which restrict or obstruct views of the listed building or rise above and behind it so that its silhouette can no longer be seen against the sky from the more familar viewpoints should also be regarded as affecting the setting, as should development which blocks long-appreciated views of important architectural landmarks.[27]

In considering whether to grant permission for a development which affects a listed building or its setting, the authority must have special regard to the desirability of preserving the building or its setting or any features of special architectural or historic interest which it possesses.[28]

(c) Intimation of Notices

Once a building has been listed, various statutory notices, orders or proposals relating to demolition or the carrying out

[25] Town and County Planning (General Permitted Development) (Scotland) Order 1992, Sched. 1, class 9(2) and TCPSA, s. 19(2)(a).
[26] TCPSA, ss. 25 and 26(1), as amended.
[27] Memorandum of Guidance (n. 4, *supra*), Appendix 1, para. 8.1.0.
[28] TCPSA, s. 54(3), as amended.

of works affecting the building must be intimated in writing by the appropriate local authority to the planning authority. If the building is owned, leased or occupied by the planning authority intimation should also be given to the Secretary of State. Written intimation may be dispensed with in cases where public safety requires demolition or other work to be carried out without delay, but intimation, even if initially oral, must be given as soon as possible before commencement of the demolition or works.[29]

(d) *Offences*

It is an offence to carry out demolition or works without listed building consent, or contrary to the conditions of a consent (above). It is also an offence to do or permit to be done any act, other than that authorised by a grant of planning permission and/or listed building consent, which causes or is likely to result in damage to a listed building (other than those buildings exempted from the provisions relating to listed building consent), with the intention of causing such damage. On summary conviction a person guilty of such an offence is liable to a fine not exceeding level 3 on the standard scale (Appendix 1). Following conviction, a further offence is committed by failure to take such reasonable steps as may be necessary to prevent any damage or further damage resulting from the offence, with a maximum fine of one-tenth of level 3 for each day on which the failure continues.[30]

(e) *Urgent Works for Preservation*

If it appears to the planning authority (or the Secretary of State) that any works are urgently necessary for the preservation of a listed building, it may execute those works after giving not less than seven days written notice to the owner of the building.[31] This power does not extend to an

[29] s. 54C.
[30] s. 55, as amended.
[31] s. 97, as substituted.

ecclesiastical building in ecclesiastical use, other than a minister's residence, or to a scheduled monument. The works may include erection of scaffolding for support or a temporary roof covering. If the building is occupied, works may be carried out only to those parts which are not in use. Scottish Office guidance encourages planning authorities to exercise these powers at an early stage when relatively inexpensive works can halt deterioration of a building and greatly improve its chances of economic re-use.[32]

A similar power may be applied by direction of the Secretary of State to an unlisted building in a conservation area which should be preserved to maintain the character or appearance of the conservation area.

Notice may also be given to the owner rendering him liable to pay the expenses of these works unless within 28 days of the date of the notice he lodges an objection with the Secretary of State on the grounds that some or all of the works were unnecessary for the building's preservation, that temporary arrangements for support or shelter have continued for an unreasonable length of time, or that the amount specified in the notice is unreasonable, or that recovery of it would cause him hardship. The Secretary of State considers the justification for such an objection and gives notice of his decision to the owner and the planning authority, if it carried out the works, together with a statement of the reasons for the decision and the amount recoverable.[33]

(f) Repairs Notices and Compulsory Purchase

A repairs notice may be served at any time on the owner of a listed building by the planning authority or the Secretary of State specifying the works considered reasonably necessary for its proper preservation, and explaining the effect of the compulsory purchase provisions.[34] The notice may be withdrawn at any time, by serving notice of the withdrawal upon any person served with a copy of the notice.

[32] Memorandum of Guidance (n. 4, *supra*), para. 3.19.
[33] TCPSA, s. 97A, as substituted.
[34] s. 105(1), as amended.

Compulsory purchase proceedings can be initiated two months after service of a repairs notice, even if the building was demolished following service of the notice. The Secretary of State may authorise compulsory purchase if he is satisfied that reasonable steps are not being taken for properly preserving the listed building, and that it is expedient to make provision for its preservation and to authorise its compulsory purchase for that purpose.[35] The compulsory purchase order may include any land required for preserving the building or its amenities, or for giving access to it for its proper control or management. This compulsory purchase power does not extend to an ecclesiastical building in ecclesiastical use, other than a minister's residence, or to a scheduled monument. Any person with an interest in the building has 28 days after service of a compulsory purchase order to apply to the sheriff for an order prohibiting further proceedings upon it. Such an order will only be granted if the sheriff is satisfied that reasonable steps have been taken to preserve the building.

Where the planning authority or the Secretary of State is satisfied that the building has been deliberately allowed to fall into disrepair for the purpose of justifying its demolition and the development of the site, a direction may be made for the payment of minimum compensation, which ignores the redevelopment value of the land.[36]

(g) Listed Building Purchase Notices

A listed building purchase notice may be served on the planning authority by the owner or lessee where the land has become incapable of reasonably beneficial use in its present state and listed building consent has been refused, granted subject to conditions, revoked or modified.[37] The notice has the effect of requiring the authority to purchase the interest in the land. The procedure is similar to that for planning purchase notices (Chapter 5).

[35] s. 104, as amended.
[36] s. 107, as amended.
[37] s. 179, as amended.

(h) Rights of Entry

The planning authority has the right to enter land in specified circumstances in connection with listed buildings,[38] including to ascertain whether work is being carried out without listed building consent, or contrary to a condition attached to a consent, and whether the building is being maintained in a proper state of repair. Entry to land which is occupied cannot be demanded as of right unless 24 hours' notice of the intended entry has been given to the occupier. A warrant authorising entry may be sought from a sheriff if admission to the land has been refused or a refusal is reasonably apprehended, or the case is one of urgency.

Building Preservation Notices

Service of a building preservation notice extends the protection afforded to listed buildings to an unlisted building, on a temporary basis, while the Secretary of State considers whether it should be listed. This notice may be served where it appears to the planning authority that the building is of special architectural or historic interest and is in danger of demolition or alteration in such a way as to affect its character. It is not competent to serve a building preservation notice in respect of an ecclesiastical building in use for ecclesiastical purposes, other than a minister's residence, or a scheduled monument.[39] While the notice is in force, the building is treated as a listed building, except that an act causing or likely to cause damage to the building will not be an offence.

The notice states that the building appears to be of special architectural or historic interest and that the planning authority has requested the Secretary of State to consider listing it, and explains its effect. The notice comes into force as soon as it has been served by the planning authority on the owner, lessee and occupier of the building. In urgent circumstances personal service may be dispensed with and

[38] ss. 265, as amended, and 97AB and 97AC.
[39] s. 56, as amended.

the notice takes effect once it has been affixed conspicuously to some object on the building. The notice remains in force for six months from the last date of service, but is discharged within this period by the listing of the building or written notification to the planning authority from the Secretary of State that he does not intend to list the building.

If the Secretary of State decides not to list the building the notice is discharged and this decision must be intimated forthwith to the owner, lessee and occupier of the building by the planning authority. Following a decision not to list the building, the planning authority cannot serve another building preservation notice in respect of the building within the following 12 months. Any enforcement proceedings will lapse, although liability will remain for non-compliance with a listed building enforcement notice committed while the notice was in force.

If the building preservation notice ceases to have effect without the building becoming listed, any person who at the time when the notice was served had an interest in the building shall be entitled to be paid compensation by the planning authority in respect of any loss or damage directly attributable to the effect of the notice.[40]

Conservation Areas

The planning authority has a duty to determine periodically which parts of its district are areas of special architectural or historic interest, the character or appearance of which it is desirable to preserve or enhance. Such areas should be designated as conservation areas.[41] The Secretary of State has a reserve power to intervene and designate a conservation area. Notice of the designation, and any variation or cancellation of a designation, is given to the Secretary of State and advertised in the Edinburgh Gazette and a local newspaper. Individual owners and occupiers of property within the area do not require to be notified. No formal confirmation of the designation is required from the Secretary

[40] s. 162(3), as amended.
[41] s. 262(1), as substituted.

of State. The authority must compile and make available for public inspection a list of particulars of conservation areas within its district.

Conservation Area Consent

Conservation area consent is required for demolition of a building in a conservation area, with exceptions including[42]:

1. a listed building (listed building consent will be required);
2. an ecclesiastical building in ecclesiastical use, other than a minister's residence;
3. a scheduled monument (scheduled monument consent will be required);
4. a building (but not a part of a building) with a total cubic content not exceeding 115 cubic metres;
5. any gate, wall, fence or railing which is less than one metre high where abutting a road used by vehicular traffic or an open space, or two metres high in any other case; and
6. any building required to be demolished in terms of a discontinuance order or enforcement notice, or by virtue of a condition of a planning permission or provision of a section 50 agreement.

Consent is obtained from the planning authority. The procedure for applying for consent and the powers of enforcement are the same as those applicable to applications for listed building consent (above). In considering the application, the planning authority must pay special attention to the desirability of preserving or enhancing the character or appearance of the conservation area (below). If the site is to be redeveloped, consent should in general only be given where there are acceptable proposals for the new building or the development of the cleared site.

[42] The full list of exceptions appears in TCPSA, s. 262A(1), as substituted and amended, and Direction "Exemption from Demolition Control in Conservation Areas," attached to S.D.D. Circular 17/1987, "New Provisions and Revised Guidance relating to Listed Buildings and Conservation Areas," Annex IV.

A number of the provisions applicable to listed building control (above) are applied to conservation area consent.[43] Conditions similar to those for listed building consents may be imposed upon the grant of conservation area consent. If consent is granted for demolition of the building, the Royal Commission on the Ancient and Historical Monuments of Scotland must be given an opportunity to record the building. Enforcement action may be taken against any failure to obtain conservation area consent, and there is a right of appeal to the Secretary of State in respect of that action. It is an offence to demolish a building without the required conservation consent.

Permitted Development Rights

Under the Permitted Development Order (Chapter 4) permitted development rights for development in conservation areas are restricted, with the result that planning permission is required for a wider range of development. For example, permitted development rights for painting the exterior of a building do not apply to buildings situated in conservation areas, with the result that planning permission will be required for the painting work if the external appearance of such a building will be materially affected as a result of that work.[44] Further restrictions may be placed on permitted development rights within conservation areas by the use of article 4 directions (below).

Planning Applications — Preservation of Character and Appearance

If the planning authority believes that a proposed development would affect the character or appearance of a conservation area, the application must be advertised in a local newspaper and a site notice displayed for at least seven days. Any comments received within 21 days of the advertisement

[43] Listed Buildings and Buildings in Conservation Areas Regulations, (n. 9, *supra*) reg. 13.

[44] Town and Country Planning (General Permitted Development) (Scotland) Order 1992, Sched. 1, class 9(2) and s. 19(2)(a).

or display of the notice must be taken into account when the application is determined.[45]

In addition, the planning authority must pay special attention to the desirability of preserving or enhancing the character or appearance of a conservation area when exercising its planning powers in relation to any buildings or land in that area, including the determination of planning applications.[46] This will include consideration of such matters as scale, bulk, height, materials, colour, vertical or horizontal emphasis and design,[47] and must be the first consideration for the authority.[48] The character or appearance of a conservation area is preserved not only by a positive contribution to preservation, but also by development which has a neutral effect and leaves the character or appearance unharmed.[49] Where a development simultaneously causes both enhancement and some detriment, the detrimental effect is a material consideration.[50] This requirement may lead planning authorities to insist on applications for detailed rather than outline planning permission for development within conservation areas.

Protection of Trees

With some exceptions, it is an offence to cut down, top, lop, uproot, wilfully damage or wilfully destroy a tree in a conservation area, even if it is not protected by a tree preservation order, unless the planning authority was given six-weeks notice of the proposed work or consented to it (see below).

Urgent Works for Preservation

The Secretary of State may direct that the power to undertake works which are urgently necessary for the preservation of a

45 TCPSA, ss. 25, as amended, and 26(4).
46 s. 262(8), as substituted.
47 Memorandum of Guidance (n. 4, *supra*), para. 4.36.
48 *The Bath Society* v. *Secretary of State for the Environment* [1991] 1 W.L.R. 1303.
49 *South Lakeland District Council* v. *Secretary of State for the Environment* [1992] 2 A.C. 141.
50 *The Bath Society* v. *Secretary of State for the Environment* (n. 48, *supra*).

listed building be extended to apply to a building in a conservation area, if satisfied that its preservation is important for maintaining the character or appearance of the area.[51] If the building is occupied, works may be carried out only to those parts which are not in use.

Proposals for Preservation and Enhancement

There is a duty placed on planning authorities to formulate and publish proposals for the preservation and enhancement of conservation areas.[52] There is some criticism that planning authorities largely ignore this duty and use the conservation area designation as a device to achieve greater control over development.

Article 4 Directions

The requirement for conservation area consent only applies to demolition of certain classes of buildings (above). The planning authority can achieve greater control over development within a conservation area (and elsewhere) by means of an article 4 direction.[53] The effect of such a direction is to remove permitted development rights under the Permitted Development Order (Chapter 4) for specified classes of development, with the result that planning permission must be obtained from the planning authority for those classes of development. The direction may apply to specified classes of development within a conservation area or other geographical areas or any particular development within a class, other than a small list of developments which cannot be restricted by an article 4 direction.

An article 4 direction may be made by the planning authority (or the Secretary of State), if it is satisfied that it is expedient to restrict permitted development rights in this way. In most cases the direction must be submitted to the Secretary of State for approval. The regional planning

[51] TCPSA, s. 97(2), as substituted.
[52] s. 262B, as substituted and amended.
[53] Town and Country Planning (General Permitted Development) (Scotland) Order 1992, art. 4.

authority should also be notified. Notice of the direction made or approved by the Secretary of State is published by the planning authority in the Edinburgh Gazette and at least one local newspaper.[54] The notice must specify any particular geographical area affected by the direction and contain a concise statement of the effect of the direction and name a place where a copy may be inspected. In the case of a direction specifying any particular development, notice must be served on the owner and occupier of the land affected. The direction comes into force on the date of publication of the first notice or date of service on the occupier or, if there is no occupier, on the owner. There is a right to compensation if an application for planning permission is refused and a development cannot proceed which other than for the direction would not have required permission.[55]

An article 4 direction made by a planning authority may be cancelled without the approval of the Secretary of State, although a notice must be published or served on the owner and occupier affected by the cancelled direction.

Trees

The planning authority has a duty when granting planning permission to ensure that adequate provision is made for the preservation or planting of trees.[56] This duty is normally discharged by imposing appropriate conditions upon the grant of permission, or making tree preservation orders.

Tree preservation orders (TPOs) may be made by the planning authority where it appears expedient in the interests of amenity to make provision for the preservation of trees or woodlands in the district.[57] The TPO will specify the particular tree, groups of trees or woodlands to which it applies and include a map showing their position. It may also provide for the prohibition of the cutting down, topping, lopping, uprooting, wilful damage, or wilful destruction of the trees without the consent of the planning authority, which

[54] *Ibid.*, art. 5.
[55] TCPSA, s. 154, as amended.
[56] s. 57, as amended.
[57] s. 58, as amended.

consent may be given subject to conditions. A TPO can secure the replanting, in a specified manner, of any part of a woodland area which is felled in the course of forestry operations. Where planning permission is granted subject to conditions requiring the planting of trees it is possible for a TPO to take effect from the time when those trees are planted. Nothing in a TPO prohibits the uprooting, felling or lopping of any tree if this work is urgently necessary in the interests of safety or is necessary for the prevention or abatement of a nuisance, provided written notice of the proposed work is given to the planning authority as soon as may be after the necessity for the operation arises, or if such work is carried out in compliance with any obligation imposed by or under any Act of Parliament.

The making of the TPO must be advertised and a copy of the order and map made available for public inspection. Notice must be served on the owners, lessees and occupiers of the land affected by the TPO, and on any person known by the planning authority to be entitled either to work any minerals in the land by surface working or to fell any of the trees affected by the TPO. A period of 28 days from date of service must be allowed for representations to be made to the planning authority.[58] The TPO does not take effect until it is confirmed by the planning authority, which must take into account any representations received. It is competent for the TPO to be confirmed subject to modifications. Following its confirmation, the TPO is recorded in the Register of Sasines or the Land Register (the property register) by the planning authority, thereby becoming enforceable against all subsequent owners of the land on which the trees stand.

In cases of urgency, a TPO may take effect immediately without previous confirmation.[59] In these circumstances, the TPO specifies the date on which it takes effect provisionally and it continues in force for six months or until its confirmation, whichever is the earlier date.

[58] Town and Country Planning (Tree Preservation Order and Trees in Conservation Areas) (Scotland) Regulations 1975 (S.I. 1975 No. 1204), as amended by Amendment Regulations in 1981 (S.I. 1981 No. 1385) and 1984 (S.I. 1984 No. 329).

[59] TCPSA, s. 59, as amended.

Where a tree protected by a TPO is removed, uprooted or destroyed in contravention of the TPO, the owner of the land must plant another tree of an appropriate size and species in the same place as soon as reasonably possible.[60] The TPO will apply to the new tree as it applied to the original tree. This replanting obligation also applies where the uprooting or felling is authorised only as being urgently necessary in the interests of safety. In the case of trees in a woodland, it is sufficient to replace the trees with the same number of trees either on or near the land on which the trees previously stood or on such other land as may be agreed with the planning authority. It is possible to apply to the planning authority to dispense with the requirement to replant trees.

The protection conferred by a TPO extends to trees in conservation areas which are not the subject of a TPO, with exceptions. These include the uprooting, felling or lopping of a tree not exceeding 75 millimetres or the uprooting or felling in a woodland of a tree having a diameter not exceeding 100 millimetres where this is done to improve the growth of other trees, the diameter being measured over the bark at a point 1.5 metres above ground level.[61]

In any prosecution relating to trees in conservation areas which are not the subject of a TPO, it will be a defence to prove that notice of the intention to do the act was served upon the planning authority and the authority consented to the work, or six weeks was allowed for them to respond before the work was carried out (there is a two-year time limit from giving such notice to do the work). The six-week period is intended to give the authority time to consider making a TPO. The planning authority must keep a register of such notices and make it available for public inspection. The replanting obligation applies.

The planning authority has the power to serve a notice on the owner of the land requiring him to plant a tree or trees of specified size and species within a specified period, in enforcement of the general replanting obligations or any conditions of a consent given under a TPO requiring

[60] s. 60, as amended.

[61] s. 59A, as inserted; Tree Preservation Order Regulations (n. 58, *supra*) reg. 11.

replanting.[62] The notice must be served within two years of the date on which the failure to comply came to the knowledge of the authority. The notice takes effect after the expiry of the period specified in the notice, which must be at least 28 days from the date of service, unless the person on whom notice is served has appealed to the Secretary of State.[63] The procedure for such an appeal is similar to appeals against enforcement notices (Chapter 7).

The grounds of appeal are that:

1. the replanting obligation or the conditions of a consent given under a TPO have been complied with;
2. in the circumstances of the case the replanting obligation should be dispensed with;
3. the requirements of the notice are unreasonable in respect of the period or the size or species of trees specified therein;
4. the planting of a tree or trees in accordance with the notice is not required in the interests of amenity or would be contrary to the practice of good forestry;
5. the place on which the tree(s) is required to be planted is unsuitable for that purpose.

There is provision for recovery of the expenses incurred by the owner in complying with the notice from any person responsible for the cutting down, destruction or removal of the original tree or trees.[64] If the steps required by the notice are not taken, the planning authority has the power to enter the land and take those steps. It is an offence to obstruct wilfully the exercise of this power.[65]

It is an offence to cut down, uproot or wilfully destroy a tree, or wilfully damage, top or lop a tree in such a manner as to be likely to destroy it, in contravention of a TPO or where the tree is situated in a conservation area.[66] Following summary conviction a fine not exceeding £20,000 may be

[62] s. 99(1), as amended.
[63] The grounds of appeal are specified in s. 99(3), as amended.
[64] s. 99(5).
[65] ss. 99A, 99B and 99C, as inserted.
[66] s. 98, as amended.

imposed, and an unlimited fine if convicted on indictment. In determining the amount of the fine the court is directed to have regard to any financial benefit which has accrued or appears likely to accrue to the offender in consequence of the offence. Any other contravention of a TPO, for example, damaging a tree short of destruction, is an offence punishable on summary conviction by a fine not exceeding level 4 of the standard scale (Appendix 1).

Advertisement Control

The display of advertisements is restricted and regulated by a separate set of controls.[67] No advertisement may be displayed without an express consent granted either by the planning authority or the Secretary of State, or a deemed consent. As with a grant of planning permission, the consent attaches to the site rather than to the applicant, and can be utilised by future persons with an interest in the site. Planning permission is deemed to have been granted for the display of an advertisement which is in accordance with the advertisement control requirements.[68]

Definition of "Advertisement"

An advertisement is defined to include any word, letter, model, sign, placard, board, notice, awning, blind, device or representation, whether illuminated or not, in the nature of an advertisement, announcement or direction, and which is employed wholly or partly for that purpose. This includes anything used or designed or adapted principally for use, for the display of advertisements, such as a hoarding or similar structure, or a balloon. Anything employed wholly or partly as a memorial or as a railway signal is excluded.[69] This definition should embrace any form of advertisement, and

[67] TCPSA, s. 61, as amended; Town and Country Planning (Control of Advertisements) (Scotland) Regulations 1984 (S.I. 1984 No. 467) as amended by Amendment Regulations 1992 (S.I. 1992 No. 1763).

[68] s. 62.

[69] s. 275(1), as amended; Control of Advertisement Regulations (n. 67, *supra*) reg. 2(1), as amended.

remove any doubt that canopies installed at shops carrying manufacturers or brand names are subject to advertisement control.[70] Similarly, anything designed or adapted principally for use as an advertisement is controlled, which will include hoardings, rotating panels, gantry or pylon signs, and free-standing structures, such as drums.

Advertisement control does not apply to advertisements[71]:

1. displayed within a building (with some exceptions);
2. on or in a vehicle normally employed as a moving vehicle, except during periods when it is being used primarily for the display of advertisements;
3. incorporated in and forming part of the fabric of a building (which does not necessarily include advertisements affixed or painted on the building), unless the building is used principally for the display of advertisements or a hoarding or similar structure;
4. displayed on land wholly or mainly enclosed with a hedge, fence, wall or similar screen and not readily visible from outside or from any part of the enclosed land over which there is public right of way or public access. This includes any railway station together with its yards and forecourts whether enclosed or not, but not public parks, public gardens or other land held for the use or enjoyment of the public, or any railway line;
5. displayed on or consisting of a balloon flown at a height of more than 60 metres above ground level;
6. displayed on or consisting of a balloon, provided the site is not within an area of special control (below), a conservation area (above), or other area designated for the purpose of conserving the natural beauty and amenity of the countryside, for example, a national scenic area (see below). No more than one such advertisement may be displayed at any one time on the site, and the site may not be used for the display of such advertisements on more than 10 days in total in any one calendar year, irrespective of which part of the site is used or who is using it for this purpose; and

[70] *Glasgow D.C.* v. *Secretary of State for Scotland*, 1989 S.L.T. 256.
[71] Control of Advertisement Regulations (n. 67, *supra*), reg. 3.

7. displayed on an article for sale or on the container or dispenser in or from which an article is sold, provided the advertisement is not illuminated and does not exceed 0.1 square metre in area.

Deemed Consent

There are six classes of advertisements for which consent is deemed to be granted without application to the authority, provided the specified conditions relating to matters such as height and area are observed (but other statutory consents may still be required).[72] Reference must be made to the statutory provisions for full details, but these classes are:

I Functional advertisements of local authorities, community councils, statutory undertakers and public transport undertakers

II Advertisements relating to the land on which they are displayed
(including identification and direction signs, and advertisements in relation to business on the premises where the advertisement is displayed)

III Advertisements of a temporary nature
(including for sale boards, and builders' signs on sites)

IV Advertisements displayed on business premises
(including references to the goods sold or services provided, and the name and qualification of the person carrying on the business)

V Advertisements within buildings
(if not exempt from advertisement control)

VI Illuminated advertisements
(displayed on business premises wholly with reference to the business, goods sold or services provided, and qualifications of the person carrying on the business).

[72] reg. 10 and Sched. 4.

Deemed consent also extends to advertisements relating specifically to elections, statutory advertisements, traffic signs, and advertisements on sites used for the display of advertisements on August 16, 1948.

In addition to the conditions attached to each class of deemed consent and the standard conditions applicable to the display of all advertisements (below), deemed consent is subject to an implied condition preventing siting or display of an advertisement so as to obscure or hinder the ready interpretation of any road traffic sign, railway signal or aid to navigation by water or air, or so as otherwise to render hazardous the use of any road, railway, waterway (including coastal waters) or airfield.[73]

There are several ways in which deemed consent can be lost or removed. Where there is deemed consent for display of an advertisement, submission of an application for express consent removes the right to display the advertisement with deemed consent, irrespective of whether the application is successful.[74] The Secretary of State has the power to remove deemed consent for the display of advertisements of a specified class or description in any particular area or in any particular case.[75]

It is also open to the planning authority to require discontinuance of the display of an advertisement with deemed consent (other than election and statutory advertisements and traffic signs), by serving a discontinuance notice, where it considers it expedient to do so to remedy a substantial injury to the amenity of the locality or a danger to members of the public.[76] The notice is served upon the person who himself, or by his servant or agent, undertakes or maintains the display of the advertisement, and on the owner, lessee and occupier of the land on which it is displayed. It specifies the advertisement or the site to which it relates, the period within which the display or use of the site is to be discontinued, and the reasons why the authority considers it expedient, in the interests of amenity or public

[73] reg. 6 and Sched. 1.
[74] reg. 10(2) and (3).
[75] reg. 11.
[76] reg. 14.

safety, that the display or use of the site should be discontinued. The notice takes effect on the date specified therein, which must be not less than 28 days after the date of service. The authority may withdraw the notice at any time until it takes effect, or, where no appeal is pending, vary its terms to extend the period before it takes effect (in contrast to most other enforcement powers, where the right to withdraw or vary a notice has been extended beyond the time when the notice takes effect).

There is a right of appeal to the Secretary of State against a discontinuance notice. Submission of an appeal prevents the notice from taking effect until the appeal has been determined. Written notice of appeal must be lodged within 28 days from the date of service of the notice.[77] The procedure is similar to that for enforcement notice appeals (Chapter 7). The Secretary of State may dismiss the appeal, quash the notice, or vary its terms in favour of the appellant.

Express Consent

In the absence of deemed consent for the display of an advertisement, an application for express consent must be submitted to the planning authority on the form available from the authority.[78] A register of the particulars of all such applications must be maintained for public inspection by the authority. The decision of the authority on the application must be notified to the applicant within two months from either the date of receipt or any longer period agreed in writing with the applicant. If consent is refused or granted subject to conditions other than the standard conditions (below), written reasons must be given for the decision.

Unlike normal planning powers, advertisement control can only be exercised in the interests of amenity and public safety.[79] Consent cannot be refused because the planning authority consider the advertisement to be unnecessary or offensive to public morals, and any consent granted cannot

[77] reg. 21(3).
[78] reg. 5.
[79] reg. 4.

limit or restrict the subject matter, content or design of the advertisement. In the interest of amenity, the authority may determine the suitability of the use of the site for the display of advertisements in light of the general characteristics of the locality, including the presence of any features of historic, architectural, cultural or similar interest. The presence of existing advertisements in the locality should be ignored. On the grounds of public safety, the authority should have regard to the safety of persons who may use any road, railway, waterway (including coastal waters), dock, harbour or airfield which is likely to be affected by the proposed advertisement display. In particular, it should consider whether the display is likely to obscure or hinder the ready interpretation of any road traffic sign, railway signal or aid to navigation by water or air. The authority should also have regard to any material change of circumstances likely to occur within the period for which the consent is required, and any other material factor.

Consent may be granted subject to the standard conditions (below) and such additional conditions as the authority thinks fit, or refused (but only on the grounds of amenity and/or public safety). Consent may be granted for display of a particular advertisement or specify the use of a particular site for the display of advertisements in a particular manner, by reference to the number, siting, size or illumination of the advertisements or the structures intended for such display, or the design or appearance of any such structure. A temporary consent may be granted, with a condition requiring removal of the advertisement following expiry of a specified period. Retrospective consent may be granted for the display of advertisements begun prior to the date of application or for the retention of advertisements displayed prior to the application.

Where the application relates to display of an advertisement within one of the deemed consent classes (above), consent cannot be refused or more restrictive conditions imposed, unless required to prevent or remedy a substantial injury to the amenity of the locality or a danger to members of the public.

Consent may be granted for the temporary display on unspecified sites within the authority's district of placards, posters or bills relating to the visit of a travelling circus, fair or similar travelling entertainment.[80] Such a consent is subject to a set of conditions which apply in addition to the standard conditions. There is no right of appeal against the decision of the planning authority on an application for this form of consent.

Every grant of express consent expires after five years, or such other period as is specified in the consent.[81] This time limit may be specified as running from the date of commencement of the display of the advertisement or from a date not later than six months after the date consent is granted, whichever is the earlier. The consent may be renewed at any time within six months before its expiry. Unless prohibited by a condition or where an application for renewal is refused, the display may continue after the time limit by virtue of a deemed consent on the same terms and conditions, subject to service of a discontinuance notice (above).[82]

An express consent may be revoked or modified by the planning authority on grounds of amenity or public safety, but only before the display of the advertisement commences or building or other operations involved in the display have been completed. The confirmation of the Secretary of State is required. A written claim for compensation may be served upon the authority within six months after confirmation of the revocation or modification order.[83]

Following a refusal of express consent or grant subject to conditions, the applicant has a right of appeal to the Secretary of State within six months from receipt of the decision. There is also a right of appeal against a deemed refusal, where the authority has failed to notify its decision within two months of the date of receipt of the application, or any longer period agreed with the applicant.[84] The appeal procedure is similar to planning appeals, except that no provision is made for using the written submissions procedure (Chapter 8). Advertisement consent appeals have been delegated by the Secretary of State

[80] reg. 27.
[81] reg. 18.
[82] reg. 19.
[83] regs. 22 and 23.
[84] regs. 20 and 21.

to reporters for decision, although some advertisement appeals may continue to be decided by the Secretary of State.[85] The Secretary of State/reporter may allow or dismiss the appeal, or reverse or vary any part of the decision by the authority whether or not the appeal relates to that part, dealing with the application as though it was made to him in the first instance. The decision on the merits of the appeal is final, but its legality may be challenged in the Court of Session using the statutory review procedure (Chapter 8), subject to a six-week time limit.

Standard Conditions

The display of all advertisements is subject to implied conditions requiring, to the reasonable satisfaction of the planning authority[86]:

1. maintenance in a clean and tidy condition of the advertisement (other than election notice) and the land upon which it is displayed;
2. maintenance in a safe condition of any hoarding, similar structure or sign, placard, board or other device used principally for displaying the advertisement;
3. removal of the advertisement when required under the regulations;
4. advance permission for display of the advertisement (other than statutory advertisements) to be obtained from the owner of the land or other person entitled to grant permission.

Areas of Special Control

The planning authority has the power to designate Areas of Special Control, within which stricter standards of advertisement control apply.[87] This power is exercised in the interests of amenity, having regard to the general characteristics of the

[85] Town and Country Planning (Determination of Appeals by Appointed Persons) (Prescribed Classes) (Scotland) Amendment Regulations 1989 (S.I. 1989 No. 577).
[86] Control of Advertisements Regulations, (n. 67, *supra*). reg. 6 and Sched.1.
[87] reg. 8. The procedure is described in Sched. 2.

area, including the presence of any feature of historic, architectural or cultural interest. The designation must be approved by the Secretary of State, who has indicated that it is not normally enough for the area to be a conservation area (above), but that this stricter control is wholly appropriate in rural areas. Once the area comes into operation, advertisements already displayed in the area (with some exceptions) may continue to be displayed for a futher six months or for the remainder of the term of any express consent, whichever is longer, and then for a further two months, after which the advertisement must be removed unless express consent is granted for its continued display.[88]

Enforcement

An enforcement notice may be served by the planning authority where it appears that any advertisement has been displayed without the necessary consent, or without compliance with a condition or limitation attached to a consent, whether express or deemed.[89] The notice is served upon the owner, lessee and occupier of the land and on any other person known to the authority to be displaying the advertisement. The notice requires specified steps to be taken, within a given period, to restore the land to its condition before the display was begun or to secure compliance with the condition or limitation. In addition, it may specify as an alternative steps to be taken to bring the display to an acceptable condition. The notice takes effect on the date specified in the notice which must be 28 days from the date of the latest service of the notice, or seven days in certain limited circumstances. Any provision in the notice requiring the use of land to be discontinued operates as a permanent restriction, notwithstanding compliance with the notice. The resumption of that use after its discontinuance will, therefore, be in contravention of the notice. Similarly, where the notice requires either demolition or alteration of buildings or works, the notice will strike at any reinstatement of those buildings

---

[88] reg. 9(3)(c).
[89] reg. 24.

or works, notwithstanding that its terms are not apt for this purpose.

Where any of the steps required by the notice have not been taken within the specified period, the planning authority may enter the land and take those steps (other than discontinuance of any use), recovering its expenses from the owner or lessee of the land.[90] The validity of this action cannot be disputed by any person who failed to exercise his right of appeal to the Secretary of State (below). Any sums incurred by the owner, lessee or occupier in complying with the enforcement notice, or in payment of the expenses of the planning authority in taking the steps required by the notice may be recovered from the person by whom the display was carried out.

At any time prior to the notice taking effect, any person on whom the notice is served may appeal in writing to the Secretary of State, indicating the grounds of appeal and stating the facts on which it is based.[91] The notice has no effect until the appeal is either determined or withdrawn. The appeal procedure is similar to the procedure for planning enforcement appeals except that there is no provision for use of the written submissions procedure (Chapter 7). The grounds of appeal are that:

1. the matters alleged in the notice do not constitute a display of an advertisement without the necessary consent or a failure to comply with any condition or limitation;
2. the notice was not served as required;
3. the specified period for compliance with the notice falls short of what should be reasonably allowed;
4. the steps required by the notice exceed what is necessary for its purpose.

In the course of the appeal the Secretary of State may correct any non-material informality, defect or error in the notice, and disregard any failure to serve the notice if neither

[90] reg. 26.
[91] reg. 25.

the appellant not the person served with the notice have been substantially prejudiced by that failure. In determining the appeal, the notice may be quashed or its terms varied in favour of the appellant.

Offences

Display of an advertisement in contravention of advertisement control is an offence, with a maximum fine on summary conviction of level 3 on the standard scale (Appendix 1), with a further offence carrying a fine of one-tenth of level 3 for each day during which the offence continues after conviction. The persons liable for such an offence are the owner and occupier of the land upon which the advertisement is displayed, or the person whose goods, trade, business or other concerns are publicised by the advertisement. It is a defence to show that the advertisement was displayed without the knowledge or consent of the accused person.[92] If the contravention of advertisement control consists of a failure to observe any condition relating to maintenance of the advertisement or its site, or to the unsatisfactory removal of the advertisement, a person whose goods, trade, business or other concern is publicised by the advertisement only commits an offence if he has failed to comply with the requirements of an enforcement notice served on him.[93]

Power to Remove or Obliterate Placards and Posters

The planning authority has the power to remove or obliterate any placard or poster displayed in its area in contravention of advertisement control, unless it is displayed within a building to which there is no public right of access.[94] This power is aimed at the nuisance caused by flyposting.

Where the placard or poster identifies the person who displayed it or caused it to be displayed, the authority must give that person written notice of its intention to remove or obliterate it on expiry of a period specified in the notice which

[92] TCPSA, s. 101(2) and (3), as amended.
[93] reg. 7(2).
[94] TCPSA, s. 101A.

must be not less than two days from the date of service of the notice. This notice period is intended to give an opportunity to convince the authority that the placard or poster is not displayed in contravention of advertisement control. Written notice is not required if the placard or poster does not give the address of the person and the authority does not know it and is unable to ascertain it after reasonable inquiry. There is a right of entry onto the land at any reasonable time, provided the land is unoccupied and it would be impossible to exercise the power without entering it.

Enterprise Zones and Simplified Planning Zones

Enterprise Zone (EZ) and Simplified Planning Zone (SPZ) schemes are intended to encourage development to take place where it is needed to promote regeneration and economic activity. This objective is achieved through the grant of planning permission, in advance, for forms of development specified in the scheme (some schemes permit all forms of development with specified exceptions), thus avoiding the need to submit an application and providing developers with a degree of certainty. In addition, EZs offer a range of fiscal benefits, typically including exemptions from local authority rates and greater capital allowances for capital expenditure incurred on construction, extension or improvement of industrial and commercial buildings. There are no automatic fiscal benefits from a SPZ scheme. Both forms of scheme have been criticised for encouraging existing businesses in the area to relocate within the zone, rather than attracting fresh employment.

An EZ is prepared by a district or regional planning authority and designated by order of the Secretary of State.[95] SPZs are promoted by the planning authority.[96] Proposals for an EZ or SPZ are advertised, giving the public an opportunity to lodge representations. In the case of an SPZ, there is

[95] Local Government, Planning and Land Act 1980, s. 179 and Sched. 32, as amended.

[96] TCPSA, ss. 21A–21E and Sched. 6A, as amended; Town and Country Planning (Simplified Planning Zone) (Scotland) Regulations 1987 (S.I. 1987 No. 1532).

provision for a public local inquiry to be held to consider any objections received (Chapter 8). The Secretary of State has powers to require the authority to consider modifications to the proposed SPZ, and to call-in the proposals for his decision. An SPZ scheme ceases to have effect 10 years after the date of its adoption or approval. No application for planning permission will be required where a development authorised by a planning permission under the SPZ scheme has commenced within the 10-year period.

Natural Heritage Areas and National Scenic Areas

The power to designate Natural Heritage Areas (NHAs) has superseded the National Scenic Area designation (NSAs).[97] As a result, no new NSAs will be created but existing ones will continue, although some may be transformed into NHAs. The statutory controls in respect of NSAs remain in force.

NHAs may be designated by the Secretary of State for Scotland on the recommendation of Scottish Natural Heritage. Such areas should be appropriate for special protection because of their outstanding value to the natural heritage of Scotland, including its flora and fauna, geological and physiographical features, natural beauty and amenity.

Scottish Natural Heritage is preparing the detailed criteria which will be used to identify appropriate areas, and no sites have yet been selected. In recommending areas for NHA designation, Scottish Natural Heritage must consult with such people as it thinks fit, and should take into account actual or possible ecological and other environmental changes to the natural heritage of Scotland; the needs of agriculture, fisheries and forestry; the need for social and economic development; the need to conserve sites and landscapes of archaeological or historical interest; and the interests of owners and occupiers of the land, and of local communities.

Notice of the proposal to designate an area as an NHA must be advertised in the Edinburgh Gazette and a local newspaper. Any representations received within three months

[97] Natural Heritage (Scotland) Act 1991, s. 6.

must be considered by the Secretary of State. Notice of the making of the designation must also be given in the same manner.

Although the NSA designation has now been superseded by the power to designate NHAs, the statutory controls applicable to NSAs remain in force.[98] NSAs are areas of outstanding scenic value and beauty in a national context, designated by the Secretary of State as appropriate for special protection (similar to the Areas of Outstanding Natural Beauty in England and Wales). There are currently 40 NSAs. Planning authorities must maintain a list available for public inspection of NSAs within their district.

When any planning powers are exercised with respect to any land within NSA, including the determination of applications for planning permission, special regard must be paid to the desirability of preserving or enhancing the character or appearance of the area. This requirement also applies to NHAs.[99] The character or appearance is preserved not only by a positive contribution to preservation, but also by development which has a neutral effect and leaves the character or appearance unharmed.[1]

To provide planning authorities with an opportunity to review development proposals, planning permission must be obtained for the following types of development within an NSA, which would otherwise have benefited from permitted development rights[2]:

> 1. erection for agricultural or forestry purposes of all buildings and structures over 12 metres high (permitted development rights have since been removed for all agricultural buildings over 12 metres high, below);

[98] *Ibid.*, s. 6(9).

[99] TCPSA, s. 262C(4), as amended.

[1] *South Lakeland D.C.* v. *Secretary of State for the Environment* (n. 49, *supra*); *The Bath Society* v. *Secretary of State for the Environment* (n. 48, *supra*).

[2] Town and Country Planning (Restriction of Permitted Development) (National Scenic Areas) (Scotland) Direction 1987, attached to S.D.D. Circular 9/1987, "Development Control in National Scenic Areas"; display of advertisements on or consisting of a balloon within an NSA will require advertisement consent — Town and Country Planning (Control of Tethered Balloon Advertisements in National Scenic Areas) (Scotland) Direction 1984, attached to S.D.D. Circular 10/1984.

2. construction of vehicle tracks for agricultural or forestry purposes except forestry tracks which are part of an approved afforestation scheme; and
3. all local roads authority roadworks outside present road boundaries costing more than £100,000.

As an additional safeguard, where the planning authority proposes to grant permission for the forms of development listed below within an NSA, it must consult Scottish Natural Heritage.[3] If Scottish Natural Heritage advise against granting permission or recommend conditions other than those proposed by the planning authority, the authority must send details of the application to the Secretary of State (and, in the case of a district planning authority, the regional planning authority). The authority cannot grant planning permission for the development until 28 days (or any longer or shorter period specified by the Secretary of State) have elapsed from the date notified to it by the Secretary of State as the date of receipt of the details of the application. This period provides the Secretary of State with an opportunity to call-in the application for his own decision.

This consultation requirement applies to:

1. schemes for five or more houses, flats or chalets except for those within towns and villages for which specific proposals have been made in an adopted local plan;
2. sites for five or more mobile dwellings or caravans;
3. all non-residential developments requiring more than 0.5 hectares of land;
4. all buildings and structures over 12 metres high, including agricultural and forestry developments;
5. vehicle tracks, except where these form part of an approved afforestation scheme; and
6. all local highway authority roadworks outside present road boundaries costing more than £100,000.

[3] Town and Country Planning (Notification of Applications) (National Scenic Areas) (Scotland) Direction 1987, attached to Circular 9/1987.

Nature Conservation

In the exercise of all statutory functions, including planning, the Government, local authorities and public bodies are required to have regard to the desirability of conserving Scotland's flora and fauna, geological and physiographical features, and its natural beauty and amenity.[4] The environmental assessment process includes consideration of the effects of a proposed development on flora and fauna (Chapter 5). Nature conservation, therefore, forms part of the planning process and there is a range of statutory designations which can be applied to control activities on land in the interests of nature conservation. It is expected that some changes will require to be made to comply with the European Community Directive on the conservation of natural habitats.[5]

Sites of Special Scientific Interest

Sites of Special Scientific Interest (SSSIs) are areas of land designated as being of special interest by reason of any of their flora, fauna or geological or physiographical features.[6] In 1991 there were over 1,300 SSSIs in Scotland. Aside from the planning consequences, the main result of the designation of land as an SSSI is the prohibition of carrying out a range of operations without the consent of Scottish Natural Heritage.

Where planning permission is sought for a proposed development which may affect an SSSI (this does not require the development site to be within or adjacent to the SSSI), the planning authority must consult Scottish Natural Heritage and consider any representations made by them in determining the application.[7] Scottish Natural Heritage's views form part of the material considerations in the determination of the application (Chapter 5), but are not binding on the planning authority. However, if the authority decides to grant

[4] Countryside (Scotland) Act 1967, s. 66 (as amended).
[5] Directive 92/43 on the Conservation of Natural Habitats and of Wild Flora and Fauna (the Habitats Directive).
[6] Wildlife and Countryside Act 1981, s. 28 (as amended).
[7] Town and Country Planning (General Development Procedure) (Scotland) Order 1992, art. 15(g).

permission contrary to Scottish Natural Heritage's recommendation, it must notify the Secretary of State and the regional planning authority.[8] Thereafter the authority cannot grant permision until the expiry of 28 days from the date of receipt by the Secretary of State, giving him an opportunity to call-in the application for decision (Chapter 5), or issue a direction restricting the grant of permission.

There is no statutory duty incumbent on the planning authority to protect an SSSI similar to that applicable to conservation areas or NSAs/NHAs, requiring special consideration to be given to preserving or enhancing the character or appearance of the area. It is also interesting to note that the restrictions on permitted development rights within SSSIs are limited to electricity cables and mineral exploration (Chapter 4). Agricultural and forestry development within SSSIs does not require planning permission, but may require to be notified to Scottish Natural Heritage as a potentially damaging operation (only grants of planning permission following an application to the planning authority provide exemption from the potentially damaging operation provisions, below).

Designation of an SSSI commences with Scottish Natural Heritage serving a preliminary notice of its intention to notify the site, on the planning authority in whose district the land is situated, every owner and occupier of that land, and the Secretary of State. The notice specifies the flora, fauna, geological or physiographical features by reason of which the land is of special interest, and any operations (known as "potentially damaging operations"), which seem likely to damage that flora or fauna or those features. Until the notice ceases to have effect, it is an offence to carry out these operations without consent (below). The notice must also specify at least a three-month period for lodging representations or objections in connection with the proposed designation. The notification ceases to have effect after nine months, unless Scottish National Heritage serve notice confirming the notification.

[8] Town and Country Planning (Notification of Applications) (Nature Conservation) (Scotland) Direction 1991, attached to Scottish Office Environment Department Circular 13/1991.

If no agreement can be reached for the withdrawal of a representation or objection lodged by any owner or occupier relating to the flora, fauna or features specified in the notice (but not the potentially damaging operations), the matter is referred to an independent advisory committee which has been appointed by the Secretary of State. Scottish Natural Heritage must then consider (but need not follow) the advice of the committee before determining whether to confirm the notification.[9] The committee also has power in some circumstances to advise Scottish Natural Heritage in respect of existing SSSIs.

Following confirmation by Scottish National Heritage of the notification of the land as an SSSI, notice is served upon the owners and occupiers and the planning authority, and the notification is registered in the Land Register for Scotland or recorded in the Register of Sasines (so that any new owner will be aware of the notification as a result of the usual searches carried out before purchase). There is no right of appeal, but it may be possible to apply for judicial review of the decision (Chapter 8).

During the preliminary notification period of up to nine months, and after service of the notice confirming the notification of the land as an SSSI, it is an offence for the owner or occupier of any land which has been so notified to carry out, or cause or permit to be carried out, any potentially damaging operation. Liability does not extend to a contractor carrying out work on the land, even where the contractor received notification of the designation by virtue of the ownership of another part of the site.[10] It is a reasonable excuse that the operation was authorised by a grant of planning permission (but not a deemed grant of planning permission for the exercise of permitted development rights), which may predate the notice by several years, or that it involved emergency work and Scottish Natural Heritage were informed as soon as reasonably practicable after the event.

This prohibition from carrying out potentially damaging operations is lifted if either the work is done in accordance

[9] NHSA, s. 12.
[10] *Southern Water Authority* v. *Nature Conservancy Council* [1992] 1 W.L.R. 775.

with a management agreement, or written consent to the proposed operation is obtained from Scottish Natural Heritage, or four months have expired from the giving of notice to Scottish Natural Heritage.[11] Thus, at most, operations can only be delayed for four months without agreement.

Management agreements between Scottish Natural Heritage and the owners and occupiers of land included in an SSSI involves the owners and occupiers agreeing to refrain from carrying out potentially damaging operations or to take positive action to safeguard the scientific interest of the site. Scottish Natural Heritage may agree to make financial payments in return for such a management agreement.

Nature Conservation Orders

A Nature Conservation Order is made by the Secretary of State for the purpose of securing the survival of particular kinds of plant or animal on a site, to comply with an international obligation, or to conserve flora, fauna, geological or physiographical features in a site.[12]

Nature Conservation Orders have a broadly similar effect to the SSSI designation, but with some differences. A Nature Conservation Order takes effect immediately on being made by the Secretary of State and can, therefore, be used where there is an urgent need for protection. In addition, the restrictions on potentially damaging operations apply to any person, whether or not authorised by the owner or occupier. Finally, the prohibition on carrying out potentially damaging operations applies for three months after giving notice to Scottish Natural Heritage, which can extend this period by offering either to enter into a management agreement or to acquire the land (in which case the three-month period is extended to the date of the agreement, or replaced by a 12-month period, or three months from the date of rejection or withdrawal of the offer, whichever period last expires). Alternatively, Scottish Natural Heritage can make a compulsory purchase order.

[11] Wildlife and Countryside Act 1981, s. 28(6), (as amended to increase original three-month period to four months).
[12] *Ibid.*, s. 29(1).

Compensation is payable by Scottish Natural Heritage for depreciation in the value of land, which is part of an agricultural unit, resulting from a Nature Conservation Order. Compensation is also available for abortive expenditure, loss or damage where the three-month time limit for potentially damaging operations is extended.[13]

The consultation and notification requirements applicable to applications for planning permission which may affect an SSSI do not appear to extend to sites which are subject to Nature Conservation Orders. In practice, consultation and notification are likely to occur.

Notice of the making of the Nature Conservation Order is advertised and served on every owner and occupier of the land affected. At least 28 days must be allowed for representations or objections to be made. A public local inquiry or other hearing is held to consider any objections which are not withdrawn. In light of the representations and objections, and the report of any inquiry or hearing, the Secretary of State considers whether the order should remain in effect, or be amended or revoked. Any person aggrieved by the decision has six weeks to challenge its validity in an application to the Court of Session, on the grounds that it is not within the statutory powers of the Secretary of State or that the statutory requirements have not been complied with (Chapter 8).[14] Once confirmed, the Order is recorded in the Register of Sasines or registered in the Land Register.

If notice of potentially damaging operations is served in advance of an inquiry into objections to the Order, but no action is taken in response to the notice the operations become lawful and free from restriction after expiry of the three-month period. In such circumstances, Scottish Natural Heritage must respond to the notice (even with a view to extending the three-month period), notwithstanding that such action may seem premature until the conclusion of the inquiry. In the situation where, by the time of the inquiry, operations were lawful and free from restriction under an Order which was primarily intended to avoid damage from

[13] *Ibid.*, s. 30.
[14] *Ibid.*, Sched. 11.

those operations, the subsequent inability of the Order to control the operations and, therefore, its uncertain efficiency, was a material consideration which should have been taken into account at the inquiry.[15]

Other Nature Conservation Designations

There are many other environmental or nature conservation designations, most of which have no direct planning consequences. Environmentally Sensitive Areas are designated for the purpose of entering into voluntary agreements for the adoption of environmentally friendly agricultural practices in return for payment.[16] Other designations include Special Protection Areas,[17] Special Areas of Conservation,[18] Ramsar sites,[19] and National and Marine Nature Reserves[20], but in most of these cases the land will first be designated an SSSI.

Agriculture and Forestry

Agricultural use and development traditionally enjoyed widescale exemption from the need for planning permission. This exemption is gradually being eroded, most recently following incidents of sheds being erected in inappropriate positions next to dwelling-houses.

Agricultural Use

A change from any use to agricultural use, or between different agricultural uses, does not require planning permission,[21] although any associated building or other work is

[15] *North Uist Fisheries Ltd.* v. *Secretary of State for Scotland*, 1992 S.L.T. 333; S.P.L.P. 36:59.
[16] Agriculture Act 1986, s. 18.
[17] E.C. Directive on Conservation of Wild Birds (79/409) — 47 in Britain (April 1992).
[18] Habitats Directive (n. 5, *supra*).
[19] Ramsar Convention on Wetlands Sites of International Importance (Cmnd. 6465) — 53 in Britain (April 1992).
[20] Wildlife and Countryside Act, ss. 35 and 36 (plans for Scotland's first marine nature reserve at Loch Sween have been shelved — *The Scotsman*, May 18, 1993).
[21] TCPSA, s. 19(2)(e).

considered separately and may require permission (below). Thus, no planning permission is required for pigs to be introduced onto land, but it is only once this agricultural use has been established that piggeries can be constructed without planning permission.[22] Fish farming is an exception to this rule, as the placing of fish cages in inland waters requires planning permission,[23] enabling planning authorities to exercise control over the visual and environmental impact of fish farms.

Provided the primary use is agricultural, no planning permission is required for ancillary uses, such as the sale of farm produce to the public on a farm. However, if produce is bought in for sale, the retail element may become a separate use in its own right and, therefore, require planning permission (Chapter 4 discusses primary and ancillary uses in more detail).

Agricultural uses include horticulture, seed or fruit growing, dairy farming, breeding and keeping livestock for the production of food, wool, skins or fur (which includes fish farming) or for the purpose of its use in the farming of land, and the use of land as grazing, meadow, or osier land, market gardens and nursery grounds and the use of land for woodlands (where that use is ancillary to the farming of land for other agricultural purposes).[24] The courts have declared that agricultural use includes the use of land for allotments, grazing horses, fox and mink farming, but not for keeping and boarding cats and dogs, installation of an egg-vending machine, keeping of animals in transit, wholesale slaughtering of animals, and the breeding and training of horses for show-jumping.[25]

Building and Other Work

Where there is an existing agricultural use, and all of the following criteria are met, planning permission is not required for the erection, extension or alteration of a building; the

[22] *Joan Jones* v. *Stockport M.B.C.* [1984] J.P.L. 274.
[23] TCPSA, s. 19(3B).
[24] s. 275(1).
[25] See the cases cited in Young and Rowan-Robinson, *op. cit.*, p. 155.

formation, alteration or maintenance of private ways; or any excavation or engineering operations[26]:

1. the land must form part of a unit occupied for the purposes of agriculture other than fish farming;
2. there must be an existing agricultural use for the purposes of a trade or business;
3. the work must be reasonably necessary for the purposes of agriculture within the unit[27];
4. the agricultural land must have an area of at least 0.4 hectares, comprised in one piece of land, except in the crofting counties where areas of separate parcels of land may be added together;
5. the work must not involve the erection, extension or alteration of a dwelling-house;
6. any building or structure to be provided must be designed for the purposes of agriculture, thereby avoiding erection of buildings used for keeping livestock, but with the appearance of dwelling-houses;
7. the ground area of any building to be erected, extended or altered, or structure (other than a fence) for the purposes of accommodating livestock, or of any plant or machinery must not exceed 465 square metres. The ground area is calculated by adding the ground area to be covered by the proposed works to the ground area of any building (other than a dwelling), structure, works, plant or machinery provided in the preceding two years within the same unit and any part of which is within 90 metres of the proposed works;
8. the height of the building, structure or works must not exceed 12 metres (three metres if within three kilometres of the perimeter of an aerodrome);
9. no part of the works must be within 25 metres of the metalled portion of a trunk or classified road; and
10. where the building or structure to be erected or worked upon is or will be used for housing pigs, poultry, rabbits or animals bred for their skin or fur, or for the storage of slurry or sewage sludge, it must be more than 400 metres from the

[26] Town and Country Planning (General Permitted Development) (Scotland) Order 1992, art. 3 and Sched. 1, class 18.
[27] *MacPherson* v. *Secretary of State for Scotland*, 1985 S.L.T. 134.

curtilage of any permanent building normally occupied by people or apt for such use, which does not form part of the agricultural unit or another such unit.

If these criteria cannot be met, planning permission will be required. A Certificate of Lawfulness of Proposed Use or Development (CLOPUD) can be obtained from the planning authority in circumstances where it is uncertain whether the criteria have been met (Chapter 4).

The following works also do not require planning permission[28]: the winning and working of any minerals reasonably necessary for agricultural purposes within the agricultural unit, provided the minerals remain within the unit and are used for agricultural purposes; works in connection with the improvement or maintenance of watercourses or land drainage works; and the winning and working of peat by any person for their domestic requirements.

Removal of more than five cubic yards of surface soil from agricultural land in any period of three months is an offence, if planning permission is required but not obtained.[29] This offence also applies to land formerly used for agriculture where that use ceased in consequence of the intention to remove surface soil. It does not extend to the cutting of peat or the removal of such quantities of surface soil as it is reasonably necessary to remove in the course of cutting turf.

Prior Notification

Even if planning permission is not required for works, it may be necessary to give the planning authority prior notification of those works, by an application to determine whether the prior approval of the authority is required. This prior notification requirement enables the planning authority to exert some degree of control over the siting, design and external appearance of a building, where planning permission is not required for its erection, alteration or extension.

The prior notification requirement applies to the erection or significant extension or alteration of a building. A building is

[28] P.D.O., Sched. 1, classes 19, 20 and 21.

[29] Agricultural Land (Removal of Surface Soil) Act 1953, s. 1, as amended.

significantly extended or altered if either the cubic content of the original building is increased by more than 10 per cent or its height is increased. A building can only be significantly altered or extended once without planning permission.

Work cannot proceed until notification is received from the authority that its prior approval is not required, or its approval is received, or 28 days have elapsed since the application was lodged and the authority has reached no decision. The work must be carried out in accordance with the approved details or, if no approval is required, in line with the details submitted with the application. In addition, the work must be carried out within five years of the date on which approval was given or if no approval was given, the date of the application.

Forestry

Similar provisions apply to forestry uses and works. Forestry use includes operations necessary to render timber marketable and disposable, even where the operations are carried on some distance from the plantation. Therefore, planning permission was not required for a change of use to use as a timber storage and transfer area.[30] Forestry works do not require planning permission unless the work involves the provision or alteration of a dwelling, the height of any building or works within three kilometres of an aerodrome would exceed three metres, or any part of the proposed development would be within 25 metres of the metalled portion of a trunk or classified road.[31] There is a similar prior notification requirement for the erection or significant extension or alteration of a building.

Designated Areas

Farming and forestry operations are often affected by some of the statutory designations examined above. For example, within NSAs the permitted development rights for the erection for forestry purposes of all buildings or structures

[30] *Farleyer Estate* v. *Secretary of State for Scotland*, 1992 S.L.T. 476.
[31] PDO, class 22.

over 12 metres high, and for construction of vehicle tracks for agricultural or forestry purposes (except forestry tracks which are part of an approved afforestation scheme) are removed. The result is that an application for planning permission will be required.

Diversification

In the current climate many farmers are considering diversifying from farming. Diversification projects will often require planning permission, for example, the conversion of farm buildings to non-agricultural use, such as holiday cottages or industrial units, the stabling of horses for riding or breeding, or the erection of houses. Use of the farmhouse for bed and breakfast may require planning permission, depending upon the number of guests and the attitude of the planning authority. As mentioned above, a shop on the farm will not require permission provided it only sells produce from the farm. In general, permission will be required for a caravan site, except for some small-scale activities.[32] Non-agricultural uses of land (but not buildings), for any purpose other than open-air markets, do not require planning permission, provided the use does not occur for more than 28 days in a calendar year. Moveable structures, such as marquees, may be placed on the land in connection with such use.[33]

Change of Use of Agricultural Land

Planning authorities are required to notify the Secretary of State, and the regional planning authority, where they propose to grant planning permission for a proposed development involving a change of use of two hectares or more of agricultural land falling within class 1, 2 or 3.1 of the Macaulay land capability classification for agriculture, and which is contrary to the adopted or approved local plan, unless no such plan has been adopted or approved.[34] If

[32] PDO, classes 16 and 17.
[33] PDO, class 15.
[34] Town and Country Planning (Notification of Applications) (Scotland) Direction 1988, attached to S.D.D. Circular 29/1988.

consulted, the Scottish Office Agriculture and Fisheries Department must have recommended that permission be refused. Following notification, the planning authority cannot grant permission until 28 days after the date of receipt by the Secretary of State of the notification. This period enables the Secretary of State to consider calling-in the application for his decision or issuing a direction to the planning authority restricting the grant of permission.

Development in the Countryside and on Green Belt Land

The high amenity value of the countryside is acknowledged in the constant pressure for housing development. In order to preserve this amenity, development in the countryside is subject to restrictive policies both at national and local level. National policy states that development in the countryside should be encouraged on suitable sites in existing settlements. The coalescence of settlements, and ribbon development should be avoided. Isolated development should be discouraged in the open countryside, except where either circumstances are clearly identified in development plans, including where a dispersed pattern of housing might be appropriate in more remote areas, or there are special needs, for example, the nature of employment requires residence in a particular location.[35] Isolated houses in the countryside are also resisted in local plans. However, there are often exceptions for single house infill within groups of buildings smaller than villages, essential houses for farm workers, replacement houses, restoration of empty or abandoned houses or conversion of redundant agricultural buildings, such as steadings. The siting and design of new housing in the countryside is also a matter of concern[36] and many authorities have published design guides to aid applicants.

Green Belt is land designated in a development plan to be left open. The purposes of Green Belt land are to check

[35] NPPG3, "Land for Housing," para. 51 *et seq*, which replaces S.D.D. Circular 24/1985, "Development in the Countryside and Green Belts," para. 3.

[36] S.D.D. PAN 36, "Siting and Design of New Housing in the Countryside."

unrestricted sprawl of large built-up areas, to safeguard countryside from further encroachment and preserve it for recreation or institutional purposes. It is also designed to prevent neighbouring towns from merging into one another, to maintain the landscape setting of towns and preserve their identity by establishing a clear definition of their physical boundaries, and to assist in urban regeneration by rendering derelict urban sites more attractive propositions for development.

The Scottish Office guidance states that there should be a general presumption against any intrusion into designated Green Belts (this is the only exception to the presumption in favour of development, Chapter 5). In particular, approval should not be given, except in very special circumstances, for either the construction of new buildings and the extension or change of use of existing buildings, for purposes other than agriculture, horticulture, woodland management and recreation, or establishments and institutions standing in extensive grounds or other uses appropriate to the rural character of the area.[37]

Minerals

Planning permission is required for mining operations, including the removal of material of any description from a mineral-working deposit, deposit of pulverised fuel ash or other furnace ash or clinker, or deposit of iron, steel or other metallic slags, and the extraction of minerals from a disused railway embankment.[38] The extraction of each shovelful constitutes a separate development, and it will therefore be rare for unauthorised mining operations to become legal.[39] There are permitted development rights (Chapter 4) in connection with mineral exploration, development ancillary to mining operations, British Coal mining development, waste tipping at a mine, and removal of material from mineral working deposits.[40]

[37] Circular 24/1985, Annex, para. 4(iv).
[38] TCPSA, s. 19(1) and (3A).
[39] *Thomas David (Porthcawl) Ltd.* v. *Penybont R.D.C.* [1972] 1 W.L.R. 1526.
[40] PDO, classes 53–66.

As a result of the unique problems of mining works, such as the length of the operations, frequent suspension for periods of time and resumption, and the harm caused to the land, the normal planning regime is supplemented by special provisions.[41] Issues such as environmental and visual impact, trade effluent and disposal of mine waste, dust, noise, subsidence, health and safety, site rehabilitation, road infrastructure and the need for the mine, will be relevant to applications for permission for mining operations. It is common for any permission to be combined with a section 50 agreement (Chapter 6), providing for restoration and aftercare of the site, and a bond to cover the cost of these works.

In connection with an application for planning permission for the winning and working of minerals, in addition to the usual notifiable parties, any person with an interest in minerals ordinarily worked for removal by underground or surface working in, on or under the land must be notified of the application as an owner of the proposed development site.[42]

Planning permision may be granted subject to a restoration condition requiring restoration of the site after the winning and working is completed, and an aftercare condition requiring steps to be taken to bring the land to the required standard for either agricultural, forestry or amenity use.[43] Unless a condition expressly specifies a shorter or longer period, the winning and working of minerals or the depositing of mineral waste must cease not later than 60 years after the grant of permission.[44]

Where the winning and working or depositing appears to have permanently ceased, the planning authority may prohibit its resumption.[45] Once the prohibition order comes into force, any planning permission for the development ceases to have effect. If the operations have been temporarily

[41] TCPSA, ss. 251, as amended, and 251A, as substituted; Town and Country Planning (Minerals) (Scotland) Regulations 1971 (S.I. 1971 No. 778), as amended by 1982 Regulations of the same name (S.I. 1982 No. 973).

[42] TCPSA, s. 24, (1A) as inserted. The PCA 1991, s. 46, will substitute a new s. 24 providing for publicity requirements to be re-enacted in regulations.

[43] s. 27A, as amended.

[44] s. 41A, as amended.

[45] s. 49A, as amended.

suspended, the planning authority may require steps to be taken for the protection of the environment during the period of suspension, to preserve the amenities of the area, to protect it from damage and to prevent any deterioration in the condition of the land. A suspension order does not prevent recommencement of development provided notice is given to the planning authority. Prohibition and suspension orders do not take effect until confirmed by the Secretary of State and registered in the Land Register or Register of Sasines.[46]

Planning authorities are under a duty to undertake periodic reviews of mineral workings to consider whether permission should be revoked or modified, or a prohibition or suspension order made.[47] Old mining permissions granted by interim development orders prior to the Town and Country Planning (Scotland) Act 1947, for which application for registration was not made by July 24, 1992, have ceased to have effect.

Crown Land

Crown land is land in which there is an interest belonging to the Queen in right of the Crown (adminstered by the Crown Estate Commissioners), or belonging to a Government department or Minister, or held in trust by the Queen for the purposes of a Government department or Minister.[48] Any Crown exemption from planning legislation no longer applies to health boards.[49]

Crown land and development is largely exempt from planning and associated controls.[50] For example, development on Crown land (other than by a person holding a private interest, such as a tenant), or which is undertaken by the Crown on any other land does not require planning permission.[51] However, all Crown bodies have agreed to adhere to a voluntary arrangement whereby notice of any

[46] ss. 49B, 49D and 49F, as amended.
[47] s. 251A, as substituted.
[48] s. 253(7).
[49] NHS and Community Care Act 1990, s. 60.
[50] TCPSA, s. 253, as amended; but see Scottish Office Environment Department Consultation Paper, "Removal of Crown Exemption from Planning Law" (November 1992).
[51] *Lord Advocate* v. *Dumbarton D.C.*, 1990 S.L.T. 158.

proposed development is served on the planning authority and treated as though it were an application for planning permission. If the Crown body and the planning authority fail to reach agreement, the proposal is referred to the Secretary of State to decide whether a planning clearance can be given.[52]

There is provision for application to be made to the planning authority for permission and other statutory consents in anticipation of the disposal of Crown land.[53] Planning agreements may be entered into between the planning authority and the Crown body to secure the use of Crown land in conformity with the provisions of the development plan, or to restrict or regulate its development or use, either permanently or during a specified period.[54] Where a material change in the use of Crown land is proposed, the planning authority may enter into an agreement deeming planning permission to be granted for the change of use, subject to a condition requiring discontinuance of the use after the land ceases to be used by the Crown.[55] After registration in the Land Register for Scotland or the Register of Sasines, the agreement will be enforceable against any party acquiring title to the land. A Tree Preservation Order made by a planning authority over Crown land will not take effect, without the consent of the Crown body, either until it ceases to be Crown land or becomes subject to a private interest.[56]

Development by Planning Authorities

To avoid the conflict of interest which would arise if the council as landowner was required to submit an application for planning permission for proposed development to itself as planning authority, there is a special procedure for authorising development by a planning authority.[57] The authority

[52] S.D.D. Circular 21/1984, "Crown Land and Crown Development."
[53] Town and Country Planning Act 1984, s. 1, as amended.
[54] TCPSA, s. 254(1), as amended.
[55] 1984 Act, s. 5, as amended.
[56] *Ibid.*, s. 2, as amended.
[57] TCPSA, s. 256, as amended; Town and Country Planning (Development by Planning Authorities) (Scotland) Regulations 1981 (S.I. 1981 No. 829), as amended by 1984 Amendment Regulations (S.I. 1984 No. 238).

must undertake the notification procedures relating to owners, agricultural tenants, and neighbours, and comply with the publicity and consultation requirements, as if it was applying for planning permission (Chapter 5). Thereafter, a notice must be published in a local newspaper stating its intention to carry out the development described in the notice, the address and times at which plans of that development may be inspected, and that representations may be made in writing to the authority within 21 days of the date of publishing.

If no representations against the development are lodged within 21 days, or such longer period as applies to the notification, publicity or consultation procedures for planning applications, planning permission is deemed to have been granted by the Secretary of State. However, deemed permission cannot be granted for the demolition, alteration or extension of a listed building or demolition of a building which would require conservation area consent, or where the Secretary of State has given a direction restricting the grant of permission for the development or class of development to which the application relates or a direction as to how an application is to be determined.

Where representations are received, or deemed permission cannot be granted, the planning authority sends a notice of intention to develop (commonly known as an NID) to the Secretary of State, together with details of the consultation exercise, and copies of representations received. Thereafter the Secretary of State may require the authority to submit an application for planning permission to him for the development, which is then treated as a called-in application (Chapter 5). If after 28 days of the receipt of the NID, or any extended period notified to the authority by the Secretary of State, the Secretary of State has not required such an application to be made, planning permission is deemed to be granted. Deemed permission enures for the benefit of the planning authority and does not transfer with the ownership of the land. In all other respects, the deemed permission has the same effect as a grant of planning permission (Chapter 5).

The Scottish Office guidance contains a presumption against an application being required where the proposed development accords with the adopted or approved local plan for the area or has not attracted a significant body of objections. Where the NID is linked to a compulsory purchase order which is to be the subject of a public local inquiry, the NID is likely to be called-in to enable consideration of the planning aspects of the proposal to be considered alongside the case for compulsory purchase.[58]

Planning authorities which wish to carry out works requiring listed building or conservation area consent must apply to the Secretary of State.[59] He has enforcement powers which can be exercised where there is development by an authority without planning permission, listed building or conservation area consent.[60]

Hazardous Substances

Previously, the development control system only provided the planning authority with the opportunity to control storage of hazardous substances on land if this storage amounted to development (Chapter 4). A new hazardous use could be introduced or an existing operation intensified without any planning permission being required. Since May 1, 1993, hazardous substances consent must be obtained from the planning authority where the aggregate quantity of the substance on, over or under the land exceeds the controlled quantity.[61] The temporary presence of a substance while in transit will be taken into account only if it is unloaded. Deemed consent for the presence of a substance could be claimed as of right until November 1, 1993.

Hazardous substances consent is obtained by submitting an application in a similar way as an application for planning permission, with owner and neighbour notification and newspaper advertisement. In determining an application, the authority will have regard to any material consideration, including any current or contemplated use of the land to

[58] S.D.D. Circular 29/1988, "Notification of Applications," paras. 17–22.

[59] TCPSA, s. 257 and Listed Building Regulations (see n. 9), reg. 11; TCPSA, s. 262(7)(a).

[60] TCPSA, s. 260(5).

[61] TCPSA, ss. 56A–560, as amended; Town and Country Planning (Hazardous Substances) (Scotland) Regulations 1993 (S.I. 1993 No. 323).

which the application relates, the use and likely use of land in the vicinity, any planning permission granted for land in the vicinity, the provisions of the development plan, and any advice received from the Health and Safety Executive or the Health and Safety Commission. Consent may be granted subject to conditions specifying the storage or use of the substance and the times between which it may be present.

The control of hazardous substances regime is similar to normal planning controls. There is a right of appeal to the Secretary of State within six months of the date of notice of the decision on the application, or from the expiry of two months (or any extended period agreed in writing with the applicant) from the date of receipt of the application. The planning authority has enforcement powers in situations where consent is required, but has not been obtained or there is a failure to comply with the terms or conditions of the consent.

Hazardous substances consent enures for the benefit of the land and is not personal to the applicant. However, unlike planning permission, the consent is revoked if there is a change of control of part of the site unless an application for continuation of the consent is made in advance to the planning authority.

The planning authority must consult the Health and Safety Executive before determining an application for planning permission, where a proposed development is within an area notified to the authority by the Executive.[62] Notification takes place because of the presence within the vicinity of toxic, highly reactive, explosive or inflammable substances. This consultation requirement applies where the development involves the provision of residential accommodation, more than 250 square metres of retail floor space, 500 square metres of office space or 750 square metres of floor space to be used for an industrial process, or is otherwise likely to result in a material increase in the number of persons working within or visiting the notified area.

[62] D.P.O., art. 15(f), as amended.

Chapter 10

PUBLIC PARTICIPATION

Planning is predominantly about controlling development in the wider public interest (a rather sweeping statement of the underlying nature of planning, but Chapter 1 discusses this matter in more detail). Therefore, it seems fitting to end this book with an examination of the extent to which members of the public can participate in the planning system. Without the interest and input from members of the public, the system cannot maintain the public confidence which it requires to function efficiently. Thus it is to be hoped that members of the public will continue to exercise their rights.

In this context, the terms "members of the public" or "third parties" are used to denote persons other than the applicant for permission/developer, the planning authority and bodies which must be consulted as part of the determination of a planning application. These persons may be local residents, and might even have been notified as neighbours of the proposed development, be members of a voluntary group such as a community council or amenity society, or concerned individuals. The planning system gives all these members of the public various opportunities to make their views known and be taken into account as part of the decision-making process.

The planning system can be divided into two parts: development planning and development control (see Chapter 2). The rights of members of the public in each part are examined below.

Development Plans

The development plan is an expression of the views of the planning authority with regard to use of the land in its district. The authority has few powers or opportunities to implement these views itself, and the provisions of the plan serve more as authoritative guidance to those wishing to develop land. The plan does not remove the need to obtain planning permission, even where a development conforms to its provisions, and those provisions form one of the material considerations taken into account by the authority when determining applications for planning permission. As explained in Chapters 3 and 5, the introduction of the plan-led system will result in a presumption that planning permission will be granted for a proposed development which is in accordance with the provisions of a development plan, unless material considerations dictate otherwise. It is in this role that the planning authority can implement its views expressed in the plan, but only to the extent of granting permission for developments which are in accordance with the plan and refusing the other applications.

The development plan is actually made up of two separate plans: the structure plan and the local plan. Both are subject to periodic review by the planning authority and alteration or replacement, the procedure for which is discussed in Chapter 3. At each stage the authority is required to publish notices in local newspapers alerting members of the public to the opportunity of inspecting proposals or draft plans and lodging representations. Information displays are often mounted in public buildings such as libraries, and public meetings may be organised. The local media may carry features on the proposals.

Members of the public should exercise every such opportunity offered to inspect proposals and lodge written representations making their views known. As replacement plans have a projected lifespan of at least 10 years, and will form the blueprint for developments during that time, it is essential that the views of the community are accurately expressed in the plan which is eventually adopted, not least because it will be difficult to resist any development which is in accordance with the plan. Inspection of the proposals will also bring to light any which have escaped the glare of publicity, but are still of importance and worthy of comment. The opportunity should also be taken to correct any factual errors. It should be appreciated that the weight given to opposition often correlates to the number of representations received, and it may be a mistake to assume that others will object and that your representations will make no difference.

Following the initial consultation stage, modified proposals will often be published. These should be inspected to check whether previous representations have been incorporated (if not, they can be repeated) or if representations should be made in relation to fresh proposals. There is no bar to lodging representations at a later stage which could have been made in connection with an earlier version of the proposals.

After the consultation stages, the finalised structure plan is submitted to the Secretary of State for approval, and the public is given an opportunity to make representations to the Secretary of State. The provision for an examination in public to be held has fallen into disuse, and there is no equivalent to the local plan inquiry.

During the replacement or alteration of a local plan, if representations remain outstanding in relation to the finalised plan, the persons or bodies maintaining those representations are given the opportunity of presenting their case at a local plan inquiry. This inquiry is chaired by a reporter appointed by the planning authority. The reporter is an independent professional normally employed by the Scottish Office Inquiry Reporters for determining planning appeals to the Secretary of State. The inquiry is, therefore, a valuable opportunity to convince a person independent of the planning authority and the plan preparation process of the need to modify the proposals. Rather than appear in person at the inquiry, it is competent to request that the reporter consider written submissions, which may take the form of the representations previously lodged with the planning authority. While the recommendations made by the reporter are not binding, the authority must give reasons for rejecting the recommendations. If the authority modifies the proposals following the report of the inquiry, the public will be given an opportunity to lodge representations in respect of the modified plan.

The legality of the decision of the Secretary of State on the structure plan, or the planning authority on the local plan, may be challenged in the Court of Session by members of the public who are persons aggrieved, using the statutory review procedure (chapters 3 and 8).[1] The treatment of third parties in the courts is discussed below.

Development Control

Development control is the term used to describe the determination by the planning authority of applications for planning permission (Chapter 5), and the taking of enforcement action against breaches of planning control (Chapter 7). While it is the former which involves most public participation, members of the public should be prepared to participate in enforcement by reporting activities which are suspected either not to benefit from planning permission or not conform with the terms and conditions of a grant of permission, rather than relying on detection by under-resourced council planning departments.

The high point of public involvement in the planning system comes with applications for planning permission, where members of the public have the opportunity to lodge representations either with a view towards persuading the authority to refuse permission for the development, or simply expressing views which seem relevant, or in support of the development. The following discussion refers principally to objections, as these are the most common form of representation.

The planning authority is required to take into account representations lodged by certain members of the public, such as notifiable neighbours, or those received following newspaper advertisement or display of site notices. However, even if the application is not advertised, any member of the public can lodge a representation which must be taken into account by the authority to the extent that it raises material planning considerations (Chapter 5).

Part of the reason for the extent of public involvement in the determination of planning applications lies in the publicity requirements (Chapter 5). In submitting the application, the

[1] TCPSA, s. 231; *Glasgow for People* v. *Secretary of State for Scotland*, 1991 S.C.L.R. 775; 1992 S.P.L.P. 35:16.

applicant is required to serve notice upon the owners and agricultural tenants of the development site, and neighbouring owners and occupiers (owners, lessees and occupiers of commercial premises). Broadly only those neighbours within four metres of the site, excluding the width of any road, must be notified. In many circumstances notice of the proposed development must be given by newspaper advertisement, and some authorities have policies of publishing advertisements beyond the statutory requirements. Site notices must be displayed if the proposed development would affect the character or appearance of a conservation area or the setting of a listed building. Finally, details of all applications must be entered in a register available for public inspection, allowing concerned members of the public to check regularly on new applications.

Prior to deciding whether to object, or writing an objection, the plans and other papers lodged with the planning authority in connection with the application should be inspected (the official notices and newspaper advertisements give few details other than the description of the proposed development). It is advisable to check with the authority by telephone that these documents are available for inspection (the application may still be in the initial processing stages), and, if so, at what location and times. Unless the application is for outline permission, or a change of use, the application should include detailed drawings of the buildings or other structures involved. Careful note should be taken of details such as the height of buildings in comparison to others in the vicinity and distance from surrounding properties, the architectural style, any loss of trees, provision for carparking, and vehicular and pedestrian access. The details of the parties notified by the applicant should be checked for any obvious omissions, which should be drawn to the attention of the authority. There should a duty planning officer present who can explain details of the drawings, and also any policies of the authority which will apply.

In addition to inspecting the drawings accompanying the application, it is important to check with the authority the time limit for lodging objections. The official notices and newspaper advertisements specify time limits, but many authorities do not strictly adhere to these limits. It should also be possible to find out the name of the planning officer dealing with the application, who will normally be prepared to discuss it.

No procedure is prescribed for lodging objections, but the objection should identify the application concerned, either by reference number, if known, or by repeating the description of the proposed development and specifying the address of the appeal site. It should be in writing, identify the objector and be signed (confidentiality can be requested). Mention should be made of any official notification of the application received by the objector, as this may oblige the planning authority to take the objection into account. Finally, the objections to the proposed development should be listed, together with the reasons for those objections and any supporting information such as plans or photographs.

The grounds of objection will, of course, depend to a large extent on the form of development proposed and the characteristics of the development site and the surrounding area. The planning authority is legally obliged to take into account all material planning considerations and ignore any other issues (even if these issues are raised by parties whose representations must be taken into account). The grounds of objection can, therefore, be compiled from the list of material considerations given in Chapter 5. The level of sophistication of the grounds of objection will depend upon the scale of the development proposed and the views of the objector. While it is not essential that each ground of objection affect the objector directly, some objectors may prefer to limit the objection to the matters most relevant to their personal position. For example, an objection may refer to a traffic problem likely to be caused to residents at one end of a street as a result of the proposed development, notwithstanding that the objector will not suffer any traffic problems.

The planning authority will acknowledge receipt of the objection. Some authorities have a practice of sending copies of objections to the applicant, with the offer of an opportunity of responding to the comments made. When the planning officer comes to consider the recommendation to be made in his report to the authority on the application, the planning considerations raised by any objections will be taken into account. A summary of the considerations (but not usually a copy of the objections) will be included in the report circulated to the councillors who will make the decision.

Objectors may wish to act further than lodging an objection. Public opposition to the proposed development can be generated by publicity and meetings. As councillors take account of the number of objections, other members of the public can be encouraged to lodge objections, possibly by the use of style letters which can be photocopied and distributed for signature. Appropriate bodies can be approached with a request for their views. The local district and regional councillors, and M.P., can be contacted and made aware of objections. If the district councillor is not a member of the committee which will decide the application, he can be asked to pass views to the councillors on that committee. If the scale or importance of the development justifies it, copies of the objection can be sent to each of the councillors who sit on the committee (the council will provide names and addresses). However, care should be taken not to burden them with too much detail and to avoid too frequent contact, which may result in loss of their co-operation. It is also advisable to delay such communications until a few days before the committee is due to consider the application, so that the views will still be fresh in the minds of the councillors at that meeting.

It is also worth maintaining regular contact with the relevant planning officer, both to check the progress of the application and to discover any problems which are being encountered which may either assist the objection, or with which the objector may be in a position to provide assistance.

Some applications involve the applicant and the planning authority entering into a section 50 agreement (Chapter 6). There may be no sinister purpose behind such an agreement, which may be necessary because normal planning powers cannot regulate the development effectively. However, there is concern about the lack of any public participation in the agreement process and the belief that developers "buy" permission by offering planning benefits over and above what is required for the development. (This belief is not borne out by the latest research.) If members of the public are concerned, and not prepared to accept reassurance from the planning department, their only option is to enlist the help of councillors to investigate the terms of any proposed agreement. When it comes to the time for a decision to be made, members of the public are entitled to attend the committee meeting, but it is unusual for them to be allowed to address the committee (although the right of address can always be requested).

Following determination of the application, some but not all authorities notify the decision to all those who lodged representations. If the application has been refused or granted subject to unacceptable conditions, the applicant has six months to lodge an appeal to the Secretary of State (Chapter 8). Any person who lodged a representation in connection with the application will be informed by the planning authority if an appeal is submitted and given the opportunity to lodge further representations (the original representations will be sent to the reporter), or to appear at a public local inquiry which will hear the appeal. Other members of the public will be alerted by newspaper advertisement of the arrangements for the inquiry. Members of the public are entitled to attend the inquiry, and may participate at the discretion of the reporter. Any person aggrieved by the decision of the reporter (or the Secretary of State) may challenge its legality within six weeks in the Court of Session through the statutory review procedure (below).

If the planning authority grants planning permission for the proposed development, objectors have no right of appeal to the Secretary of State. Their only remedy is to petition the Court of Session for a common-law judicial review of the decision. The limited value of such a remedy is discussed below. Other forms of challenge, such as a complaint to the ombudsman, will not prevent the development from proceeding, and are therefore of limited value.

The lack of an opportunity for members of the public to challenge the merits of a decision to grant planning permission may seem unsatisfactory, but it must be remembered that until the introduction of planning control in 1947 landowners could do as they pleased with their land. For this reason, it has been consistent government policy that there is a presumption in favour of development, and the planning authority must show reasons why development should not proceed (Chapter 5). To allow members of the public a right of appeal against a grant of permission would unduly restrict the rights of landowners, and be contrary to that presumption. Such a right of appeal would also play havoc with developers who often have a tight timescale for a development, and would incur substantial losses if a project was delayed by an appeal lodged by a member of the public. Even if such losses could be claimed against that person following dismissal of the appeal, most members of the public have insufficient assets to make this worthwhile, and the danger of becoming liable for such losses would dissuade members of the public from utilising the right of appeal in the first place. Unfortunately, members of the public must accept that there is no second chance if they fail to persuade the planning authority that permission should be refused, unless there is a legal flaw in the decision which can be challenged in court.

Members of the Public in Court

Following an unsatisfactory planning decision, members of the public often assume that it can be challenged in the courts. Indeed, any person aggrieved by a decision to adopt/approve a development plan, or by the decision of the Secretary of State on appeal, has the right to challenge that decision in the Court of Session through the statutory review procedure, and there is a similar possibility of challenge against a decision of the planning authority on a planning application by the common-law judicial review procedure. These procedures are discussed in detail in Chapter 8.

Members of the public rarely appreciate the limitations on what can be achieved through the court procedures. The right of challenge only extends to the legality of the decision, and not its planning merits. It is not enough to show that the decision was wrong. A successful challenge requires proof that the authority (or the Secretary of State) incorrectly exercised their powers by taking into account irrelevant matters or by ignoring relevant factors, or that their decision was irrational, or the procedure adopted for making the decision was unfair (Chapter 8). For example, provided the authority takes all relevant factors into account, the court will not interefere with the weight it chose to place on each factor, unless its decision is irrational. Even if the decision is shown to be illegal, the court has the discretion not to grant any remedy, for example, if it decides that the same decision would have been reached in any case. Furthermore, the remedy most likely to be granted is the quashing of the decision. This results in the matter being referred back to the planning authority for a fresh decision to be made. Providing the authority avoids making the same mistake twice, it is likely that it can reach the same decision as before. A successful judicial review may, therefore, be a pyrrhic victory.

Ironically, lodging a comprehensive objection to the application reduces the likelihood of a successful judicial review. The full nature of the objection will alert the planning authority to all the material considerations. It will be difficult to prove that some of the grounds of objection were ignored, as opposed to considered and overruled. Thus the objection will prevent the authority from failing to take into account a relevant consideration and therefore remove one of the grounds for judicial review. This line of reasoning should not dissuade objectors from raising all the grounds of objection, as a successful objection will avoid the need for court action. It is easier for third parties to win (i.e. refusal of planning permission) in the factual arena of the planning authority, than the legal arena of the Court of Session.

If the previous paragraphs paint a bleak scenario, members of the public seeking to challenge a decision should be cheered by the favourable attitude of the Court of Session shown in recent years towards the status (known by lawyers as standing) of third parties to bring such challenges. The details of the legal requirements of standing are discussed in Chapter 8. Two cases are particularly worthy of note.

In the first, a member of the public (L) had complained to the planning authority that he had not been notified of the submission of an application in accordance with the neighbour notification procedures and reserved his right to object to the proposed development once he had received such notification. The authority informed the applicants of the position, and, without informing L, subsequently granted permission for an amended application in which the boundaries of the development site had been redrawn to avoid any obligation to notify L as a neighbour. The Court of Session quashed this decision on the grounds that L had been unfairly deprived of his legitimate expectation of being able to lodge an objection. While neither the applicant for permission nor the authority had failed to comply with the statutory procedures, the procedure adopted by the authority was unfair because it prejudiced L's rights as a member of the public.[2]

The other decision worthy of note possibly goes even further towards protecting third-party rights in the development control process. An application for planning permission was submitted which described the proposed development as a roadside petrol station and service area. This description was repeated in the notices served on neighbours and in the newspaper advertisements. However, the plans submitted with the application showed a separate petrol station for each of two roadside sites and a 40-bedroom lodge, two restaurants and three car parks. A member of the public applied to the Court of Session for the decision to grant permission for the development as shown on the plans to be quashed. The court upheld the application on the grounds that the inadequate description had deprived him of an opportunity to lodge representations which might, at least in his view, have affected the result.[3]

The significance of the decision in *Cumming* can only be appreciated from a detailed examination of the facts. The member of the public was a businessman who was likely to lose business to the bedroom-lodge part of the development. It seems that the omission of the lodge from the description caused him to assume wrongly that he had no objection to the development, although inspection of the plans would have corrected this misassumption. There was some uncertainty whether he could have produced any planning arguments against the development which would have influenced the decision. Perhaps the most telling fact is that he was eventually given full notice of the true extent of the development and given an opportunity to lodge representations before the decision was taken on the application. Despite all of these factors, the Court of Session upheld his

[2] *Lochore* v. *Moray District Council*, 1992 S.L.T. 16; 1991 S.P.L.P. 34:78.
[3] *Cumming* v. *Secretary of State for Scotland*, 1993 S.L.T. 228.

right as a member of the public to expect the description contained in an application for planning permission to give full and fair notice of the extent of the development for which permission is sought.

Such a favourable decision cannot be expected at all times, but these two decisions emphasise the importance which the Court of Session now appears to place on third-party rights in planning.

Conclusion

Although the Court of Session has recently shown a more positive attitude towards allowing members of the public to challenge planning decisions, the role of the court is limited to reviewing the decision challenged to ensure that it has been reached within the law. Members of the public have no opportunity to challenge the planning merits of a grant of planning permission or the adoption of development plan. This emphasises the importance of mounting an effective campaign at the earliest stage.

APPENDIX 1

STANDARD SCALE OF FINES

[From October 1st, 1992]

Level	*Amount*
1	£200
2	£500
3	£1,000
4	£2,500
5	£5,000

[Criminal Justice (Scotland) Act 1991, s.17(1)]

APPENDIX 2

BAD NEIGHBOUR DEVELOPMENT

(1) the construction of buildings for use as a public convenience;

(2) the construction of buildings or other operations, or use of land
   - (a) for the disposal of refuse or waste materials, or for the storage or recovery of reusable metal
   - (b) for the retention, treatment or disposal of sewage, trade waste, or effluent other than
     - (i) the construction of pumphouses in a line of sewers;
     - (ii) the construction of septic tanks and cesspools serving single dwellinghouses, or single caravans, or single buildings in which not more than 10 people will normally reside, work or congregate;
     - (iii) the laying of sewers; or
     - (iv) works ancillary to those described in sub-paragraphs (i) to (iii);
   - (c) as a scrap yard or coal yard; or
   - (d) for the winning or working of minerals;

(3) the construction of buildings or use of land for the purposes of a slaughterhouse or knacker's yard or for the killing or plucking of poultry;

(4) the construction or use of buildings for any of the following purposes:
bingo hall
building for indoor games
casino
cinema
dance hall
fun fair

gymnasium (not forming part of a school, college or university)
hot food shop
licensed premises
music hall
skating rink
swimming pool
theatre, or
Turkish or other vapour or foam bath

(5) the construction of buildings for or the use of buildings or land as
   (a) a crematorium, or the use of land as a cemetery;
   (b) a zoo, or wildlife park, or for the business of boarding or breeding cats or dogs;

(6) the construction of buildings and use of buildings or land for motor car or motor cycle racing;

(7) the construction of a building to a height exceeding 20 metres;

(8) the construction of buildings, operations, and use of buildings or land which will
   (a) affect residential property by reason of fumes, noise, vibration, smoke, artificial lighting or discharge of any solid or liquid substance;
   (b) alter the character of an area of established amenity;
   (c) bring crowds into a generally quiet area;
   (d) cause activity and noise between the hours of 8 p.m. and 8 a.m.; and
   (e) introduce significant change into a homogeneous area.

[Town and Country Planning (General Development Procedure) (Scotland) Order 1992, Schedule 7]

INDEX